D0710521

WITHDRAWN
UTSA LIBRARIES

The German Historical School
in American Scholarship

A Study in the Transfer of Culture

The German Historical School in American Scholarship

A Study in the Transfer of Culture

By Jurgen Herbst

KENNIKAT PRESS
Port Washington, N. Y./London

THE GERMAN HISTORICAL SCHOOL IN AMERICAN SCHOLARSHIP

Copyright © 1965 by Cornell University
Reissued in 1972 by Kennikat Press by arrangement
Library of Congress Catalog Card No: 79-159072
ISBN 0-8046-1666-3

Manufactured by Taylor Publishing Company   Dallas, Texas

To the memory of my father

HERMANN HERBST

of the

BIBLIOTHECA AVGVSTA

Preface

SCHOLARSHIP and science, like most human endeavors, are given their distinguishing character by the specific time and place in which they are pursued. The perennial quest for truth can never be observed in pristine purity, as it is inseparable from the varying modes of civilization in which it occurs. The realization of this fact first prompted me to take a look at the scholarship and science of both Germany and the United States, and I decided to investigate the ties between scholars in Germany and America that came into existence during the nineteenth century. In a general way, the influence of European upon American scholars has always been acknowledged. We have spoken of the predominantly British cast of American education during the colonial period, the impact of French science during and after the Revolution, and the model provided by the German states for American secondary and university education during the nineteenth century. More recently, there has been the reverse phenomenon of American influence upon educational systems abroad. We know that such systems have their similarities and their differences, and that through the activities of scholars, scientists, teachers, and students these systems interact with one another. Yet despite several excellent studies—such as, for example, Howard Mumford Jones' *America and French Culture*—our information on the transfer of culture from the Old to the New World is still fragmentary and limited.

The case investigated here is the rise and decline of the German historical school of social science in the United States between the founding of The Johns Hopkins University in 1876 and the outbreak of war in Europe in 1914. By the German historical school of social science in America I mean those men in university departments of history, political science, economics, and sociology who had been trained in Germany and who regarded themselves as disciples of the German historical school. My concern has been with what these scholars discovered in Germany that they deemed worthy of introduction into American higher education.

In the pages that follow I have set out to describe how the institutions and concepts of German *Wissenschaft* made their appearance in the United States. Although I am mainly concerned with the closing decades of the nineteenth century, I have decided to devote large portions of the first four chapters to a more general discussion of relevant topics in German and American educational history in the nineteenth century, and all of Chapter 8 to twentieth-century issues. I did this because I believe that the full measure of a historical epoch or event can appear only when it is viewed as a moment in time that has both its past and its future.

My readers will not, I hope, anticipate a full treatment of the subject covering the years before 1876 or after 1914. Much as I am concerned with the nineteenth-century German historical school of social science, I have intended neither to write of German historicism *per se* nor to engage in a survey of German intellectual history. I have purposely restricted myself to a discussion of the thought and work of historians and social scientists. Thus I write of Ranke and Schmoller, and not of Goethe and Herder. As a matter of fact, I have found that although the German-trained American students of history and social science often referred to their German "masters" of the historical school, they did so only rarely to the great proponents of historical thought in literature and philosophy. It was only in the 1920's and 1930's, when the Crisis of Historicism became a topic of debate in America, that *Historismus* and its problems were seen in the wider perspective of society and culture. I thus decided to postpone my discussion of this subject until Chapter 8.

I trust I shall not be understood as saying that everything new in the American academic world after 1876 was German, or as offering a general history of American higher education and social science. I have intended to focus on those things that were German in their origin— to show how they were imported and modified, and the problems that arose in the process. After a sketch of the *Wanderjahre*, that migration of thousands of students to the German lecture halls, and of the academic changes that ensued in America, I have turned my attention to the twin pillars of the older college curriculum, moral philosophy and religion, and the extent to which they were hostile or hospitable to the empiricism of the new scholarship. I may say here that the reception given to the concepts and methods of empirical scholarship was more favorable than I had previously supposed.

In Chapter 5 I deal with what I regard as the heart of

the matter—the attempt of several German-trained social scientists of the historical school to re-create in their own country, and to harmonize with its traditions, the legacy of German *Wissenschaft*. Since my findings are based on the published work of five German-trained American social scientists, they have all the shortcomings of a selective approach. Finding it impossible to make a thorough study of all German-trained American social scientists, I singled out five men who, judging by the scope of their published writings and by the reputation they have enjoyed among their contemporaries, appeared most nearly to represent their separate disciplines, and who for the major part of their careers were active at rather dissimilar universities. The five are the historian Herbert Baxter Adams of The Johns Hopkins University; the Columbia political scientist John W. Burgess; the Wisconsin economist Richard T. Ely; Albion Small, sociologist at the University of Chicago; and the Harvard professor of social ethics Francis Greenwood Peabody.

It was from blueprints drawn after the German academic pattern, transported across the ocean by these scholars and many of their compatriots, that the ground was prepared for a successful reorganization of American institutions of higher education. A similar attempt to introduce the methodology and ideology of German social science met with failure. If social science was indeed a historical discipline, there was no possibility of ignoring its roots, blithely teaching in America what one had learned in Germany. Such an enterprise was bound to fail, even if the historical school in Germany had not itself succumbed to what has already been spoken of as the Crisis of Historicism.

Through an analysis of the methodology and ideology of the German historical school, I seek to relate the school's rise and decline in America to its internal strengths and weaknesses. I am quite aware that this approach cannot yield a full explanation, since much could be said of the historical school in relation to other schools and currents of social thought, such as Social and Reform Darwinism, or Comtean and behaviorist positivism. But these relationships are separate chapters in the history of American social science, and to discuss them would not, I believe, add substantially to our understanding of the historical school as a system of thought in its own right. Throughout this book I have generalized to the extent of treating the influence of the historical school as synonymous with the German influence on American social science. It must be acknowledged at the outset, of course, that not all German scholars and not all American students in Germany were disciples of the historical school. (Chapter 6 offers some statistics on this matter.) I believe, however, that the generalization is both valid and useful, since the ideology and methodology of the historical school were far more characteristic and pervasive than any other German influence.

What I have hoped to illuminate, finally, is the complex phenomenon of cultural transfer, exemplified by the effect of German historical scholarship on American social science between 1876 and 1914, as it is documented in the work of certain scholars. The reasons for the rise and decline of the historical school in America constitute the problem with which I am mainly concerned. Whether the historical school is dead and gone, whether it has been transformed in both Germany and America, and differently so in the two countries, are matters worthy of inquiry. To these questions I have suggested some answers of my own in the final chapter. My primary intention, however, has been not to propound an answer to the problem but, as clearly as I could, to set forth the problem itself. It is my hope that others may feel challenged to amplify, modify, or correct my conclusions, since no investigation of five scholars—however representative they may have been, and however perceptively I may have read their works—can be more than an outline sketch of a development in which the thought and experience of hundreds of others were involved.

JURGEN HERBST

Middletown, Connecticut
April, 1964

Acknowledgments

THIS study was first suggested to me by Professor
Howard Mumford Jones in a seminar at Harvard University on the History of American Civilization. I cannot
adequately assess the debt I owe Professor Jones for his
teaching and counsel and above all for the example of
inspired scholarship and personal concern by which my
own efforts to inquire, teach, and write have been encouraged and sustained. I have benefited likewise from the
exacting standards and criticisms of Professor Bernard
Bailyn, whose contributions to the study of American
educational history and whose interest in my topic cannot be too highly prized. Whatever value my study may
have will be due in large measure to these men. For its
defects and errors I willingly carry the blame, since I
alone am responsible.

To Professor Barry Karl of Washington University, St.
Louis, is due a special word of thanks for showing me how
to write literate English, with a thoroughness that ferreted
out errors of reasoning as well.

I am further indebted to friends and colleagues who
gave me the benefit of their critical reaction to earlier
drafts of my manuscript, and to those infrequently praised
university press readers who, unknown though they are

to the author, saved him from many an inexcusable blunder. From among very many others I wish to single out Professors Norman O. Brown of the University of Rochester and Rosalie Colie of the State University of Iowa, who gave encouragement when it was needed most. I have no words to express the gratitude I owe my wife, who through many months and years suffered patiently the incivilities of a writing husband, and who yet never failed to give her much-needed comments and support.

Finally, I wish to thank Mrs. Dorothy Hay of Portland, Connecticut, for her faithful service in typing the manuscript; the American Council of Learned Societies for a grant-in-aid; the Danforth Foundation for a faculty summer study grant; and the Harvard Graduate School of Arts and Sciences and Wesleyan University for their financial support of my project.

J. H.

Abbreviations

The following abbreviations are used in the footnotes and bibliographical notes:

AAU	American Association of Universities
AEA	American Economic Association
AHA	American Historical Association
AHR	American Historical Review
AJS	American Journal of Sociology
APSA	American Political Science Association
ASS	American Sociological Society
JHSt.	Johns Hopkins University Studies in Historical and Political Science
MVHR	Mississippi Valley Historical Review
NEA	National Education Association
PSM	Popular Science Monthly
PSQ	Political Science Quarterly
USBE	United States Bureau of Education

Contents

Preface vii

Acknowledgments xiii

Abbreviations xv

1 American Students in German Universities 1

2 The American College and the Problem of
  Professional Education 23

3 German *Wissenschaft* and American Philosophy 53

4 German Theological Science and American Religion .. 73

5 The Science of History and Politics 99

6 The Sciences of Society: Political Economy
  and Sociology 129

7 Scholarship and Social Action 161

8 The German Influence and American Social Science ..203

9 A Closing Word 231

  Bibliographical Notes 235

  Index 249

The German Historical School
in American Scholarship

A Study in the Transfer of Culture

1

American Students in German Universities

Auf reicht mir Stab und Wanderkleid
der fahrenden Scholaren.
Ich will zur schönen Sommerszeit
ins Land der Franken fahren!
—STUDENT SONG

BETWEEN the years 1820 and 1920 nearly nine thousand American students set sail for Europe to enter the lecture halls, seminars, and laboratories of German universities.[1]

---

[1] The statistics on American students in Germany have been gathered chiefly from the annual reports of the U.S. Commissioner of Education and of the German universities. Especially valuable are B. A. Hinsdale, "Notes on the History of Foreign Influence upon Education in the United States," *Report of the Commissioner of Education for the Year 1897–1898*, I (Washington, 1899), 610–613; Daniel B. Shumway, "The American Students of the University of Göttingen," *German-American Annals*, n.s., VIII (Sept.–Dec., 1910), 171–254; William W. Goodwin, "Remarks on the American Colony at the University of Göttingen," *Proceedings*, Mass. Hist. Soc., 2nd series, XII (1897–1899), 366–371; and Johannes Conrad, *The German Universities for the Last Fifty Years* (Glasgow, 1885). The figures given in the text are at best approximate. The available records are spotty, and do not follow a uniform system of accounting. For the most part they include only officially matriculated students, and thus leave out auditors

1

The magnitude of this transatlantic migration would be sufficient to arouse the historian's interest even if he were not immediately concerned with the consequences entailed for the development of American education. The motives of the students for going abroad; their choice of university and of subject; the reasons behind their predilection for Germany rather than for England or France; and their reactions to what they found there—such are the matters to be taken up in this chapter.

When President Frederick A. P. Barnard of Columbia College wrote in 1886, with a touch of sadness and hurt pride, that

in past years it has seemed to be an impression almost universally prevailing among the young men graduating from American colleges with aspirations for making a career in a learned or scientific profession, or in the educational field, that a residence of one or more years at a German university was indispensable to anything like signal success,[2]

and gentleman scholars on the Grand Tour. Whereas for the century beginning in 1820 an over-all compilation of matriculated students based on the statistics used here would run to about 9,000, Charles F. Thwing in *The American and the German University* (N.Y., 1928, p. 40), estimated the number to be close to 10,000. I believe the smaller figure to be more accurate, since allowance should be made for counting more than once those students who matriculated at more than one German university. Furthermore, during the earlier years students from the United States were frequently lumped together with *Amerikaner* from both North and South America, or with *Nordamerikaner* from Canada. I have given a more detailed statistical analysis in my thesis, "Nineteenth Century German Scholarship in America: A Study of Five German-Trained Social Scientists," typescript (Harvard University, 1958), pp. 32–50.

[2] In William F. Russell, ed., *The Rise of a University*, Vol. I (N.Y., 1937), p. 376.

he was reporting what was hardly questioned anywhere in the United States. Most college graduates believed that first-rate professional training in the more specialized scholarly and scientific disciplines was not to be obtained from American colleges, universities, or polytechnical institutes, but was reserved for those privileged to drink at the fountain of German scholarship. Germany's university seminars, laboratories, libraries, and research institutes, its scholarly and scientific associations, its scientific publications, and—last but not least—its colloquia and drinking bouts, its celebrated academic freedom, and its awesome and rigorous scholarly discipline, were revered throughout the nineteenth century by aspiring physicians and chemists, and by all young men who took seriously Bacon's adage that knowledge was power, including many who hoped by means of learning to set the world right. Thus Bliss Perry wrote: "That Germany possessed the sole secret of scholarship was no more doubted by us young fellows in the eighteen-eighties than it had been doubted by George Ticknor and Edward Everett when they sailed from Boston, bound for Göttingen, in 1814."[3] John William Burgess likewise followed the call to the seats of German higher learning, in order to prepare himself there for his self-appointed task of "teaching men how to live by reason and compromise instead of by bloodshed and destruction."[4]

Ticknor and Everett arrived in Göttingen in 1815 to continue their literary studies. In the following year Joseph Cogswell joined his fellow countrymen to prepare

[3] *And Gladly Teach* (Boston, 1935), pp. 88–89.
[4] *Reminiscences of an American Scholar* (N.Y., 1934), p. 29.

3

for the career of an explorer with studies in the natural sciences. Two years later George Bancroft went to Göttingen for advanced instruction in theology and history.[5] For some students with romantic notions of reviving the medieval tradition of the wandering scholar, the motive was more superficial. Others thought of travel itself as an educational experience, or looked upon it as part of a gentleman's upbringing, and chose Germany as best suited to satisfy all or some of these requirements. Our four New Englanders all traveled widely through Germany, and each paid a visit to Goethe in Weimar—a pilgrimage to be recalled as one of the high points of their German experience, an added enhancement to the benefits of their studies.

American students in Germany naturally expected their foreign residence to give them an advantage in the competition for a position at home, although, especially toward the end of the century, the expectation was not always fulfilled. In 1880, Richard T. Ely, arriving in the States with a Heidelberg *Dr. phil.*, had to wait a full year before he could obtain a position on the faculty of The Johns Hopkins University.[6] Nevertheless, the prestige lent by the German sojourn and still more by the German doctorate was real, and if it did nothing else, it served to bolster the young American's assurance and self-esteem.

By the turn of the century, however, the magic spell of the German universities began to wane as the new American graduate schools of arts and sciences outgrew their

[5] For an account of Ticknor, Everett, Cogswell, and Bancroft in Germany see Orie W. Long, *Literary Pioneers* (Cambridge, 1935), *passim*.

[6] R. T. Ely, *Ground under Our Feet* (N.Y., 1938), p. 65.

dependence on German models and patterns. During the 1880's and 1890's many of these graduate schools were directed by men who had spent their apprentice years in Germany, and now were loath to see their students go off to foreign places. The longer these men taught, the more they had come to realize that German methods and approaches were inadequate when applied to American materials and when practiced in an environment indifferent, if not hostile, to German academic and social thought. American scholars in philosophy, scientific methodology, and the social sciences found the canons of German idealism and of the historical school restrictive, and were led to take a second, more critical look at their German experience. Professor David Kinley wrote from Berlin in 1901:

I think far less of Germans, German education and German educational institutions than I did six months ago! I cannot help feeling that they (especially the *Prussians*) are a narrow people, outwardly polite, but at heart somewhat coarse. I wonder why American students come here to study in any lines except such as Germanic philology, Roman jurisprudence, German history, art, and other subjects in which the material can be found only here. It seems to me that in all technical education, and in university subjects like Economics, chemistry, all history *except* German, mathematics, literature, etc., etc., Germany has nothing to offer that our students cannot get better in our own country.[7]

World War I finally eclipsed the already dwindling luster of all things German, scholarship not excepted. The massive influence of German academic practice and thought

[7] See letter to Herbert B. Adams in W. Stull Holt, ed., "Historical Scholarship in the United States, 1876–1901," *JHSt.*, LVI (1938), 690–691.

had come to an end. The ebbing of the American student migration to Germany was a response not only to the law of supply and demand, but also to changing cultural and social currents in both countries. To these more complicated matters we shall return in later chapters.

Before 1870 most of the American students in Germany had been drawn there by the desire for professional training in the natural sciences, particularly chemistry and medicine—a preponderance that may be explained by the almost total absence of professional schools of medicine in America. The deplorable status of American medical training was still evident in the 1890's, when Americans contributed the largest contingent of foreign medical students in Germany, even though in 1892 the number of American medical students was less than half the number of Americans registered in the philosophical faculty.[8] Reforms in American medical education, begun at Chicago in 1859 with the introduction of a three-year graded curriculum, and continued with President Eliot's reorganization of the Harvard Medical Faculty in 1871, tended toward professional standards. By 1893 The Johns Hopkins Medical School and by 1901 the Harvard Medical School required an academic degree for admission.[9] As American medical education gradually raised its sights, the number of students going abroad for medical training declined. Next in numbers to the students of medicine were the students of law, who—surprising though it may seem—up until the 1880's actually outnumbered those in

[8] See *Report of the Commissioner of Education for the Year 1891–1892* (Washington, 1894), I, 341–342.

[9] Abraham Flexner, *Medical Education in the United States and Canada* (N.Y., 1910), pp. 11–12.

the field of theology. But although neither Roman nor canon law was directly relevant to the practice of law in America, it must be remembered that the desire for professional training was accompanied by the appeal of whatever was foreign and unfamiliar. In the absence of academic legal training in the United States, German law studies were esteemed both as general education and as the best professional preparation for a gentleman lawyer. This conclusion is supported by statistics indicating that the majority of the American law students at Göttingen before 1850 came from the South, where the tradition of the gentleman lawyer was particularly well established.[10] Southerners had all the more reason to seek out such German teachers of civil and public law as Niebuhr and Savigny and their followers, in that the historical school of jurisprudence represented by these men was opposed to the Enlightenment concepts of natural law and natural rights, and thus provided support for the "peculiar institution" of slavery. Hugh Swinton Legaré praised Niebuhr as "the first to lay his hand upon that key of the Past—the effect of races upon the revolutions of society, and the character of governments." [11]

For young men who expected to become clergymen the need for advanced studies abroad appeared less acute, since their undergraduate studies had emphasized religion and further theological studies were not required of them. Furthermore, the ill repute in America of the higher criticism, which flourished among German biblical scholars

[10] See Shumway's statistics in *German-American Annals,* Vol. VIII.

[11] *Writings of Hugh Swinton Legaré* (Charleston, 1846), Vol. I, p. 505.

7

at the time, was more likely to jeopardize than to improve the standing of any American clergyman who had been exposed to it abroad. A change in the American attitude toward German theology did not occur until nearly the end of the century, after the theory of evolution had ceased to be regarded as a threat to traditional religious beliefs. Once German criticism had been accepted by American biblical scholars, the hold of German theology on American academic theological scholarship became dominant, and remained so until after the turn of the century.

Soon after 1870 American students of the liberal arts and the social sciences began going to Germany in large numbers. By 1878 they outnumbered those of law and of theology,[12] and in the final three decades of the century they more than doubled the volume of the American student migration to Germany. As the nation became industrialized, there was a need for specialists, scholars, and teachers trained in economics and statistics, and in allied areas of the social sciences and humanities. The universities of Germany continued to provide that training until around 1900, when American universities largely took over the task of professional education. Thereupon a critical reaction against German social science began, and the German influence upon the ideas and teaching methods of social science in America came to an end.

But why, one may ask, did Americans between 1870 and 1900 prefer the universities of Germany to those of other European countries, and specifically those of France and England? Why, for example, in 1895 were only thirty

[12] See *Report of the Commissioner of Education for the Year 1878* (Washington, 1880), p. clxi.

American students enrolled at the Sorbonne, whereas there were more than two hundred at Berlin?[13] Initially it had been the glowing reports of Ticknor and his friends at Göttingen and of early German-trained natural scientists and physicians that favored the predilection for study in Germany. Added to this were the inducements which German universities offered to foreign students. Matriculation was a mere formality; the only thing required was previous enrollment in a reputable college. Successful attendance at seminars for as little as two years, an acceptable thesis, and the passing of a comprehensive oral examination were rewarded with the Doctor of Philosophy degree. The ease with which the German doctorate could be obtained became notorious; in 1901 the Association of American Universities declared that doctoral examinations in the United States "in nearly all cases . . . were more rigorous than the examinations held at the University of Berlin." [14] It requires no special insight into the minds of students to fathom the appeal of the German universities under such conditions!

Besides, from Germany the winds of new doctrine were blowing. It was there that the romantic rebellion against the Enlightenment had begun. In theology and philosophy a new idealism was in protest against the philosophical sensationalism of the English, against Scottish realism and French rationalism. Philological scholarship had transformed history from a mere chronicle into a critical science. American students of moral philosophy were of-

[13] John H. Wigmore, ed., *Science and Learning in France* (1917), p. 354.

[14] AAU, *Journal of Proceedings and Addresses* (1901), pp. 11, 38.

fered, at first, the cameralistic studies of German scholars, and later the statistical bureaus and seminars that shifted the discussion of public ethics from the abstract level to solid, down-to-earth facts and figures. All these developments were highlighted by the reputations of individual German scholars. Kant and Hegel were internationally known in philosophy; Helmholtz, Du Bois-Reymond, and Koch in natural science; Treitschke, Droysen, Adolph Wagner, and Johannes Conrad in history and social science.

Political developments, too, had worked in favor of Germany. Prussia's support of the North during the Civil War had won her much sympathy in Unionist circles.[15] Not unlike the United States, the German empire was passing through a turbulent period of unification. Americans frequently compared their own Civil War to the Prussian wars of 1864, 1866, and 1870–1871, which led to the consolidation of a large national state, and which for many Americans thus demonstrated a universal tendency in the development of nationalities. Since the three decades after the Franco-Prussian War witnessed an almost parallel rise of the United States and Germany to world power, accompanied by similar internal industrial and social problems, it is easy to understand the desire of American students to meet with and learn from the Germans on their home ground.

No other European country could offer this peculiar combination of institutional, political, and personal attractions. By comparison France suffered from a centralization

[15] See John W. Burgess, "Germany, Great Britain, and the United States," *PSQ*, XIX (March, 1904), 9.

of its university system that drew its best teachers to Paris and impoverished the provincial universities. In French universities, moreover, a nine-year course of studies with annual examinations led to a doctorate that conferred the right to practice one's profession in France. American students, even though they had no such professional goal, were expected to follow the same curriculum. Not until 1896, with the introduction of so-called university degrees, were foreign students allowed to qualify for a diploma after a shorter period of study.[16] Finally, in the eyes of many Americans, everything French was still tinged with abhorrence of the Enlightenment's "infidels" and the suspicion of lax morality. There were those, Herbert Baxter Adams tells us, who considered Paris "an unsafe place for a young man." [17] If Americans did nevertheless go to France, they went in the hope of obtaining "a point of view, a sense of proportion, the meaning of the intellectual life and standards of taste in judgment and appreciation" which, in the view of Nicholas Murray Butler, was but a "frame on a picture." The substance of the picture itself had been provided by "the drill, the discipline and the training in patient thoroughness" of the universities of Germany.[18]

England, though it attracted more American students than did France, was likewise no match for Germany's drawing power. Here science and learning flourished outside the universities, but not within them. Scientists in Victorian England, one author remarked, "were, for the most part, isolated individuals, inquiring into the secrets

[16] Wigmore, ed., *Science and Learning*, pp. 351-353.
[17] In Holt, ed., "Historical Scholarship," *JHSt.*, LVI, 99–100.
[18] Butler, *Across the Busy Years*, Vol. I (N.Y., 1939), p. 133.

of nature for their private edification, pride, or wealth. Owing little or nothing to the state, they cared little or nothing for the state"—and in their isolation from the social and political life of the nation they did little to reform or advance the English institutions of higher learning.[19] "There is to be found among those to whom Oxford confides the business of education, an infinitely smaller proportion of men of literary reputation, than among the actual instructors of any other university in the world," Sir William Hamilton had written in 1831.[20] The universities, he went on, did not concern themselves with public affairs but were "merely a *collection of private schools.*" [21] Lord Bryce told Americans that English professors were "so much occupied in preparing men to pass examinations as to give, except in two or three branches, but little advanced teaching," [22] and Sir William added that teaching was regarded as a task "which every 'graduated dunce' might confidently undertake." [23] The English ideal of the scholar as gentleman could scarcely attract those Americans who viewed advanced training abroad as direct preparation for a professional career. Furthermore, Americans balked at signing the Thirty-nine Articles of the Anglican church—a requirement for admission as a candidate for a degree at Oxford, Cambridge, and Durham which was not abolished until June, 1871, and which thus

[19] George Haines IV, *German Influence upon English Education and Science, 1800–1866* (New London, 1957), p. x.

[20] Sir William Hamilton, *Discussions on Philosophy and Literature, Education and University Reform* (N.Y., 1853), pp. 397–398.

[21] *Ibid.,* p. 394.

[22] James Bryce, *The American Commonwealth,* 2nd rev. ed., Vol. II (London, 1890), p. 558.

[23] *Discussions,* p. 421.

hindered the English universities in the competition for American students.[24]

The German universities, while they thus outdistanced those in other countries, each established its own particular claim to excellence. Halle and Göttingen were the first to attract the attention of Americans. In the eighteenth century, the correspondence of Cotton Mather with August Hermann Francke, a leading German pietist theologian and founder of the Halle orphanage school, and the influence of the latter on Jonathan Edwards and George Whitefield, had already made the name of Halle familiar to American men of learning.[25] In Philadelphia a graduate of Halle, John Christopher Kunze, had established his German *Seminarium* in 1773, and from 1780 to 1784 he had taught classical languages in German at the University of Pennsylvania.[26] Another Pennsylvanian, the American Lutheran leader Henry Melchior Mühlenberg, had been a teacher at the Halle orphanage, and in 1763 had sent his three sons to Halle, thereby setting a pattern that was to involve hundreds of young Americans a century later.[27] Between 1800 and 1850 a total of sixteen American students were enrolled at Halle. During the 1880's the number applying for admission rose to one hundred, and throughout the nineties an average of sixteen applied every year. Most of these came to study philosophy, theology, philology, and—after 1870—political economy. The theology students at Halle—among

---

[24] Thwing, *The American and the German University*, p. 76.

[25] See Henry A. Pochmann, *German Culture in America, 1600–1900* (Madison, 1957), pp. 19, 37–38.

[26] *Ibid.*, p. 45.   [27] *Ibid.*, p. 43.

them Henry Boynton Smith (1837) and Francis Greenwood Peabody (1872–1873)—came to hear Friedrich August Gottreu Tholuck, who continued the pietistic tradition begun by Francke. For the economists, after 1872 the seminar of Johannes Conrad became a gathering place where many of the American leaders in the "new economics" of the 1880's and 1890's were trained. Henry Carter Adams, Richard T. Ely, Simon N. Patten, Edmund J. James, Roland Falkner, Joseph French Johnson, Henry Rogers Seager, Frank Albert Fetter, and Samuel McCune Lindsay all studied under Conrad at one time or another.[28] In 1896 Conrad's American students gave him recognition by electing him an honorary member of the Academy of Social Science at Philadelphia, and by awarding him an honorary LL.D. degree at Princeton.

Göttingen's American reputation likewise dates to the eighteenth century. So far as is known, its first visiting American was Benjamin Franklin, who went there in 1766 for a meeting of the Royal Society of Sciences. The visits of Ticknor, Everett, Cogswell, and Bancroft owed their inspiration largely to the scholarly correspondence, from 1795 to 1812, of the Hamburg historian and geographer Christoph Daniel Ebeling with William Bentley of Salem. This exchange of letters, which eventually brought Ebeling's outstanding library of Americana to Harvard College,[29] further increased the fame of Göttingen's late-eighteenth-century historical school, whose chief expon-

---

[28] Karl Diehl, "Johannes Conrad," *Jahrbücher für Nationalökonomie und Statistik,* CIV, 3rd series, Vol. 49 (June, 1915), p. 753.

[29] Pochmann, *German Culture,* pp. 52–54.

ents were Gatterer, Schlözer, and Johann von Müller.[30] By their assiduous cultivation of philological investigations and by the application of these methods to their research, these men had prepared the ground for the critical method in the historical and social sciences. The tradition of this school was carried on by the philologists Eichhorn, Dissen, and Welcker, and by the historians Heeren, Saalfeld, and Planck[31] under whom the four early students from New England first encountered it. By 1825, however, scholarly progress in the natural sciences had caught up with the advances of the historical school. Carl Friedrich Gauss' pioneering work in mathematics was now matched by the comparable achievements in physics of Wilhelm Weber, and in chemistry of Friedrich Wöhler. From then until after the end of the century Göttingen was the favorite training ground of American chemists, mathematicians, physicists, and physicians. The recorded attendance of American students at Göttingen jumped from 34 between 1825 and 1850 to 95 in the fifties, 118 in the sixties, 167 in the seventies, 225 in the eighties, and 316 in the nineties, falling to 230 during the first decade of the twentieth century. Among Göttingen's teachers outside the natural sciences who attracted American students during the second half of the century were the philosopher Lotze, the historian Waitz, the jurist Zachariä, and the statistician and geographer Wappäus.[32]

Although Halle and Göttingen were the first to attract

[30] See Herbert Butterfield, *Man on His Past* (Cambridge, 1955), pp. 36ff.

[31] Long, *Literary Pioneers, passim.*

[32] Cf. Götz von Selle, *Die Georg-August Universität zu Göttingen,* 1737–1937 (Göttingen, 1937), *passim.*

American students, it was the University of Berlin to which the largest number of Americans came during the nineteenth century. Of all American students in Germany between 1820 and 1920, about half spent at least one semester at Berlin.[33] From 55 students during the second quarter of the nineteenth century the number rose in the 1880's to 1,345, and then declined to 900 in the 1890's. During these two decades there were hardly ever fewer than one hundred Americans in attendance during any one semester. The peak was attained in the winter semester of 1896–1897, when 180 Americans matriculated. For an American, Berlin had many attractions. Philosophers and historians had broadcast the fame of its university. Schleiermacher, Fichte, Hegel, and Schelling, its outstanding philosophers before 1850, had been succeeded by Trendelenburg and Zeller. Ranke, Droysen, Mommsen, and Treitschke were the giants of a revitalized historical science. The admiration of von Gneist for English constitutional law endeared him to American students in that field. The lectures and seminars of Pfleiderer in theology, Lepsius in Egyptology, Curtius in archaeology, Jacob and Wilhelm Grimm in Germanic philology, Hermann Grimm in art history, and Adolph Wagner in political economy, all became favorite meeting grounds for young Americans. Along with the achievements of its philosophical faculty, Berlin could boast an excellent medical faculty, including the pathologist von Virchow and the physiologist Du Bois-Reymond, with whom we may associate the physicist Helmholtz. The social sciences benefited greatly in the 1860's from the founding of the

[33] Thwing, *The American and the German University*, p. 40.

Royal Statistical Bureau, as well as from the university's position at the center of the social, political, and cultural affairs of Prussia and—after the victorious conclusion of the Franco-Prussian War—of the German empire.[34] American students were quick to appreciate the excitement of Berlin's parliamentary debates, the charm and magnificence of its opera, the splendor and pomp of army parades, and the thrill of watching the mounted Emperor ride past. "We glorified the army and celebrated the anniversaries of her victories. We were the most loyal of all the Kaiser's subjects," wrote one American.[35] Such things were to be found neither in republican America nor in Halle, Göttingen, or Bonn. Although after 1870 an occasional American rebel expressed disgust with both the high cost of living and the extravagance of Berlin's *nouveaux riches,* as well as with her superannuated, "crotchety, opinionated, illiberal" professors,[36] the city remained a natural choice for the students of history and politics and for others as well.

Of the remaining universities it will suffice to mention briefly the place of Leipzig and Heidelberg in the American student migration to Germany. At Leipzig, as at Halle, philosophy and theology, together with history and political economy, were the chief subjects studied by Americans after 1870, although Leipzig also attracted a large proportion of American medical students. During the 1870's the average annual attendance of Americans at

[34] Cf. Max Lenz, *Geschichte der Königlichen Friedrich-Wilhelms Universität zu Berlin,* 4 vols. (Halle, 1910–1918).

[35] F. F. D. Albery, "Imperial Berlin," *The Bachelor of Arts,* IV (Feb., 1897), 10.

[36] James M. Hart, *German Universities* (N.Y., 1874), p. 374.

17

Leipzig was greater than at Halle and Göttingen, and remained second only to Berlin. For Anglo-American students of theology during the eighties Franz Delitzsch offered a special *Vorlesung*. Historians turned to Georg Voigt and Heinrich Wuttke, and social scientists to Wilhelm Roscher, the founder of the older German historical school of national economy.[37] At Heidelberg, where the fame of the social scientists Bluntschli, Knies, and Erdmannsdörffer was an attraction, there was an average annual attendance of twenty-one Americans during the 1880's and of twenty-eight during the 1890's. Under Bluntschli Americans studied international law, and were taught the comparative case method in political science. Knies and Roscher—founders of the historical school in political economy—and Erdmannsdörffer all stressed the inseparability of economics, history, and political science. Through their American students, notably Herbert B. Adams and Richard T. Ely, the Heidelberg trio was to exert a strong influence on social science teaching in American universities. To complete this survey of German universities it is well to mention those at München, Strassburg, Freiburg, Bonn, and Jena. American students could certainly have been found at every German university as well as at various professional schools of agriculture, dentistry, veterinary medicine, mining, forestry, business, and technology. However, the universities discussed in greater detail here were undoubtedly those most attractive to American students.

The primary appeal of the German universities was

[37] Cf. Rudolf Kittel, *Die Universität Leipzig und ihre Stellung im Kulturleben* (Dresden, 1924).

quite clearly in their specialized scholarship. An American student chose to enroll at a particular German university because of the reputation of the scholars in some particular department. But after he had actually entered its portals, what he found even more exhilarating than the professional opportunities it provided was the prevailing sense of freedom.

I had the feeling [wrote Richard T. Ely] that I had entered into a new heritage of freedom, and a certain joyous expansion was one of the most pronounced feelings which I experienced. There was a free and large spirit on the part of the professors . . . to which I had not been accustomed. I felt that . . . there was room for growth and encouragement of the development of individuality, which was something new to me." [38]

For these young Americans, the German concept of academic freedom as an integral part of higher education was something new.

While the professional education provided by German universities did indeed offer a variety of skills and tools to whoever wanted them, this *Lernfreiheit* left the student free to avail himself of the opportunity or to let it pass. It inspired those who took their studies seriously to enter upon the scholar's quest of truth for its own sake, and to discover for themselves the implications of scholarship for individual and social life. At its best Germany gave young Americans a commitment to scholarship as a profession. A craftsman's regard for technical expertise, an unfailing respect for accuracy, and a concern for the application of knowledge and skills to social ends characterized this commitment. For many Americans their

[38] In *AEA Quarterly*, 3rd series, XI (April, 1910), 68–69.

German experience marked a turning point in their attitude toward work and life.

In Germany there were no tutors to supervise student activities. There was no college to serve as a home or provide board and room. The university consisted of libraries, laboratories, lecture halls, and institutes. It had neither dormitories nor common dining halls. Students roomed in private homes and ate their meals either in their rooms, with their landladies' families, or at inns. Perhaps the fundamental difference from America was that in Germany students were no longer regarded as schoolboys, but as men responsible for their own affairs. They themselves decided how often to attend classes. This was particularly true of the public lectures, and somewhat less so when it came to the more rigorously prescribed work in seminars and laboratories. Students were expected to show good manners and observe the rules of gentlemanly behavior. Discipline was a matter left largely to themselves. Again, since the university's purpose was to give professional rather than general education, a great variety of subjects were offered, and students selected those which appeared best to serve their own needs. A final comprehensive examination measured the student's knowledge; when to take it was once again a matter for the student, with the advice of his professors, to decide. Thus there were no fixed graduation classes as in America. Rather, a German student was known simply as *stud. phil., stud. jur., stud. theol.,* or *stud. med.,* according to the faculty in which he was enrolled.

This student freedom came as a jolting surprise to many a young American in Germany. Moreover, it was not restricted to the academic life, but extended to other spheres as well. G. Stanley Hall relates, for example, that he was "mildly shocked" when he saw one of his professors —a theologian at that—drinking beer with his family and watching the dancing in a public resort.[39] This was a far cry from the exhortations of college moral philosophy on the other side of the Atlantic. It nevertheless seems remarkable how easily and quickly American students adjusted themselves to their newly found freedom.

This adjustment was facilitated partly by the comparable background given American and German students by their previous training. Education in the German *gymnasium* had been just as rigorously regulated as in American colleges. Daily drill and recitation in classical and modern authors, mathematics and natural science, history and geography, and modern languages were the intellectual fare of the *gymnasia*. There the students were "pupils"—children who were expected to memorize lessons and to obey their teachers in conduct and manners. After nine years of this, all pupils hopeful of attending a university were required to sit for a comprehensive examination. Those who passed were awarded a "certificate of maturity," as a token that, having ceased to be "pupils," they were now men worthy to be entrusted with personal freedom and capable of taking responsibility. Once he had sown his wild oats, the German university student was expected to turn his mind to scholarly duties of his own free will, uncoerced by regulations or supervision.

For a German, then, the freedom of the university and the discipline of the *gymnasium* were two different but

[39] G. Stanley Hall, *Life and Confessions of a Psychologist* (N.Y., 1923), p. 187.

complementary aspects of education.[40] An American found it natural to view the *gymnasium* as the German equivalent of the college, whose sequel, after the first exuberant taste of freedom, was devotion to scholarly labors. For many an American student, this academic freedom became the cornerstone on which the whole of his professional education rested.

The emphasis on vocational preparation, however, tended to dampen uncritical praise of Germany's ideal of free science. Americans soon learned that much of the talk of scholarly dedication to the pursuit of truth was part of a venerable tradition that went back to the days of Wilhelm von Humboldt, when Prussia had lent her power and prestige to the support of scholarship. Although for Germans the tradition could be a potent stimulus, all too often Americans found German students more concerned with their future careers than with the advance of science and learning. German students selected their courses not for the new insights they promised, but because they would be useful professionally. The goal of most German students was not the admired degree of *Dr. phil.* but the passing of state-administered civil service examinations. The *Dr. phil.* degree was a necessity only to an academic career, while to others the prestige it assured was social rather than professional. Thus, desirable though it was for many American students who hoped for academic preferment at home, the scholarly ideals represented by the degree appealed far less to German students who looked forward to a career outside the universities.

[40] Cf. Heinrich von Sybel, *Die deutschen Universitäten* (Bonn, 1874).

22

2

The American College and the Problem of Professional Education

> The combination of recitations of the English and American colleges with the academic freedom of the German universities can only aggravate instead of relieving the difficulty of working an organization which is neither a college nor a university.
> —Noah Porter, 1878

PRESIDENT NOAH PORTER of Yale, a one-time student at Berlin, did not object to professional education on the graduate level. Yet he feared that the German-trained professors would permeate all levels of higher education with their zeal for professionalism and academic freedom, and thus wreck the autonomy and integrity of the undergraduate college. The latter, he held, was the equivalent of the German *gymnasium*, which knew neither professionalism nor academic freedom; and anyone who in Germany proposed "that the gymnasia should be transformed into universities . . . would be received with derision." [1] This was, however, precisely what he saw the German-trained professors as advocating when they sought to apply German ideals to undergraduate education. Nor was Porter wrong in this assumption. As trained professionals the returning scholars made possible the rapid growth of American graduate education in the 1880's and 1890's, and to a very large extent were responsible for the shaping of the new institutions for training the professions. As teachers they introduced German ideals into undergraduate as well as graduate education. In this chapter we shall be concerned with the effect of the returning scholars on old and new educational institutions, and with the problems thereby entailed.

The American college was the institution threatened most directly by the German concept of professional education. In the nineteenth century most colleges had been private institutions under denominational sponsorship, offering a prescribed curriculum for a liberal education in the arts and sciences. The men who brought home the challenge from Germany had all been college graduates themselves, and, because the colleges could not provide their graduates with professional training, were already disposed to be critical. On the part of the colleges there had been a certain pride in never having intended to offer training in any of the professions, but rather, in the words of the famous Yale Report of 1827, "to lay the foundation which is common to them all." [2] This foundation was

[1] *The American Colleges and the American Public,* new ed. (N.Y., 1878), pp. 107–108. See also Ralph H. Gabriel, *Religion and Learning at Yale* (New Haven, 1958), p. 159.

[2] "Original Papers in Relation to a Course of Liberal Education," *The American Journal of Science and Arts,* XV (1829), 308.

offered as a single uniform curriculum. Latin and Greek were taught in the expectation that familiarity with the heroes of antiquity and exercises in translation would elevate and discipline the mind. Such translations were the means of learning logic, grammar, and rhetoric, which in turn received practice in literary societies and oratorical contests. These studies were supplemented with training in mathematics, geology, natural philosophy—which consisted of the rudiments of physics and chemistry—botany, zoology, and astronomy. As the student passed from these **required** fundamentals to more advanced studies in mental and moral philosophy, the consciously didactic purpose of a college education became evident, reaching its culmination with the senior course in moral philosophy. This was commonly taught by the college president, who was usually an ordained minister, and who might deal with anything from prices and wages to the doctrine of purgatory. But although its content varied with the interests and inclinations of the teacher, its purpose was invariable: to impress upon the students' minds the realization that life had a moral purpose. Given this didactic emphasis, the graduation certificate was not a claim to any specific vocational or professional competence. Rather, it testified that its bearer had been duly instructed in grammar, logic, rhetoric, and natural science, and had been given a Christian education which emphasized the educated citizen's responsibility for the public good.[3]

Behind this curriculum was an educational philosophy based on what was called the "faculty psychology." The

[3] See George P. Schmidt, *The Liberal Arts College* (New Brunswick, 1957), pp. 45–47; R. Freeman Butts, *The College Charts Its Course* (N.Y., 1939), pp. 116–155, *passim*.

human mind, according to this doctrine, consisted of many faculties, the most important being reason, feeling, and will. A college education was intended to supply "the *discipline* and the *furniture* of the mind; expanding its powers, and storing it with knowledge." All its faculties were to be so trained "as to give them the fair proportions which nature designed." The colleges offered a balanced mental fare, and fed it impartially to all their students.

Those branches of study should be prescribed [wrote the Yale scholars in 1827], and those modes of instruction adopted, which are best calculated to teach the art of fixing the attention, directing the train of thought, analyzing a subject proposed for investigation; following, with accurate discrimination, the course of argument; balancing nicely the evidence presented to the judgment; awakening, elevating, and controlling the imagination; arranging, with skill, the treasures which memory gathers; rousing and guiding the powers of genius.[4]

The prescription of a uniform curriculum was thus no accident, but the conscious and deliberate result of a philosophy of education prevalent in nineteenth-century America.

Teaching methods only added to the uniformity and monotony of college life. An instructor read from a textbook or commented on the passages he had assigned. Students were required to recite each time a class met. Andrew D. White reported of his student days at Yale, "The instructor sat in a box, heard students' translations without indicating anything better, and their answers to questions with very few suggestions or remarks."[5] "Study

[4] "Original Papers," pp. 300–301.
[5] *The Autobiography of Andrew Dickson White* (London, 1905), I, 26.

and recitation, investigation and discussion, from early morning till night and deep into the night, every day in the week, except Sunday, when we had to hear two sermons as well as attend prayers in the morning as every other morning in the week, with no diversion except the Thursday evening prayer meeting," complained John W. Burgess of his Amherst student life in the 1860's.[6] Students found themselves

> in the same round condemn'd each day
> to study, read, recite and pray.

No wonder that the typical reaction was a constant urge to defy or circumvent authority. "We were school-boys," wrote one of them, "chiefly concerned with memorizing rules and exceptions, regimented in recitations, and without training of the eye or hand." [7]

The belief in mental discipline was accompanied by a corresponding reliance upon physical discipline. College professors riding herd on bands of lusty "school-boys," probably regarded their approach to teaching as entirely justified. "To lay the foundation of a superior education," reads the Yale Report, "is to be done at a period of life when a substitute must be provided for *parental superintendence*." [8] Professors acting *in loco parentis* saw to it, or tried to, that all the daily activities of their students were regulated and ordered. With its stated times for meals, classes, prayers, and study, college life resembled that of soldiers in their barracks. Petty regulations, close sur-

[6] *Reminiscences of an American Scholar* (N.Y., 1934), p. 58.

[7] Francis G. Peabody, *Reminiscences of Present-Day Saints* (Boston, 1927), p. 26.

[8] "Original Papers," p. 300.

veillance, academic inflexibility and traditionalism were evident everywhere. Whether it was the students' behavior that brought on these disciplinary measures, or their enforcement that brought on the students' unruliness, is a moot question. Professors all too often took the part of drill sergeants or police investigators. Of Harvard's President Walker it was once sadly remarked that he applied "his gigantic mind . . . to determining whether Bill knew his lessons." [9] Unfortunately this waste of talent was all too common.

But despite the monotony and rigid discipline that burdened college life, and the curb upon intellectual curiosity that was all too often imposed by denominational dogma, the nineteenth-century college had its bright sides too. The cameraderie of irrepressible youth often developed into lifelong friendships, and there was inspired teaching by the superior men of its faculty. The close contact of teachers and students often made it possible to realize the goal of providing guidance for life. The college succeeded in imparting moral standards both through fostering a common spirit among its students and through the personal impact of its teachers. "I did not find at Cambridge any better opportunities than I had found at New Haven," reported Daniel Coit Gilman, "but in both places I learned to admire the great teachers." [10] Professors set an example by their opinions, their enthusiasms, and their performance of civic duties outside the campus. Thus many a young man who had gone to Germany to sit at the feet of world-famous scholars still looked back with warmth to the memory of Andrew Pea-

[9] Peabody, *Reminiscences*, pp. 26–27.
[10] *The Launching of a University* (N.Y., 1906), pp. 8–9.

body at Harvard, of Theodore Woolsey or Noah Porter at Yale, of Julius Seelye at Amherst, of Charles Murray Nairne at Columbia, Henry Robins at Colby, John Bascom or Mark Hopkins at Williams.[11] In the influence of its great teachers the American college made its most enduring bequest.

Between the uniformity and discipline of the American college and the freedom of the German university the contrast was sharp indeed. The returning Americans, almost to a man, were determined to bring about the same educational opportunity and student freedom in their own country. To be sure, specialized instruction was not entirely lacking in America. It could be obtained at the polytechnical institutes of Troy and Worcester, and at the Massachusetts Institute of Technology. At Yale the Sheffield Scientific School, at Harvard the Lawrence Scientific School, and at Dartmouth the Chandler School of Science offered a curriculum leading to a Bachelor of Science degree. Law and medical schools were in some places associated with colleges; in others they existed as independent, private institutions. The Morrill Act of 1862 had given stimulus to engineering and agricultural schools. But the training at these institutions, the German-trained scholars felt, was neither "free" nor advanced enough to correspond to the German ideal. In spirit and form it was collegiate and vocational.

The German-trained students wasted little time in

[11] Peabody, *Reminiscences*, p. 31; White, *Autobiography*, I, 28; Burgess, *Reminiscences*, pp. 52–57; Richard T. Ely, *Ground under Our Feet* (N.Y., 1938), p. 34; Albion Small, "Fifty Years of Sociology in the United States," *AJS*, XXI (May, 1916), 729; G. Stanley Hall, *Life and Confessions of a Psychologist* (N.Y., 1923), p. 157.

diagnosing what they considered the basic weakness of American specialized education, namely the absence of the *philosophische Fakultät* as the institutional embodiment of the scholarly quest for truth. The German scholar professed not to be affected by financial rewards or by coercive or restraining powers outside the academic halls. His was the *libertas philosophandi*, the freedom to investigate, to think, and to speculate in whatever direction his inquiries might lead him. For the German-trained students who returned to America in search of an academic position, the idea of the professor's freedom to investigate and to teach began to overshadow their earlier enthusiasm for the student's corresponding freedom to learn. The two freedoms, *Lehrfreiheit* and *Lernfreiheit*, of course went together and were both contained in the concept of the *libertas philosophandi*. But for a new *Dr. phil.* at the very outset of his academic career, the important thing was the *Lehrfreiheit* of the philosophical faculty—which, John Burgess told his fellow professors, was "the life and glory of the University . . . , the foundation of everything further. Without it Theology becomes a dreary dogmatism, Law a withering letter, and Medicine a dangerous empiricism." [12] To "Germanize" American higher education meant nothing less than to prepare the ground for what was subsequently to become the Graduate School of Arts and Science.

Although the philosophical faculty in Germany was the one mainly responsible for preserving the freedom to investigate, research was an activity that permeated every one of the professional faculties and was in fact the real

[12] *The American University: When Shall It Be? Where Shall It Be? What Shall It Be?* (Boston, 1884), p. 16.

business of the university. The very teaching that American students received away from home depended on and flowed out of research. Now that they were teachers themselves, however, the claims of research competed with those of instruction. Research, wrote G. Stanley Hall, was

the very highest vocation of man. We felt that we belonged to the larger university not made by hands, eternal in the world of science and learning; that we were not so much an institution as a state of mind and that wherever and to what extent the ideals that inspired us reigned we were at home; that research is nothing less than a religion; that every advance in knowledge to-day may set free energies that benefit the whole race to-morrow.[13]

In the halls of American colleges the new "religion of research" had a heretical sound; and it tended not only to overshadow the commitment to teaching but also to blur the image of the German philosophical faculty as a bulwark against vocationalism, an "ism" German students called the *Brotstudium*.

It has already been noted how vocationalism minimized the German student's freedom to learn. It may now be added here that the "religion of research" often became the professorial corollary to vocationalism, and that certain of the German-trained professors in the American universities recognized and sought to limit the danger in the short shrift it gave to teaching. Reflecting on their German experience, these men asked whether the new graduate schools could carry on two tasks simultaneously and with equal success. Could they train future teachers, civil servants, scientists and other professionals, and still

[13] *Life and Confessions*, p. 338.

pursue the disinterested search for truth? A closer examination of this question will occupy us in Chapter 7. Here
we shall deal with the confident assertion by many of
the German-trained scholars that they could best avoid
a conflict of interest by turning the search for truth itself
into a professional aim, by making scholarship a profession uniting research and teaching, and by instructing the
first generation of native-trained American scholars in the
spirit of academic freedom.

Young both in age and in spirit, and full of enthusiasm
for their newly acquired skills, the new generation of
German-trained scholars were missionaries, even crusad-
ers, and without doubt they were inspiring teachers and
guides. Their students, too, were young men, less imma-
ture and ignorant than college freshmen, and as graduates,
near enough their equals in age to permit the foreign-
trained teachers to look upon them not as boys to be
taught but as junior colleagues. The instructors of graduate students came, indeed, to view themselves as masters
in research rather than schoolmasters. Before a problem
in research the minor differences of age and experience
melted away altogether, and student and professor were
united in the labors and joys of discovery.[14] There was,
in effect, a revival of the medieval conception of the
scholar as both a student and a professor. Within the
community of scholars the distinction between the graduate student and the beginning instructor was blurred,
as both became fellows associated in the task of research.

This development led to the practice of granting graduate fellowships. New in American academic life, this was
at least in part an adaptation of German academic prac-

[14] See Ely, *Ground under Our Feet*, p. 286.

tice. The American graduate fellow was roughly equivalent to the German *Privatdozent*, the aspirant to a professor's chair, who in Germany was required to have the *Dr. phil.* degree before he could teach. American universities could ill afford so strict a requirement; and although the desire to limit fellowships for research to postdoctoral applicants was marked from the beginning,[15] in practice the fellowships went predominantly to those who had not yet obtained the doctorate. The Johns Hopkins University granted twenty such fellowships annually during its early years, and many institutions followed its example. Frequently the fellowships involved both research and teaching duties; and as John Burgess observed, they were intended "to combine the excellences of the English fellowship system and the German Privatdocent system."[16] Invariably they placed a premium on research and on teaching based on research or guaranteed by the teacher's capacity therefor.

When The Johns Hopkins University inaugurated its fellowship program, the move did not meet with universal approbation. In 1883 Harvard's President Eliot protested vigorously against the practice of "paying students to come."[17] David Starr Jordan of Stanford warned that fellowships tended "to turn science into almsgiving,"[18] and Harry Pratt Judson of Chicago described them as "a species of protective tariff on domestic learning."[19] Never-

[15] See AAU, *Proceedings of Second Conference* (Feb., 1901), pp. 38–46.

[16] *Reminiscences*, pp. 199–200.

[17] See G. Stanley Hall, "American Universities and the Training of Teachers," *The Forum*, XVII (March, 1894), 152.

[18] "University Building," *PSM*, LXI (Aug., 1902), 336.

[19] AAU, *Proceedings of Second Conference*, p. 39.

theless the practice spread, spurred on by eager proponents, most of whom looked back upon a year or two in German universities. G. Stanley Hall, for example, expressed the opinion that "a 'fellow' should be the very apple of the eye of the university." [20] Jordan, despite his misgivings, came to recognize the fellowship system as a *fait accompli,* cogently observing that "in a matter of this kind it is not possible for a single institution to stand aloof from its associates," and that to minimize the competitive struggle of universities for fellowship students all that could be done was "to demand an adequate return in laboratory or other assistance from each fellow." [21] Although as late as 1901 contemporaries were still divided on the merits of the fellowship system, in the later judgment of the Johns Hopkins historian, "Probably no expenditure of ten thousand dollars in American education has ever had so large and so enduring a return from the investment." [22] In themselves, of course, fellowships could not assure excellence in either research or teaching. But they could and did open paths for outstanding scholars and teachers.

Perhaps the best-known academic innovation inaugurated by German-trained instructors of graduate students was the seminar. Both an institution and a teaching device, the seminar was first introduced in research departments devoted to language and history. "A limited number of students, whose merits and adequate preparation are

[20] *Ibid.,* p. 43.
[21] "The College and the University," *Science,* n.s., XXVII (April 3, 1908), 533.
[22] John C. French, *A History of the University Founded by Johns Hopkins* (Baltimore, 1946), p. 41.

ascertained, are in the *seminarium* drilled in the manner usual in college lecture-rooms in England, but with the special object of qualifying them for original investigation and for the higher teaching posts," Professor Gildersleeve of Johns Hopkins wrote, quoting from the Owens College Extension Commission.[23] In philological seminars exegesis and textual criticism and the preparation of research papers were to develop the skill in investigation and presentation needed by the future university scholar. In history the same objectives were sought by turning the students loose with original sources, which they were encouraged to analyze and interpret. "As pedagogy," Henry Adams reported from Harvard, "nothing could be more triumphant. The boys worked like rabbits, and dug holes all over the field of archaic society; no difficulty stopped them; unknown languages yielded before their attack, and customary law became familiar as the police court." [24]

The adoption of the seminar method in the social sciences was well-nigh universal. In history Charles Kendall Adams introduced it at Michigan in 1869, and Henry Adams followed at Harvard the next year. At Cornell, it was inaugurated by Moses Coit Tyler, Charles Kendall Adams, and Herbert Tuttle. At Harvard, Ephraim Emerton and Edward Channing continued the path first marked out by Henry Adams, and at Johns Hopkins the historical seminar was inspired by Austin Scott and George Bancroft. John Burgess utilized the seminar method in his School of Political Science at Columbia, and at Harvard

[23] *Essays and Studies: Educational and Literary* (N.Y., 1924), p. 112.

[24] *The Education of Henry Adams* (N.Y., 1931), p. 303.

Edward Channing, Albert B. Hart, Charles Gross, and Archibald C. Coolidge introduced it for the study of government. Henry Carter Adams taught seminar courses in political economy at Cornell and Michigan; F. W. Taussig and Charles Dunbar did so at Harvard. The list could easily be enlarged. There can be no doubt that the seminar as a method and an institution was an integral part of the new graduate education, and that it was due to men who had studied in Europe, and primarily in Germany, or who had been converted to the German ideals by their teachers and colleagues.

Just what the pioneers of the seminar regarded as its superior virtues has been best expressed by Herbert Baxter Adams. First of all, the seminar was unthinkable without a room and a library of its own. Adams' historical seminar collection at Johns Hopkins began with the statistics and archives of the American colonies and states, Congressional journals, and presidential papers. To these were added statutes and parliamentary reports from England, and in 1892 the private collection of the Heidelberg law professor Johann Bluntschli. That these books were moved into a room vacated by the biological laboratory was regarded by Adams as a propitious omen:

The influence of the newly acquired environment had, perhaps, some effect upon the development of the historical seminary. It began to cultivate more and more the laboratory method of work and to treat its book collections as material for laboratory use. The old tables which had once been used for the dissection of cats and turtles were planed down, covered with green baize, and converted into desks for the dissection of government documents and other materials for American institutional history. Instead of cupboards for microscopes, instruments, and apparatus—instead of show-cases for bottled snakes and monkey-skeletons, the visitor now beholds book-cases full of books, pamphlets, manuscripts and coins under glass, a growing museum of prehistoric, Egyptian, and classical art. These collections are frequently used for purposes of historical illustration. The idea that the sources of history are more extensive than all literature, begins to dawn upon the student as he explores the environment of his seminary library which is also a seminary-museum.[25]

Adams' association of the seminar and its library with the museum of a laboratory indicates his eagerness to promote the "scientific" outlook on historical study and research training. "The seminary is still a training-school for doctors of philosophy; but it has evolved from a nursery of dogma [*i.e.*, the *seminarium* of scholastic theology] into a laboratory of scientific truth." Again, "The Baltimore seminaries are laboratories where books are treated like mineralogical specimens, passed about from hand to hand, examined, and tested." [26] The seminar as a teaching method was deliberately modeled after the laboratory approach of the natural sciences. Research was to begin with the detailed examination of physical objects that could be measured, weighed, analyzed, and compared, and thus humanistic and social studies were to become "scientific."

The results of research were then set down in written reports to be discussed in the seminar, and eventually to be presented to fellow scholars elsewhere in the form of dissertations and monographs. In the publication of re-

[25] "Seminary Libraries and University Extension," *JHSt.*, V (1887), 455.

[26] "Methods of Historical Study," *ibid.*, II (1884), 64, 103.

search results, too, the scientific ideal prevailed. New factual knowledge and properly documented data were sought. The emphasis was on the discovery and classification of new materials, and on publication. Monographs thus tended to become catalogues of facts, heavily footnoted, and they were published with ever increasing frequency so as to keep pace with the flood of new facts. Little attention was paid to style or to principles of selection and discrimination. Facts *qua* facts were held to be of equal significance. The shortcomings of this kind of scholarship were later to become obvious. In the judgment of a modern literary scholar,

The enormous possibilities of production, of production in quantities, and of a standardization of the products were aids to victory [for the new scholarship], for bulk in production was an industrial ideal, and the convenient grading of teachers was a practical necessity. The useless antiquarianism, the dreary factualism, the pseudoscience combined with anarchical skepticism and lack of critical taste characteristic of this scholarship must be apparent to almost everybody today.[27]

The continued regular publication of the results of research led to the founding of scholarly and scientific periodicals, once more of the German example, by professional associations, university presses, or university departments. In the past American scholarly journals— beginning with the venerable *Transactions* of the American Philosophical Society founded by Benjamin Franklin in Philadelphia and the *Memoirs* of the American Academy of Arts and Sciences in Boston—had been supported by

[27] René Wellek, "Literary Scholarship," in Merle Curti, ed., *American Scholarship in the Twentieth Century* (Cambridge, 1953), p. 113.

gentleman scholars, scientists, and amateurs, joined together in nonprofessional societies. The new publications became at once more specialized, more rigorous in their adherence to professional standards, and more academic in tone. This at any rate held true for the natural and humanistic studies, and with some qualifications for the social sciences as well. Professor Schurman of Cornell set forth the objectives of the new scholarly periodical literature in the opening editorial of the *Philosophical Review*, written in 1892:

The *Review* will aim at the organization, the diffusion, and the increase of philosophical knowledge and activity in America. It will reflect, in properly classified summaries, the light now scattered throughout the philosophical periodicals of the world; it will present full and critical notices, by recognized experts, of all new books as they appear; it will furnish an arena for the free discussion of philosophical topics or writings; and it will be an organ through which investigators may make known to their fellow-laborers the results of their researches and reflections.[28]

The emphasis on the collection, presentation, and diffusion of research scholarship through periodical literature characterized every academic field. The titles of a few of the more important of these publications will suggest something of their scope, as well as their sponsorship. In 1869 the American Philological Association began issuing its *Transactions*, and the American Social Science Association its *Journal*. The *Transactions of the Modern Language Association* followed in 1884, and two years later the American Historical Association launched its *Papers* and the American Economic Association its *Publications*.

[28] *Philosophical Review*, I (1892), 5–6.

The American Philosophical Association, the American Political Science Association, and the American Sociological Society brought out their respective *Proceedings* in 1902, 1904, and 1906. In 1911 the Association of American Geographers entered the field with its *Annals*. From universities came the *American Journal of Philology* (Johns Hopkins, 1880), the *Political Science Quarterly* (Columbia, 1886), the *Quarterly Journal of Economics* (Harvard, 1886), the *Educational Review* (Columbia, 1891), the *Psychological Review* (Princeton, 1894), and the *American Journal of Theology* (Chicago, 1897). University departments sponsored monograph series of their own, such as the Papers of the American School of Classical Studies at Athens (1882), the Johns Hopkins University Studies in Historical and Political Science (1883), the Harvard Studies in Classical Philology (1890), the Pennsylvania Philosophical Series (1890), and the Columbia Studies in History, Economics, and Public Law (1891). The titles listed here are no more than a selection, typical yet by no means representative of the great variety of scholarly periodicals whose aim was to give to higher learning the professional character it had in Germany.

We have already mentioned the role of the associations in the production of scholarly literature. But this was not their only function. They tended, either deliberately or merely by virtue of their existence, to weaken the claim of a college as the locus of professional identity, and to give the scholar a new *persona* as a practitioner of his discipline. Thus he began to think of himself less as a teacher, and more as a historian, a biologist, or an anthropologist. The associations functioned like guilds in setting standards of admission and performance on a national scale. This was a new departure, since the manifold philosophical, historical, literary, and scientific societies of pre-Civil War America had been open "to those from every walk and station of life who sought admission," and had been largely local in membership and in the character of their work.[29] Now enrolling in a graduate seminar often became the minimum requirement. A doctoral degree was preferable, but best of all was a published contribution to knowledge. The associations, by virtue of their prestige in an age that had come to value specialized competence, came more and more to direct the course of university scholarship and research. They provided a national forum for professional discussions.

Yet the older American tradition of nonspecialized, nonprofessional, gentlemanly study did not disappear altogether, nor was it to be without its effect on the new research scholarship. In the social sciences especially, there were lively debates between academic specialists and interested amateurs, between devotees of research and disciples of various reform causes. When the American Historical Association was founded in 1884, the initiative had been taken by John Eaton and Frank B. Sanborn, who were president and secretary, respectively, of the American Social Science Association, and by Charles Kendall Adams of the University of Michigan, Moses Coit Tyler of Cornell, and Herbert B. Adams of Johns Hopkins. The professed task of the Social Science Association had been, in Sanborn's words, "to discover and amend what

[29] Ralph S. Bates, *Scientific Societies in the United States* (N.Y., 1945), p. 84. On the localism of historical societies see David D. Van Tassel, *Recording America's Past* (Chicago, 1960), esp. ch. 10.

is wrong in the habitual life of men," [30] and it had devoted many, if not most, of its energies to questions of reform. It had supported the reform of the Civil Service and of the administration of criminal justice; the establishment of public libraries and of industrial and nautical schools; the distribution of reproductions of art objects to schools, the publication of a handbook for immigrants, and public health training. It helped bring about the Children's Aid Society of New York, the National Conference of Charities, the National Prison Association, the American Public Health Association, and similar ventures. Eaton and Sanborn welcomed their scholarly colleagues' desire to launch the American Historical Association as a professional group, yet the emphasis they envisioned was bound to be less academic and more practical than what the professors had in mind.

As it turned out, the officers of the old Social Science Association were to be the losers in the controversy. Eaton and Sanborn, holding that "the tendency of scholarship in this country was toward excessive specialization," wanted the Historical Association to be incorporated as a section of the Social Science Association. The professors, spearheaded by Herbert B. Adams, advocated "a national society upon an independent basis." [31] The "independents" won after they had expressed a desire to cooperate fully with the scholars in other branches of social science. Adams became the Association's first secretary and retained that post until ill health forced his resignation in

[30] "The Work of Twenty-Five Years," *Journal of Social Science*, XXVII (Oct., 1890), xlv–xlvi.

[31] H. B. Adams, "Secretary's Report," *Papers of the AHA*, I (1886), 12–15.

1900. "It has never been questioned," J. Franklin Jameson observed in retrospect, "that the main influence in the movement was that of Herbert Adams." [32]

Under Adams' leadership the Association preserved its independent character but slowly came to accept more of the philosophy of the Social Science Association. The change occurred gradually, and can be seen in the changing emphases of Adams' own work. An early exponent of the ideal of German scientific scholarship, and a pioneer of the seminar in history, who in 1883 produced the first volume of the Johns Hopkins University Studies, Adams also emulated the German scholar's direct participation in government to the extent of strongly advocating civil service reform, the founding of a civil service academy, and the incorporation of the American Historical Association by the Congress of the United States. The latter action, which took place in 1889, "tended to place an expert body in the position of adviser to the government in historical matters [and] was no small gain in a democratic country," as Mr. Jameson correctly observed.[33] To Adams the tie between the Association and the government in Washington became for a time a key element of his work. In 1895, when in order to increase the national influence of the Association's work, his colleagues decided to hold their annual meetings at various cities outside of Washington, Adams demurred. But he changed his mind after concluding that America was not Germany, and that scholarship in a democracy could not have the aristocratic pattern of scholarship in the *Reich*. Rather,

[32] "The American Historical Association, 1884–1909," *AHR*, XV (Oct., 1909), 4.
[33] *Ibid.*, 15.

the scholar in America must address himself directly to the people. He must not fear to leave his study or the exclusiveness of his professional organization. Adams' final endorsement of the Association's movement away from Washington was symptomatic of a genuine change of heart, and it was one of which the old Social Science Association members heartily approved.

The American Economic Association had a similar development. What Herbert Adams accomplished for the historians, Richard T. Ely, associate in political economy at Johns Hopkins, achieved for his own field. Ely, who came from a family of reformers, had studied in Germany, and like Adams, he had experienced the tensions between religion and science, between philanthropy and scholarship, and between reform and disinterested research. But unlike Adams he was convinced at the very outset of his career that reform and study should be combined. Science, to Ely, was the fusion of the will to act and the command to study. It was to bring about this union that Ely formed the American Economic Association. His proposals at the first meeting in 1885 drew the fire of the "old" economists, adherents of laissez-faire, who regarded their work as "purely scientific," untouched by any consideration of reform. Ely was forced to accept a compromise, and the Economic Association began its activities with the understanding that historical and statistical studies of actual economic conditions were the province of economic science.

As secretary of the Association Ely had to mediate between the claims of the old and the new, reform-conscious school—not an enviable lot. When in order to emphasize the area of agreement he stressed the scientific character of the Association and its roots in the historical and statistical work of German scholars, Simon Patten retorted that he assumed "too simple a state of affairs. . . . We were not German students but American thinkers that united to form the Association." [34] When he asserted that the Association had been "greeted with enthusiasm precisely because it is not colorless, precisely because it stands for something," [35] members of the old school accused him of trading scholarship for propaganda. Even friends of the new school objected to the Association's "putting excessive stress upon projects for improving economic activities, and often for improvement of activities which were less economic than something else, while they were neglecting the crying fundamental need of probing into the deeper nature of human society, human resources, and human wants." [36]

The Historical and the Economic associations were both caught in the crossfire of scholarship and reform. Research science was the legacy of Germany, reform the heritage of the American Social Science Association. The attempt to fuse German and American traditions marked the development of social science in late-nineteenth-century America. It was in evidence again when the political scientists and the sociologists separated themselves from the Social Science Association. The Political Science Association intended "to advance the scientific study of Politics, Public Law, Administration and Diplo-

[34] Ely, "Recollections on the Life and Work of Professor Simon N. Patten," *American Economic Review,* XIII, Supplement (March, 1923), 261.
[35] *Publications of the AEA,* I (March, 1886), 19.
[36] Albion Small, "Fifty Years," *AJS,* XXI (May, 1916), 768.

macy." This was to be done by encouraging research, by providing annual opportunities for discussion, by aiding the collection of source materials, by publishing important papers, and by bringing together academic teachers and "those who are more immediately responsible for the solution of the many pressing political problems of the day." [37] The American Sociological Society, founded for "the encouragement of sociological research and discussion, and the promotion of intercourse between persons engaged in the scientific study of society," likewise joined research to reform. Through the Society, said Lester Ward, "sociology, established as a pure science," entered "upon its applied stage, which is the great practical object for which it exists." [38] Although the reform activities of scholars in these societies varied with their interests and their philosophical disposition, the ideal of research scholarship united them all. It is not surprising, then, that research scholars of all disciplines made a concerted effort to obtain higher standards for the academic profession.

The scholars who formed these associations were teachers as well as investigators, and they did not banish pedagogical concerns from their discussions. On the contrary, they frequently spoke out on the subject of teaching. It was a committee of the American Historical Association that in 1890 published *The Study of History in Schools*, a document that was to shape the high school history curriculum for over two decades.[39] After asserting

[37] *Proceedings of the APSA*, I (1905), 27, 46.

[38] *Publications of the ASS*, I (1906), 9.

[39] Report to the American Historical Association by the Committee of Seven (N.Y., 1899). See also Arthur S. Bolster, Jr., "History, Historians, and the Secondary School Curriculum," *Harvard Educational Review*, XXXII (Winter, 1962), 40–43.

that secondary education ought to fit boys and girls to become, not scholastics, but men and women who know their surroundings . . . , that the most essential result of secondary education is acquaintance with political and social environment, some appreciation of the nature of the state and society, some sense of the duties and responsibilities of citizenship,

the report acknowledged that "the great majority of schools are not fitting-schools for college." Nevertheless, the report drew up "a scheme of college entrance requirements" as requested by the American Historical Association.[40] The authors of the report considered teaching and research to be two inseparable and complementary aspects of the scholar's work. This was the attitude, also, of the college deans and university presidents who took an active part in the associations of professional educators. In 1896 Nicholas Murray Butler of Columbia, and in 1903 Charles William Eliot of Harvard, as presidents of the National Education Association, argued that high school teachers were members of the same genus as university professors. These noted educators saw nothing provincial or parochial in problems of secondary school administration, nor were they ready to sacrifice either college or high school teaching on the altar of research and professional training. In their concern for teaching they were likewise against segregating the graduate schools in some region beyond the yard, the quadrangle, or the campus, to lead a life of academic seclusion. They recognized that the whole process of education was one, that teaching and research as well as the different levels of education were all closely interrelated.

As specialization progressed the number of associations

[40] *The Study of History*, pp. 17, 121, v.

47

was augmented by those of teachers and administrators at various institutional levels. In the area of graduate education this step was marked by the founding in 1900 of the Association of American Universities, which was called into being by the presidents of Harvard, Columbia, Johns Hopkins, and the universities of Chicago and California. In addition to these institutions, the Catholic University, Clark, Cornell, Stanford, Princeton, Yale, and the universities of Michigan, Pennsylvania, and Wisconsin became charter members of the Association. Their initial concern was "to protect the dignity of our Doctor's degree." [41] The members thus proposed to adopt uniform standards, by means of which they would not only improve the international reputation of American universities, but also raise the level of collegiate studies at home. At their fifth meeting the delegates turned to the relation of the undergraduate colleges to the graduate schools. Most of the scholars present agreed that the college and the university graduate and professional schools were two stages of one institution. As David Starr Jordan put it, "The university furnishes the college its inspiration; the college furnishes the university its life." [42] Professional training, although pre-eminently the task of the university, was not to be excluded entirely from the college. President Eliot argued forcefully that a truly liberal education could not exist in a vacuum. The student was to be a citizen, and it was as such that he prepared for his life's work. His professional interests made his collegiate studies meaningful and could not arbitrarily be separated from them. The discussions reflected a desire to weld together the

[41] AAU, *Journal of Proceedings and Addresses* (1901), pp. 11, 38.
[42] *Ibid.* (1904), p. 29.

new research-minded professional instruction with the collegiate tradition of a liberal education. The educational statesmen assembled at these meetings wanted to avoid the exclusively professional-technical cast of German higher education, while they hoped to revive in America the German ideal of the *libertas philosophandi* through a mutual interpenetration of the professional temper of graduate education with the ideal of a liberal arts education. The German graduate school and the American college were each to offer its most cherished traditions to the other.

The attempt to relate the old-time American college to the new, German-inspired graduate schools thus brought about a movement for college reform. From the new graduate schools at Johns Hopkins, Clark, Catholic University, and Chicago; from the graduate departments of such long-established colleges as Harvard, Yale, and Columbia; and from the midwestern and western state universities came an impetus that was to shake the undergraduate colleges to their foundations. Organized facilities for graduate instruction and training in research might be set up in separate buildings and be independently administered. But the "university idea" leaped over ivied walls and across dividing lanes to challenge the traditions of the college itself. What, after all, was a college? the German-inspired professors asked. Was it a *gymnasium?* That was what its enforced general education would make it; and if so, it would be better to call it by name. A university it certainly was not—or at any rate not yet. Young men fired by a new idea can be headstrong and impatient. "I confess," wrote John W. Burgess, "that I am unable to divine what is to be ultimately the position of the Colleges which cannot become Universities and which will not be Gymnasia. I cannot see what reason they will have to exist." [43] With the onset of German-style graduate education in the America of the 1870's the college was challenged to take stock of itself. The whole weight of the German-inspired university problem fell on the college. To build universities meant in fact to reform the colleges. And with this reference to the subject of college reform we shall bring this chapter to a close.[44]

It will be remembered that President Porter had expressed his skepticism concerning the desirability or even the possibility of admitting German ideals of professional education and academic freedom to the colleges. His colleagues Jordan and Eliot not only endorsed the German ideals, but thought it neither wise nor fruitful to draw a sharp dividing line between college and graduate school. They agreed with the Germans that research, training for research, and teaching in the spirit of the liberal arts and the *libertas philosophandi* were indissoluble. The academic profession as they defined it owed its existence to the fusion of research and teaching, of discipline and freedom, of vocational instruction and liberal education. The history of American higher education bears out the contention of Jordan, Eliot, and the German-trained scholars. But it also shows how wide a gulf may yawn between ideal and actuality. That professional education in practice may be no more than a glorified vocationalism, the Ameri-

[43] *The American University*, p. 5.
[44] For a discussion of college reform see my article, "Liberal Education and the Graduate Schools: An Historical View of College Reform," *History of Education Quarterly*, II (Dec., 1962), 244–258.

can students had already observed in Germany; thus President Porter's hesitation was not unjustified. Later chapters will consider in greater detail the ambiguities of the German influence on the professional education of social scientists in America.

3

German Wissenschaft
and American Philosophy

If the worst side of the American college is the philosophical, its best is the scientific department.

—G. STANLEY HALL, 1879

RICHARD T. ELY once said that he went to Germany with visions of finding "the absolute truth" of the philosophers, only to discover that what he had learned was simply "to look and see." Instead of Truth, he had found the scientific methodology of observation, experiment, and induction.[1] The discrepancy revealed by Ely's remark may be partly explained in historical terms. As the nineteenth century drew to a close the Germany of the philosophers had given way to that of the scientists. The increasing importance of research, and the transformation of Germany's universities from centers of teaching into laboratories of investigation, had contributed to this change. American students were both fascinated and alarmed by the process as they witnessed it, but they nevertheless proceeded to set it in motion at home. This chapter will describe the changing methodological as-

[1] *Ground under Our Feet* (New York, 1938), pp. 40–41.

sumptions of nineteenth-century German scholarship, and indicate how the rising prestige of *Wissenschaft* affected the teaching of philosophy in American colleges.

The flowering of German scholarship in the nineteenth century had been the result of converging methodological traditions in philosophical, historical, and scientific inquiry. It received its first impetus from the philosophy of Immanuel Kant, whose major contribution had been to differentiate the real world from the realm of phenomena, and to give an *a priori* demonstration of the underlying rationality of the universe. The rational nature of the real world was to be known intuitively and to be proved by logical analysis. Man could gain an understanding of the phenomenal world through empirical study, and could test that understanding by the strict application of logical analysis to his observations. This rational approach to the "real" and the "phenomenal" became known as the critical method. When exponents of orthodox Protestantism at the Prussian universities of Halle and Berlin accepted the rational philosophy, they assured the continuance of the critical spirit in German philosophical scholarship along with a relative freedom from religious attack and a reliance on rational methods of inquiry.[2]

However, the critical method of the philosophers was only one of several that existed side by side. The classicists and linguists had developed a rigorous canon of historical inquiry into the origin of words and concepts, and of comparative philology. The analysis of language became the key to an understanding of history and culture, and

[2] Cf. Max Lenz, *Geschichte der Königlichen Friedrich-Wilhelms Universität zu Berlin* (Halle, 1910), I, 17–18.

the study of literature to an understanding of human motives. Training in the methods of philology became indispensable for historians and theologians. While textual analysis—known among biblical scholars as the lower criticism—was regarded as strictly empirical, the work of interpretation, or the higher criticism, demanded an awareness of the author's purpose, such as was to be gained through the historical study of literature. The methods of the philologist thus ushered in the vogue of biblical and historical criticism, which in turn gave rise to the historical schools in economics and politics.

At the end of the eighteenth century the concept of *Geisteswissenschaft* sprang from the convergence of the methods of philosophical, philological, and historical criticism. It encouraged German scholars to go beyond factual research and rational analysis, and led to the hypothesis of the fundamental unity of all branches of knowledge. To discover the common characteristics of historical phenomena, to formulate the laws governing them, and in a supreme effort of ratiocination to abstract from these data and laws the underlying reality of the cosmos, became the exalted task of speculative philosophy. Even natural scientists paid homage to this philosophical concept. Baconian empiricism and Newtonian mechanism did not prevent them from arranging their data under some comprehensive scheme of natural philosophy. Such a scheme granted that the mechanism of cause and effect might be reconciled with the assumption of a teleological world order; thus Schelling, the foremost German natural philosopher, defined nature as unconscious reason in the process of becoming, struggling to gain consciousness of itself.[3] Within the realm of *Geisteswissenschaft* proper, the crowning masterpiece is to be found in Hegel's philosophy of history. Here concrete historical data, and Reason as the essence of history, were fused in a single imposing system. In their methodology the German speculative philosophers steered a precarious course between reliance on verifiable facts and the postulation of governing principles, between the claims of human reason to self-sufficiency and the demands of traditional piety for the recognition of a divine purpose in history. Kant had separated reality from appearance and had distinguished between intuitive and empirical knowledge; his successors now sought to reassert the unity of all things by means of speculative philosophy.

By 1815, however, the continental European revolt against speculative philosophy was in the air. It began in the natural sciences, with the repudiation of natural philosophy. The German chemist Wöhler's synthesis, in 1828, of an organic compound from inorganic substances, was symbolic of the tendency.[4] From then on, natural scientists hesitated to speculate about the relation between the organic and the inorganic, or about the nature of the universe, and preferred to seek the answers to their problems in laboratory research. In the social sciences the historical school of the nineteenth century led the reaction against the pretensions of speculative philosophy in favor of empirical investigation, verification, and induction.

[3] See Wilhelm Windelband, *Die Geschichte der Neueren Philosophie* (Leipzig, 1911), I, 299–319; II, 252.

[4] See John T. Merz, *A History of European Thought in the Nineteenth Century* (Edinburgh, 1896), I, 188–192.

Just as the *Naturwissenschaften* came to depend on empirical research and, eventually, upon logical-mathematical analysis, the *Geisteswissenschaften* depended upon the methods of historical and rational criticism. In the universities these scholarly procedures gradually removed the last vestiges of speculative philosophy and *Naturphilosophie*. The modern age of scholarship, dated by Rudolph von Virchow from the return of Alexander von Humboldt to Prussia in 1827, followed by the death of Hegel in 1831, was to be dominated by empirical research and by the use of logic and mathematics in the analysis of data.[5] During the second half of the century the same methods were applied to social science. The "philosophic age" receded into history; the "scientific age" had arrived.

The scientific spirit, rather than speculative inquiry into the nature of truth, had come to shape the American students' concept of a *Wissenschaft* imbued with a concern for human motives and purposes, as embodied in the higher criticism in philology, biblical scholarship, and historical inquiry. This balanced concern for both scientific facts and human values appealed to the students in American colleges. The old-time college curriculum had placed a premium on accurate and detailed knowledge of facts, and on a retentive memory; its moral philosophy course, on the other hand, had been concerned with values. The German universities with their *Wissen-*

---

[5] "The Founding of the Berlin University and the Transition from the Philosophic to the Scientific Age," *Annual Report of the Board of Regents of the Smithsonian Institution . . . to July 1894* (Washington, 1896), pp. 681–695.

schaft did likewise; but they had gone on to make factual studies "scientific," and to embrace a moral philosophy far more comprehensive than that taught in the denominational colleges.

How, then, did the ideals of *Wissenschaft* affect the teaching of philosophy in American colleges? In moral philosophy—the division which is all the more fittingly our main concern since in its heterogeneous subject matter it was the precursor of the social sciences [6]—by 1820 the colleges had adopted the deistic heritage of the Enlightenment. The Newtonian alliance of experience with reason, and the rational ethics of deism provided the philosophical background for class discussions. The mechanistic Newtonian universe, set in motion by Paley's "watchmaker" God, gave sanction to a system of ethics in which actions were evaluated according to their consequences. However, although rationalism, deism, and utilitarian ethics were familiar concepts to American college men, they received only qualified acceptance. The clergymen who served as college presidents and moral philosophers saw rationalism as dangerously close to materialism, deism as smacking of "French infidelity," and utilitarianism as insufficiently attentive to the place of "good will" in ethical considerations. The moral philosophers, intent upon character training and committed to Protestant Christianity, thus looked for more nourishing fare.

[6] See Gladys Bryson, "The Emergence of the Social Sciences from Moral Philosophy," *International Journal of Ethics*, XLII (April, 1932), 304–323; "The Comparable Interests of the Old Moral Philosophy and the Modern Social Sciences," *Social Forces*, XI (Oct., 1932), 19–27, and "Sociology Considered as Moral Philosophy," *Sociological Review*, XXIV (Jan., 1932), 26–36.

They found it in the common-sense realism of the Scottish philosophers Francis Hutcheson, Thomas Reid, Dugald Stewart, and Adam Ferguson. This philosophy had arisen in the Scottish universities of the eighteenth century, and was a direct reaction to the skepticism of Hume, the materialism of the Enlightenment, and the rationalism of the deists. Its originators had rejected the traditional philosophic debate between realists and idealists as irrelevant to the actual problems of daily life. Viewing man and the objects that impinge upon his consciousness as given and real, the Scottish realists sought to isolate empirically the indivisible elements of nature, which they assumed to be indubitably present and to be subject to simple natural laws. Analogous to these simple patterns in the natural world there were, they believed, equally simple and definable rules for the conduct of human affairs. Natural science would discover the laws of nature; psychology would help to define the rules of human conduct.

The Scottish realists were moralists at heart. "Right ethical relationships were not only the ultimate but the immediate desiderata of their study." [7] They believed that a sure knowledge of good and evil, supplementary to that given in revelation, could be obtained independently through science and philosophy. To them "moral science" was not a threat to revelation. They sought to rejuvenate the theology of the Scottish Kirk by empirical observation of the human consciousness, as well as by the intuitive reliance on an innate moral sense, and regarded as self-

[7] Gladys Bryson, *Man and Society* (Princeton, 1945), p. 244.

evident the existence of moral laws. These moral laws, although they existed *a priori*, were also empirically verifiable.[8]

What attracted the American college moral philosopher to the Scottish philosophy was that it served as a bulwark in defense of religion. Its appeal to common sense made it easy to teach—and therefore all the more attractive, no doubt, to busy college presidents. It lent itself equally to any of the Protestant denominations that had established colleges in the United States.[9] Philosophically, its insistence on the dichotomy between subject and object implied a logical rejection of both pantheistic and materialist monism and upheld the authority of revelation. While its reliance on experience and reason carried on the heritage of the Enlightenment, the one thing needful had been added: it allowed for the demands of revealed religion.[10]

With the widespread use in American colleges of Francis Wayland's *Elements of Moral Science* (Boston, 1835) as the textbook for the moral philosophy course, the Scottish philosophy became dominant. Aiming to be "simple, clear, and purely didactic," Wayland's intuitive ethics stressed conscience, duty, and intentions, in place of Paley's ethics of prudence and Locke's emphasis on the consequences of

[8] Cf. James McCosh, "The Scottish Philosophy as Contrasted with the German," *Princeton Review*, July, 1882, p. 333.

[9] Woodbridge Riley, *American Thought from Puritanism to Pragmatism and Beyond* (N.Y., 1923), pp. 118–122, and Henry A. Pochmann, *German Culture in America, 1600–1900* (Madison, 1957), p. 661.

[10] Cf. Wilson Smith, *Professors and Public Ethics* (Ithaca, 1956), pp. 36–43.

actions as the criteria for moral judgment. From the 1830's into the 1880's the Scottish philosophy continued to dominate in American colleges. At Harvard (where it had already been taught by Levi Hedge from 1795 to 1832), James Walker from 1839 to 1860, and Francis Bowen from 1853 to 1889, were its exponents. Francis Wayland himself taught at Brown until 1855; at Yale, Noah Porter was active until 1892, and at Princeton, James McCosh—the leading American exponent of common-sense realism—until 1888.

Scottish realism did more, however, than provide a scholarly philosophy acceptable to the pillars of religious orthodoxy. Its emphasis on empirical observation of consciousness also stimulated scientific investigation, in the particular form of psychology. Whereas the philosophers of the Enlightenment had proclaimed the equal validity of natural and moral laws, and the Scottish realists had aimed at the elucidation of a "moral science," American professors and churchmen saw to it that both natural and moral science were subordinated to revealed religion. Nevertheless the framework of denominational theology and moral philosophy allowed room for empirical investigation. Introspection and observation were regarded as the tools of the common-sense realists. Even outside the classroom, the unsophisticated methods of the Scottish school found ready acceptance in a society eager for practical application of scientific inquiry in any form. Although it is true, as Herbert Schneider has suggested, that religious orthodoxy blighted the scientific endeavors of the common-sense school in America, the empirical-logical methods advocated by it also helped prepare the ground for the work, after the Civil War, of Joseph Henry, Willard Gibbs, and Charles S. Peirce.[11] Despite the hostility of orthodox clergymen and professors, natural science survived and even developed under the shadow of denominational supervision.

Besides being compatible with religion and science, the Scottish philosophy in America proved to be a handy—if not especially keen—weapon to be brandished against the gathering forces of German speculative idealism and native transcendentalism, especially as these, fortified by Continental "higher criticism," appeared to threaten traditional religion. Doctrinally the orthodox champions of the common-sense philosophy retreated into the stronghold of facts and reason, which they regarded as the only true support of revelation. From their position they assailed religious emotionalism on the one hand, and the "profanities" of historical criticism on the other. They condemned the preoccupation of German critical philosophers with "phenomena"—rather than with "facts"—as scientifically unsound and conducive to agnosticism.[12] Nurtured on "indubitable facts," Francis Bowen of Harvard brushed away the "German mania" of speculative philosophy as "sheer midsummer madness." [13] American common-sense philosophers in general had no love for German speculative philosophy, and those who knew anything of German scholarship took their stand with the representatives of the "scientific age."

[11] See Herbert W. Schneider, A History of American Philosophy (N.Y., 1946), p. 247, and Harvey G. Townsend, Philosophical Ideas in the United States (N.Y., 1934), pp. 96–98.

[12] See James McCosh, "The Scottish Philosophy," p. 339.

[13] "Locke and the Transcendentalists," Christian Examiner, XXIII (Nov., 1837), 175.

What was most important about the Scottish philosophy was that it provided a basis for the moralism so characteristic of the nineteenth-century American reform movements. Duty, perceived intuitively and without consideration of the consequences, was regarded as the motive force in the individual's commitment to improving the public weal. The refusal to separate the sphere of private morality from that of public duty was typical of the Scottish moral philosophy and its uncompromising code of civic responsibility. "The moral philosophers earnestly believed and taught that moral purity in a man's intentions determined the morality of his public actions." [14] The supreme authority, for them, lay in the voice of the individual conscience, which thus determined the actions of society. It was the concept of individual responsibility for public events that distinguished Scottish moral philosophy from the utilitarianism of Paley, and the college moralists from the transcendentalist followers of Emerson and Thoreau. Moral philosophers could see no use for transcendentalism, since it was normative for lone individuals and could not be accommodated to serve the pious orthodoxy of middle-class society.[15] The concept of the individual's moral obligation to society, which replaced the mechanistic philosophy of Newton and Locke, remained a potent force in American ethical thinking throughout the nineteenth century.

This concept, which called for reform within the framework of denominational religion, gave instruction in moral philosophy a dynamic inner tension, which kept it lively but at the same time served as an invitation to other

[14] Smith, *Professors*, p. 4.   [15] *Ibid.*, pp. 190–193.

systems of thought. In the area of strictly religious teaching, the challenge of the new thought proved fatal. Put on the defensive, orthodox college professors sought to smother new ideas, and "made traditional doctrine so lifeless and static that a new theological turn was virtually inevitable." [16] But while orthodox denominational instruction suffered a mortal blow, the clash of opposing ethical systems lent vitality to the moral temper of much college teaching.

The common-sense philosophy, not unlike the early-nineteenth-century *Geisteswissenschaft,* relied on and sought to harmonize reason, intuition, and experience as sources of knowledge, while maintaining that none of these in itself could constitute a guarantee of revealed truth. In nineteenth-century America rational theology led to Unitarianism, and intuitive religion to transcendentalism, both of which drew upon the data of experience. When such moral philosophers as Nathaniel W. Taylor of Yale and President Walker of Harvard deserted orthodox Calvinism in favor of Unitarianism, the Calvinists could not but despair. The Unitarian emphasis on reason and introspection was bound to concentrate attention on man rather than God. As Albion Small later put it, theology, "the science of the character and purpose of God," was slowly being replaced by a science "of God's image, or the science of human welfare." [17] In this guise the "moral science" gained a new lease on life.

The Unitarians, confronted in their turn with the heresy

[16] Sydney E. Ahlstrom, "The Scottish Philosophy and American Theology," *Church History,* XXIV (Sept., 1955), 269.

[17] "Religion and Higher Education," *The Watchman* (Oct. 10, 1889), p. 1.

of the transcendentalists, managed for a time to keep the new doctrine of natural revelation and of the humanity of Christ out of the college classrooms. They were profoundly shocked by Emerson's Harvard Divinity School address in 1838, in which the sage of the transcendentalists told his audience:

Whilst the doors of the temple stand open, night and day, before every man, and the oracles of this truth cease never, it is guarded by one stern condition; this namely, it is an intuition. It cannot be received at second hand . . . . The stationariness of religion; the assumption that the age of inspiration is past, that the Bible is closed; the fear of degrading the character of Jesus by representing him as a man; indicate with sufficient clearness the falsehood of our theology.[18]

Such was the boldness of this attack that the transcendentalist message became anathema for church and college alike. Emerson was not invited to speak at Harvard again until 1865, and it was not until 1869, upon the initiative of the new president, Charles William Eliot, that Emerson was asked to teach a graduate course on "The Natural History of the Intellect." Only then were the students allowed to hear Emerson's criticism of the "pale negations of Boston Unitarianism."

Toward Hegelianism the American college was initially as inhospitable as it was toward transcendentalism. With one exception—the teaching of President Frederick A. Rauch at Marshall College, Mercersburg, Pennsylvania, from 1836 to 1841—Hegelian idealism did not take root in American colleges. Its most notable flowering was in

[18] "An Address," *The Complete Essays and Other Writings of Ralph Waldo Emerson* (N.Y., 1950), pp. 71, 80.

St. Louis at the meetings of a discussion group of educators and politicians. It was not until the 1870's that it found its way into the universities, and then chiefly as a system of social thought. What differentiated Hegel's social philosophy from the common-sense school, as well as from transcendentalism, was the value it assigned to the group as contrasted with the individual. As a system of ethics it supplemented the individualism of Locke, and prepared the ground for collectivistic theories in politics, sociology, and economics. The editors of the *Journal of Speculative Philosophy* explained the new departure thus:

The idea underlying our form of government had hitherto developed only one of its essential phases—that of brittle individualism. . . . Now we have arrived at the consciousness of the other essential phase, and each individual recognizes his substantial side to be the State as such.[19]

The appearance of Hegelian social thought in the colleges was connected with the resurgence of nationalist sentiments during and after the Civil War. It coincided with the disappearance of moral philosophy into the emerging separate disciplines of history, political science, political economy, and sociology.

During the sixties and seventies Julius H. Seelye impressed upon his students in the moral philosophy course at Amherst that history was "the grandest study in the world." Just as did moral philosophy, it comprehended every human activity and furnished insight into man's nature as both a moral and a social being.[20] George Bancroft, by 1886 the dean of American historians, was en-

[19] Vol. I (1867), p. 1.

[20] See Herbert B. Adams, "History in American Colleges," *Education*, VII (Oct., Nov., 1886), 94, 180.

dorsing this proposition; historians, he told the American Historical Association, were "nearest of kin to the students of moral philosophy.[21] To view and to evaluate man as a member of a group rather than as an individual invited reliance on a nonindividualistic philosophy such as was offered by the Hegelians. Once the post-Civil War migration to German universities had begun, the results were soon evident. John W. Burgess, a former student of Seelye, earned the nickname "Weltgeist" by telling his Amherst students that the state, "the *ultima Thule* of political history," was "the human organ least likely to do wrong." [22] The economist Richard T. Ely taught "that it is a grand thing to serve God in the State which he in his beneficent wisdom instituted, and that to betray a trust in the divine State is as heinous an offence as to be false to duty in the divine Church." [23] At Chicago the sociologist Albion Small demonstrated the applicability of the Hegelian dialectic to social and intellectual history: "Conventionality, [*i.e.*, laissez-faire individualism] is the thesis, Socialism is the antithesis, Sociology is the synthesis." [24] In the hands of such teachers the Hegelian dialectic explained and superseded individualistic moral philosophy, ushering in a more socially minded instruction in ethics, which was advanced by the new disciplines of social science.

[21] "Self-Government," *Papers of the AHA*, II (1888), 7.

[22] See Thomas Le Duc, *Piety and Intellect at Amherst College* (N.Y., 1946), p. 53; Burgess, *Reminiscences of an American Scholar* (N.Y., 1934), p. 254, and *Political Science and Comparative Constitutional Law* (Boston, 1890), I, 57.

[23] "Co-operation in Literature and the State," in William E. Barns, ed., *The Labor Problem* (N.Y., 1886), p. 16.

[24] Small and Vincent, *An Introduction to the Study of Society* (N.Y., 1894), p. 41.

The emphasis on the group rather than on the individual, on social science rather than on moral philosophy, was further strengthened by the appearance of Darwinian thought. As one student remarked, Darwinism, like Hegelianism, "implied a shift of emphasis from the individual to the group or species." [25] This was not, of course, a foregone conclusion. Natural selection and survival of the fittest could be applied to individuals as well as to groups. Herbert Spencer and his American disciple, William Graham Sumner, treated sociology as a modern, scientific corroboration of laissez-faire individualism. In the hands of devout college professors, evolution became the vehicle of a beneficent Providence that ruled the world by the law of love. Against a background of nationalism and Hegelianism, the doctrine of the struggle for survival applied to the emergence of national states became an argument for the inevitable rightness of the outcome. Darwinian thought thus could and did take either an individualistic or a collectivistic form. In either instance it relied upon the prestige of natural science, and foreshadowed a new evolutionary ethics.

Science now claimed a place in the curriculum equal to that of philosophy. The psychological observations of the Scottish school, the inductive logic of John Stuart Mill, the work of Darwin in natural science and of Comte in social science all contributed to the rising prestige of empirical studies. This prestige was transferred with little hesitation to the great systematizers, who had based their theories on what they saw as empirically verified facts.

[25] David F. Bowers, "Hegel, Darwin, and the American Tradition," in Bowers, ed., *Foreign Influences in American Life* (Princeton, 1944), p. 158.

In the place of Hutcheson, Reid, Stewart, Ferguson, Paley, Locke, Wayland, and McCosh—philosophers all—the new guiding minds became those of men like Hegel, the philosopher-historian; Pfleidererer, the theologian; Wundt, the psychologist; Darwin, the naturalist; Comte and Spencer, the sociologists; and Herbart, the pedagogue. The change, to be sure, was not abrupt. Advocates of the old and the new schools taught side by side, and more often than not offered a mixture of philosophical doctrines. Eclecticism was rampant, and G. Stanley Hall's 1879 description of philosophical instruction at American colleges may be accepted as reasonably accurate:

Some of the professorlings of philosophy are disciples of disciples of Hopkins, Hickok, Wayland, Upham, Haven. Most have extended their philosophical horizon as far as Reid, Stewart, Hamilton. Many have read Mill's *Examination of Hamilton*, chapters of Herbert Spencer, lectures of Huxley and Tyndall, and epitomes of Kant, Berkeley, Hegel, and Hume. Others, fewer in number, have studied compendious histories of philosophy like Schwegler and Ueberweg, have read Mill's *Logic* and Taine, have dipped into Kant's *Critique*, and have themselves printed essays on Spencer, Leibnitz, Plato, etc., in religious periodicals, have perhaps published compilations on mental or moral science, and are able to aid the sale of small editions of their works by introducing them into their own classes as text-books. Others, fewer yet, . . . have had thorough training, and are doing valuable and original work.[26]

The "valuable and original work" to which Hall refers was that of the laboratory investigator. Quite obviously the

[26] "Philosophy in the United States," *Mind*, IV (Jan., 1879), 90–91.

devotees of science, Hall among them, were not content to share the limelight with the philosophers, but aimed to make science the crowning subject of the academic curriculum.

It was in connection with the claim of science to leadership within the colleges that the impact of the German university on American academic life made itself felt with all its force. Four New England men—Ticknor, Everett, Cogswell, and Bancroft—had introduced German thought to Boston intellectuals. Kant's and Hegel's philosophies were understood by few, and were taught in the colleges, if at all, as moral or political doctrine. As the eighties drew to a close, German philosophy, without ever having found a real home in the American college, began to recede in importance before the new scientific outlook that had captured the universities of Europe. "It was no mere coincidence," writes Pochmann, "that the Plato club, the American Academe [both of Jacksonville, Ill.], the Philosophical Society [of St. Louis], the Concord School, the *Journal of Speculative Philosophy*, the *Journal of the American Akademe*, and the *Bibliotheca Platonica* all came to an end within the short period of five years (1887–1892)." [27] Indeed, the scientific empiricism of German scholarship took on increasing importance. The German critical methods in theology and history, and the German laboratory science, that had invaded American colleges, could be grafted upon the Lockean empirical tradition and upon the *a posteriori* methodology of the Scottish school. In short, one could teach history or government as an

[27] Pochmann, *German Culture*, p. 302.

empirical, inductive study without necessarily endorsing the Hegelian *Geschichtsphilosophie.*

Although it cannot positively be said that German science stamped out the teaching of moral philosophy, there is no doubt that the scientific spirit of Germany's universities helped bring about its demise. Moral philosophy as taught in American colleges was a hodgepodge of doctrines and subjects, held together by a prevailing ethical concern. German scholarship insisted on rigorously defined, specialized subject matter, taught by experts trained in investigation. It called for the division of the field of moral philosophy into what were to be known as the social sciences. Philosophy itself had to become a distinct field and as *Wissenschaft* had to untie itself from the apron-strings of religion. Science was to be both specialized and objective—that is, devoid of all non-scientific assumptions and concepts. The questions traditionally raised in the moral philosophy course were to be answered more competently, because more scientifically, within the newly specialized departments of philosophy, psychology, religion, history, government, political economy, and sociology. Thus science, pursued in its various divisions, was expected to become the arbiter in problems of ethics.

4

German Theological Science and American Religion

> All untrammeled scientific investigation, no matter how dangerous to religion some of its stages may have seemed, for the time, to be, has invariably resulted in the highest good of religion and of science.
>
> —ANDREW D. WHITE, 1875

WHEN President White of Cornell University, in his Cooper Institute lecture, "The Battle-Fields of Science," delivered himself of the sanguine opinion quoted above, he hoped to end forever the attacks of orthodox zealots against nonsectarian scientific teaching at Cornell.[1] It was widely held that science subverted the truth of Scripture, and that evolution contradicted the biblical story of creation. But science, White maintained, had no such intent and led to no such results. Nature and man both were God's creations, and the scientific study of nature and man only led to a deeper understanding of the work of God. There could be no different and con-

[1] *The Autobiography of Andrew D. White*, I (London, 1905), 425.

tradictory accounts of the creation. White went on, in the best tradition of the Scottish common-sense philosophy and of faculty psychology:

God's truths must agree, whether discovered by looking within upon the soul, or without upon the world. A truth written upon the human heart to-day, in its full play of emotions or passions, cannot be at any real variance even with a truth written upon a fossil whose poor life ebbed forth millions of years ago. This being so, it would also seem a truth irrefragable, that the search for each of these kinds of truth must be followed out on its own lines, by its own methods, to its own results, without any interference from investigators on other lines, or by other methods. And it would also seem logical to work on in absolute confidence that whatever, at any moment, may seem to be the relative positions of the two different bands of workers, they must at last come together, for Truth is one.[2]

White, in his optimism, had oversimplified the problem. If we are to take at all seriously the aims both of the Scottish common-sense philosophy and of the scientific methodology of the German seminars and laboratories, we must begin by admitting that the claims of science were far greater than White's remarks would suggest. The methodology of scientific observation and induction was to be applied to all subject matter, not excepting religion itself. For White as president of a nonsectarian university the problem implicit here did not arise, simply because religion was not taught as an academic subject in the undergraduate college. But matters were far different in the theological seminaries and divinity schools of the United States. Here the claims of science as the only al-

[2] *The Warfare of Science* (N.Y., 1876), pp. 8–9.

lowable methodology, added to the results obtained by an empirical study of religious phenomena, produced a revolution. Here the threat of the "infidel" was not indifference to religion due to a fascination with science; rather, it was a direct attack on inherited doctrines by "scientifically" trained professors of religion. The invasion of the training grounds of the Protestant ministry in America by the scientific approach to religion, and what that approach owed to the influence of German teaching and scholarship, will be the subject of this chapter.

Of the scholars mentioned in the preceding chapters, George Bancroft gave possibly the fullest and most far-sighted estimates of early-nineteenth-century German theology. In Göttingen in 1819 he found the professors of theology—particularly J. G. Eichhorn, the Old Testament critic—steeped in what he saw as rationalist atheism. "I have nothing to do with it," Bancroft assured President Kirkland of Harvard. The Göttingen theologians, he reported,

form a very peculiar body. They have no idea of the sublimity or sanctity of their science. 'Tis reduced to a mere matter of learning. I never heard anything like moral or religious feeling manifested in their theological lectures. They neither begin with God nor go on with him, and there is a great deal more religion in a few lines of Xenophon, than in a whole course of Eichhorn. Nay, the only classes, in which I have heard jests so vulgar and indecent, that they would have disgraced a jail-yard or a fishmarket, have been the theological ones. The bible is treated with very little respect, and the narratives are laughed at as an old wife's tale, fit to be believed in the nursery.[3]

[3] Quoted in Orie W. Long, *Literary Pioneers* (Cambridge, 1935), pp. 115, 120–121.

Yet once the initial shock was over, Bancroft learned to appreciate the critical method and piety of the German theologians. He exempted from his censure the work of his teachers "in so far as it is merely *critical.*" In fact, he became so enamored of the biblical critics that he thought of devoting his life to "raising among us [in America] a degraded and neglected branch of study, which in itself is so noble, and to aid in establishing a thorough school of Theological Critics." Although Bancroft never carried out this plan, a lasting appreciation of critical philological and historical studies had been aroused—despite his bitter scorn for the rationalists at Göttingen. He deplored their bad manners; he found them dull and trite in conversation and degraded by love of money. At Berlin, however, things were better. Here it was Schleiermacher above all who awoke his unstinting praise:

Language flows from his lips most fluently and uninterruptedly. He is the best extempore speaker I have ever heard. . . . In the pulpit his whole appearance is full of dignity. . . . I honour Schleiermacher above all the German scholars with whom it has been my lot to become acquainted.[4]

As a background for Bancroft's comments, a brief glance at German biblical criticism is in order here. The German critics were concerned with God's word as given to them in Scripture. They dealt with the Bible as literature, and took as their starting point the grammatical and philological analysis of the text. They hoped to arrive at the original wording, and in order to do so it was necessary to detect the errors of copyists and the accretions of later authors. Careful attention to the rules of grammar and

[4] *Ibid.,* pp. 115, 114, 120, 132–133.

syntax made it possible to clarify disputed texts and to establish the exact wording of the original. All this was the work of the lower critics. The higher critics, utilizing historical rather than philological criticism, then applied the findings of literary and historical scholars to an interpretation of the biblical text.[5]

The program of these biblical critics was based on the assumptions of eighteenth-century neology—namely, that since reason could be applied to revelation, a biblical word could be given a new meaning as a result of rational analysis. The neologists shared the hope of Enlightenment thinkers that proper methods of study would make the truth known. Their primary concern was with method rather than with philosophy. Nevertheless they were frequently understood to have denied altogether the authority of revelation, and to have replaced the God of revelation with a God of reason. This was Bancroft's charge against the Göttingen professors. However, although as scholars the neologists and other biblical critics were not concerned with theological systems, as individuals they subscribed to varying beliefs. They agreed in affirming simply that the truth about the Christian faith could be obtained only through a study of the Bible as a historical and literary document.

Such was the program of the biblical critics which Bancroft came to accept so long as it was "merely critical." The higher criticism, which he enthusiastically endorsed as he encountered it in the teaching and preaching of Schleiermacher, fused philological analysis with textual interpretation in an investigation of the lives and pur-

[5] Cf. George B. Gray and Francis C. Burkitt, in *Encyclopaedia Britannica*, 11th ed. (Cambridge, 1910), III, 857–865, 886–887.

poses of the biblical authors. For these critics the problem was no longer Who was Jesus? or What did the biblical authors actually write? Rather, it became the nature of Jesus as portrayed by Matthew, Mark, Luke, or John, and the purpose behind the portrayal. That purpose could not be known without a knowledge of the writer's personality and career. The meaning of Christ for John, for example, became identical with John's religious experience, which must be understood in order to explain his message. Thus, under the influence of German idealistic philosophy and historiography, religious experience and evangelistic purpose served as touchstones for the higher critics.

In Berlin Bancroft admittedly fell under the spell of Schleiermacher's teaching that religious experience was an inward matter, a feeling antecedent to thought, to be received and described but not rationally explained. The critics belonging to Schleiermacher's school regarded their own investigations as primarily historical. For them the emotional experience on which religion was based was an empirically verifiable historical fact. Schleiermacher himself saw religious experience as the antidote to speculative philosophy and theology. Although religion was experienced individually, the experience was shared by believers in the church, and found expression through the activity of both the intellect and the will. When hostile theologians attacked the mystical basis of Schleiermacher's religious experience as subjective, Schleiermacher answered by stressing this experience as a historical fact, shared by many and institutionalized in the church, while agreeing with the empirical idealists that religion might legitimately be studied as a phenomenon of the individual human consciousness. This approach brought him fame as the great conciliator of rationalism and supernaturalism.[6]

Bancroft's warm response in 1819 and 1820 to the work of German critics foreshadowed the reactions of a large group of American scholars. The work of German theologians, "in so far as it is merely critical," and Schleiermacher's personal piety, were both attractive to rebels against the prevailing orthodox Calvinism. They welcomed Schleiermacher's concept of a God of grace and love rather than of sovereign justice and righteous wrath. The appointment of the Unitarian Henry Ware to the Hollis professorship at Harvard in 1805 showed that liberal views were not confined to Germany alone. Among the Congregationalists the followers of Jonathan Mayhew and Samuel Hopkins were assured of God's disinterested benevolence and that man was partly able to achieve his own salvation. Yale's Nathaniel W. Taylor insisted on the freedom of man's will in accepting or rejecting salvation, and thereby weakened the Calvinist doctrines of a sovereign God, and of election, total depravity, and regeneration. Horace Bushnell, repelled by the reasoning of theologians, decided to shun "logical deductions and systematic solutions" and, stressing "the more cultivated and nicer apprehension of symbol," to give theological studies "a more esthetic character," thereby "drawing them as [sic] much closer to the practical life of religion."[7] For him the personal revelation of Christ, rather than any process of reasoning, was the source of truth. Bancroft's

[6] Cf. K. S. Latourette, *The Nineteenth Century in Europe: The Protestant and Eastern Churches* (N.Y., 1959), pp. 12–16.

[7] *God in Christ* (Hartford, 1849), p. 92.

reactions to the theology of Göttingen fit into a pattern at home—the pattern not of traditional Calvinist orthodoxy but of liberal reform.

The appeal of biblical criticism was not, however, to theological liberals alone. Orthodox Trinitarian Calvinists appropriated it as a useful weapon against the Unitarians. Between 1810 and 1852 Moses Stuart of Andover actually undertook what Bancroft only thought of doing—namely to found an American school of biblical criticism. In 1819, the year of Bancroft's sojourn at Göttingen, Stuart commented on the use and value of the lower criticism.[8] He began by noting the agreement between Congregationalists and Unitarians on the Bible as the revealed word of God. Thus, he argued, when

> . . . God condescends to speak and write, for men, it is according to the established rules of human language. What better than an enigma would the scriptures be, if such were not the fact? An *inspired interpreter* would be as necessary to explain, as an inspired prophet or apostle was to compose, the books of Scripture.

Here Stuart hoped to find further agreement with Channing, the spokesman for the Unitarians, who had written that God, "a wise teacher discovers his wisdom in adapting himself to the capacities of his pupils, not in perplexing them with what is unintelligible."[9] Stuart continued:

> From this great and fundamental principle of all interpretation, it results that the grammatical analysis of the words of any passage; *i.e.* an investigation of their meaning in general,

---

[8] *Letters to the Rev. Wm. E. Channing*, 2nd ed. (Andover, 1819).
[9] In Walter G. Muelder and Laurence Sears, eds., *The Development of American Philosophy* (Boston, 1940), p. 120.

of their syntactical connexion, of their idiom, of their relation to the context, and of course their *local* meaning; must be the essential process, in determining the sense of any text or part of Scripture. On this fundamental process, depends the interpretation of all the classics, and of all other books; from this result laws which are uniform, and which cannot be violated, without at once plunging into the dark and boundless field of conjectural exegesis.[10]

The lower criticism, moreover, was scientific. It yielded uniform laws which were applicable to both sacred and profane writings. On scientific grounds Stuart proposed to lay the ghost of intuition and speculation:

Admitting then the fundamental principles of grammatical interpretation, to be the best and surest guide to the sense of any writer; I must never supersede these, by *supposing* or *conjecturing* that some peculiar principles or motives influenced this writer. If it can be *proved* that he was under the influence of these; or this can be even rendered probable; of course, such a fact must have its proper influence upon the interpretation of him. But until this can be shown, the *general* laws of grammatical interpretation are our only guide.

If it could be proved, however, that a sacred writer was indeed under the influence of some such peculiar principle or motive,

then I must revert at once to the question, Is the book divine? Can it be so, if there is contradiction? This question I may settle, (on my responsibility to God,) as I please. But I have no right to violate the fundamental rules of language.[11]

The science of grammar thus became the arbiter of disputed theological questions.

[10] *Letters*, pp. 52–53.   [11] *Letters*, pp. 52–55.

So far as Stuart was concerned, orthodox Christianity had nothing to fear from the science of grammar:

I abide by the simple declarations of the New Testament writers, interpreted by the common laws of language. My views reconcile all the seeming discrepancies of description, in regard to Christ, without doing violence to the language of any. I can believe, and do believe, that the sacred writers are consistent, without any explanation but such as the laws of interpretation admit and require.[12]

Stuart also noted, however, that in the hands of fallible men the scientific tool of biblical criticism did not always produce results agreeable to orthodoxy. Eichhorn, he reported, held the account of the creation and the fall of man to be "merely a poetical, philosophical speculation of some ingenious person." Ammon, Thiess, Heinrichs, Meyer, and Baur explained away everything miraculous. De Wette even rejected the divine origin of the Bible.[13] But Stuart was little troubled by any of these. He rejected their results, but he appreciated their method.

On points which are not concerned with the special doctrines of Christianity; in illustrating critical and literary history, philology, natural history, and grammatical exegesis—in a word every thing literary or scientifical that pertains to the Bible; who can enter into any competition with recent German writers? . . . *Egyptii sunt, spoliemus; They are Egyptians, let us take their spoils.* Shall I not accept the good which they proffer me; and proffer me in a more scientific manner, and well digested, lucid, established form, than I can elsewhere find? Without hesitation, I answer, Yes." [14]

---

[12] *Ibid.,* p. 155.   [13] *Ibid.,* pp. 163–168, *passim.*
[14] *Ibid.,* pp. 171, 173.

Stuart's essay amounted to a confirmation that the lower criticism had been accepted by orthodox Congregationalists. They utilized the lower criticism to vindicate on "scientific" grounds the position of supernaturalism which was their creed. It gave the authority of science to their condemnation of Unitarian rationalism. How important the notion of science was to orthodox Presbyterians, and how indispensable they regarded the support of "science" for their theology, may be seen from the remarks of Stuart's colleague Leonard Woods of Andover, who told the Unitarians that

the only mode of reasoning, which can be relied upon to lead us to right conclusions, is that which is pursued in the science of Physics. Regulating ourselves by the maxims of BACON and NEWTON, we inquire, not what we should expect the properties and laws of the physical world would be, nor whether this or that thing can be reconciled with the infinite wisdom and goodness of God; but simply *what is fact? What do we find from observation and experience, that the properties and laws of nature really are?*

Woods contended that theology differed from physics only in that in addition to the facts of observation and experience it knew the facts of revelation. He concluded that God's word, the Bible, taught that man was by nature unholy. Observation and experience agreed. Thus the agreement of all three authorities proved the truth of the orthodox position. Not only was the Unitarian belief in the natural goodness of man untrue; the reasoning on which it was based was actually unscientific.[15]

While orthodox Congregationalists were making use of

[15] *Letters to Unitarians* (Andover, 1822), pp. 18–21.

the lower criticism and of "scientific" exegesis against the Unitarians, the latter, led by Henry Ware and Andrews Norton, were employing both the lower and the higher criticism to refute the Congregationalists' Trinitarian doctrine and their assertion of man's depravity. Henry Ware agreed with Woods that theologians ought to study facts; but for the study of facts he argued that the lower criticism alone was insufficient. "In ascertaining what is taught by observation and experience," he wrote, "there is room for inquiry, discussion, and diversity of opinion. . . . So extensive, various, and complicated are [the facts], that the great difficulty is to settle the question, what observation and experience to teach." As for the facts of God's revelation, they were conveyed in human language and transmitted by imperfect men. Thus it happened "that the question, what God has declared by revelation, is one that is not to be answered by adducing a single, clear, and decisive declaration. The answer is to be furnished by an extensive and close investigation." [16] Andrews Norton was to describe the nature of this investigation.

An industrious student of English and German philosophy and theology, Norton took his cue from the Scottish philosophy and from Locke's *Reasonableness of Christianity*. He went beyond Stuart in accepting the higher criticism—although he might have added with Bancroft, "in so far as it was merely critical." He had no love for German idealistic philosophy, and discounted Schleiermacher as a romantic "veil-maker." With the higher critics he asserted that language was by nature ambiguous and

[16] *Answers to Dr. Woods's Reply in a Second Series of Letters Addressed to Trinitarians and Calvinists* (Cambridge, 1822), pp. 38, 39.

conventional, and thus had to be interpreted. Merely working "with the assistance of a lexicon and grammar" was not enough. Textual interpretation required as its first step a knowledge of the biblical languages, and it further required the interpreter's "power of sympathizing" with the author he interpreted—though sympathy was never to be allowed to deteriorate into pantheistic speculation. Thus Norton struck out both against a narrow-minded reliance on the lower criticism and against the speculative tradition among the higher critics. "We at once reject the literal meaning of the words, and understand them as figurative, because, if we did not do this, they would convey some meaning which contradicts common sense." Here Norton showed his own position. The higher criticism was welcome and useful where it shattered the literalism of orthodox supernaturalists or buttressed the arguments for Christianity in the rational tradition of Butler, Paley, and Locke. It was to be repudiated where it was de-rationalized by German speculative pantheists or by the transcendentalist apostates.[17]

Norton was quite aware that the German higher critics did not agree among themselves on every aspect of their philosophy. There were the Hegelian critics, who claimed the basis of rationalism for their speculative systems; there were the critics of the Tübingen school, who viewed their work as historical rather than philosophical; and there

[17] "Inaugural Discourse on the Extent and Relations of Theology," and "Remarks on the Modern German School of Infidelity," in *Tracts Concerning Christianity* (Cambridge, 1852), pp. 61–98, 277ff.; *A Statement of Reasons for Not Believing the Doctrines of the Trinitarians*, 12th ed. (Boston, 1880), pp. 138–155, *passim.* The "Inaugural Discourse" was delivered in 1819; the *Statement* was first published in 1833.

were the followers of Schleiermacher, who emphasized subjective religious experience. For Norton the Germans were nevertheless all speculative idealists. The Hegelian notion of a Reason evolving itself through history, and the Schleiermacherian harping on emotional experience, alike smacked of "moonshine and cobwebs." Thus Norton, the disciple of Scottish common sense and British rationalism, would have none of the German idealists.

Much to his distress, however, they found eager devotees in Unitarian Cambridge. Charles Follen, who taught ethics at the Harvard Divinity School from 1828 to 1830, expounded German theology to his students, among whom were George Ripley and Theodore Parker.[18] Ripley, revolted by Norton's rationalism and charmed by the spiritualism of the German idealists, had soon thrown the Unitarian clergy into an uproar over the question of miracles—as lively an issue at Cambridge as it was in Germany. Ripley raised it innocently enough when he sought to acquaint his compatriots with the ideas of Herder and Schleiermacher. He wrote that Herder had argued the impossibility of establishing the truth of any religion on the ground of miracle, and that Schleiermacher had established the truth not by relying on miracles but by basing religion on science and on the promptings of the heart.[19] This was in 1835. A few months later, in November, 1836, Ripley put the matter in a form that could no longer be ignored. "We hold it to be an unsound method," he wrote in the *Christian Examiner*, "to make a

[18] See G. W. Spindler, *Karl Follen: A Biographical Study* (Chicago, 1917), pp. 174–175.

[19] See Ripley on Herder and Schleiermacher in the *Christian Examiner*, XIX (Nov., 1835), 172–204; XX (March, 1836), 1–7.

belief in [miracles] the essential foundation of Christian faith, or the ultimate test of Christian character." It may be noted that it was the method he considered unsound, not the belief in miracles *per se*. Sound method demanded a scientific investigation, and miracles as facts were "to be settled by historical considerations, including that of the character and position of their author. . . . Let the study of theology commence with the study of human consciousness"—and thus Ripley came out in favor of the methods of the higher critics.[20] Once again he appealed to Schleiermacher, who "has found no representative in our own theological progress." [21]

That the issue was originally one of methodology rather than of dogma was understood by Ripley's antagonists as well as by his friends.[22] Had it remained precisely that, it might for a time have involved Unitarian professors and ministers in academic dispute. But as the debate moved from method to dogma it spread from Unitarian colleges and seminaries to set off the transcendentalist revolt. Among the churches it disclosed what Ripley called "a radical difference in . . . philosophical views." On the one side stood the orthodox Unitarian clergy led by Norton, who were largely steeped in the empirical philosophy of Locke and the common-sense school of Scotland. On the other side were Ripley, Brownson, Parker, and Emerson, transcendentalist spokesmen who were all more or less— but mainly less—well acquainted with the philosophy of

[20] *Christian Examiner*, XXI (Nov., 1836), 253–254.
[21] *Ibid.*, XX (March, 1836), 5.
[22] See Norton, Ripley, and James Freeman Clarke in the *Boston Daily Advertiser*, Nov. 5 and 9, 1836; also in *The Western Messenger*, III (April, 1837) 576–579.

German idealism from Kant to Herder and Schleiermacher. As Ripley saw it, the orthodox were bound "to a dead letter," whereas the idealists espoused "the living and practical faith of the heart." [23]

Ripley, distressed and angered by the rationalist diatribes of Norton, had in fact moved to a position diametrically opposed to Norton's. He now took his stand with the German idealists, and like Norton indiscriminately lumped together Goethe, Schiller, Schleiermacher, Herder, and De Wette. In 1838 he began to bring out the Specimens of Foreign Standard Literature, a series that was to include translations of Cousin, Jouffroy, Constant, Goethe, Schiller, Eckermann's *Conversations,* Menzel, De Wette, and various German poets. Brownson heralded its appearance with the pronouncement, "We must bring in France and Germany to combat or neutralize England, so that our national spirit may gain the freedom to manifest itself." [24] Ripley himself from then on was to rely chiefly on German literature and philosophy, and to relegate science, including the science of theology, to a subordinate position. He had exchanged empirical idealism for idealism pure and simple, and not infrequently treated the speculative idealists as the sole spokesmen for German scholarship—all because of Norton's devotion to the empiricism of Locke and the Scottish philosophers. Norton indignantly wrote off the transcendentalist movement as a "restless craving for notoriety and excitement. . . . It owes its origin in part to ill understood notions, obtained by blundering through the crabbed and disgusting obscurity of some of the worst German speculatists, . . . re-

[23] *Boston Daily Advertiser* (Nov. 9, 1836).
[24] *Boston Quarterly Review, I* (Oct., 1838), 433–444.

ceived by most of its disciples at second hand." [25] And in his own way Norton was right. Transcendentalism, whatever its merits, did not accurately represent the message of German theology.

Because of Norton's tenacious commitment to British rationalism on the one hand and the transcendentalists' espousal of German speculative idealism on the other, Unitarian theologians were never able to come to grips with the message of German scientific theology. They succeeded in banishing transcendentalism from their pulpits, and continued to reject as sheer pantheism a faith that was not supported by an empirically derived and rationally defended theology. They accepted the lower criticism as a scientific tool and the higher criticism as an instrument of rational analysis. It was not until well into the second half of the century that the Unitarians took a closer look at the historical disciplines of the higher criticism.

In the meantime, however, the Congregationalists at Andover and Union seminaries had begun to discover the historical criticism and Schleiermacher's religion of experience. After Stuart's acceptance of the lower criticism, they had for a time been loath to pursue their German studies much further. The Andover trustees disagreed with Stuart's description of the Germans as "Egyptians" whose spoils were to be taken. For them *Danaos sunt,* and *Timeo Danaos ut dona ferentes.* In 1850 they were rudely disturbed by the thesis set forth in Professor Edwards A. Park's essay, "The Theology of the Intellect and that of the Feelings." Park held that the theology of the intellect —logical, plain, instructive, precise in thought and style— "is adapted to the soul in her inquisitive moods, but fails

[25] *Boston Daily Advertiser* (Aug. 27, 1838).

to satisfy her craving for excitement," whereas the theology of the feelings—preferring the individual statement to the general; satisfied with vague, indefinite representations; sublime, impressive, obscure, rather than accurate—aimed "not to facilitate the inferences of logic, but to arrest attention, to grapple with the wayward desires, to satisfy the longings of the pious heart." [26]

Park would appear to have taken his text from Schleiermacher, and orthodox Congregationalists immediately charged him with "gross error and self-contradiction, and . . . with the subversion of the whole system of revealed truth." To them the theology of the feelings was a heresy that Park—and Bushnell before him—had copied "from the neologists of Germany," who had pronounced the language of the Bible to be figurative rather than literal. The chief accusation of the orthodox Calvinists was that Park had divorced faith from reason when he based faith on individual emotional experience. That experience, and all that arose therefrom, threatened any system of rational theology, and could only lead to heresy. What, the orthodox theologians asked, had become of Andover, the seminary established to strengthen "the true faith," if now, "ere a generation has passed away, it has become, in a large degree at least, the seat and propagandist of a worse form of error than that which it was mainly designed to oppose?" [27]

It could be argued that the theology of the feelings

[26] *Bibliotheca Sacra*, VII (July, 1850), 535, 537. The essay has been reprinted in Joseph L. Blau, ed., *American Philosophic Addresses, 1700–1900* (N.Y., 1946), pp. 627–658.

[27] B. B. Edwards, *Review of Professor Park's Theologies of the Intellect and of the Feelings* (n.p., n.d.), pp. 3, 37, 58.

rested on experience, and that experience was a matter of history, regardless of whether it could be subjected to rational analysis. Thus a historical rather than a rational theology was called for. This was the assertion, twenty years after Park's essay, of Egbert C. Smyth, another Andover professor, in a lecture significantly entitled "From Lessing to Schleiermacher, or from Rationalism to Faith." [28] With it the higher criticism may be said to have arrived among the Congregationalists. Unhampered by Unitarian rationalism, the Andover Congregationalists found in the theology of Schleiermacher a synthesis of scientific history and Christian faith. In that theology, according to Smyth, "the testimony of history becomes a fact of consciousness, and what is first accepted as a probability becomes a living certainty." [29] Where historical investigations of the origins of Christianity threatened orthodox dogma, "Andover again turned to religious experience as a way of escaping the devastating effects of [historical] criticism on an historically grounded faith." [30]

At Union Seminary Henry Boynton Smith, trained at Halle and Berlin from 1838 to 1840, likewise saw Christ as pre-eminently the Saviour experienced through faith. Against the destructive impact of historical criticism, and the rationalism of neologists, Hegelians, and Unitarians, Smith argued that the higher criticism was not only scientific but superior to the subjectivism of the Transcendentalists, because it dealt with historical "facts." These facts, Smith wrote, were the stone against which the

[28] Reprinted in *Christianity and Scepticism: Boston Lectures* (Boston, 1870), pp. 276–311.
[29] *Ibid.*, p. 307.
[30] D. D. Williams, *The Andover Liberals* (N.Y., 1941), p. 97.

speculative pantheism of Hegel "fell . . . and was broken."
A historical theology that accepted religious experience as
a scientifically observable and verifiable fact "tells us
how far the redemptive purposes of God have been accomplished in the actual course of human events." [31] History was thus the vindication of faith. Smith built what he
saw as an empirical philosophy of history upon the cornerstone of the intense personal experience of Christ.
His grandiose concept of history as the unfolding of
revelation prompted George Bancroft to write admiringly,
"In church history you have no rival in this hemisphere,
and you know I am bound to think history includes dog-
matics and philosophy and theology." [32]

Ultimately, historical criticism dominated American
academic theology because it was regarded as scientific
and at the same time gave recognition to Christian piety.
In Schleiermacher Americans saw the fusion of an Ed-
wardsian strain of holiness with respect for empirically
verifiable facts. During the second half of the century the
historical-scientific approach in theology gained the upper
hand among Congregationalists, Presbyterians, and Unitarians as well. At the same time the desire to treat religion
as an observable and measurable phenomenon of human
experience caused much despair among traditionalists,
who viewed such an attitude as destructive to faith: "The
Bible or the mathematics as the basis of preaching,—in
the long run it must come to that," Frederick Henry

[31] Smith, *Faith and Philosophy: Discourses and Essays* (N.Y.,
1877), pp. 55, 59.

[32] Quoted in *Henry Boynton Smith: His Life and Work*, ed. by
his wife (N.Y., 1881), p. 167.

Hedge warned in 1864.[33] The new theologians were determined to prove this prediction false.

The spread of the scientific-historical method in American theology is typified by the Unitarian thinking at the Harvard Divinity School, where biblical criticism followed the path marked out by Andrews Norton and Francis Bowen. At first, Lockean empiricism and common-sense philosophy served to block the advance of German idealism; but as the century progressed a new foe appeared: the theory of evolution, in the agnosticism of Spencer and the materialism of Haeckel, laid exclusive claim to scientific authority, and thus became a threat to the status of theology. Under Charles Carroll Everett, dean of the Divinity School after 1878, the Harvard Unitarians found an ally in German higher criticism and spiritualism. They now accepted both Schleiermacher and Hegel, who, as Everett put it, "may be called the pillars of Hercules, through which entrance was made into the broad ocean of modern theological speculation." [34] Norton's earlier distinction between rationalist and idealist critics now became meaningless, and the whole of German philosophy was welcomed in the fight against materialism and mechanism. For Everett, however, the most potent weapon in the German arsenal was spiritualism, as he found it in Hegel, Fichte, and Schleiermacher.[35]

[33] In "Antisupernaturalism in the Pulpit," *Christian Examiner*, CCXLV (Sept., 1864), 152.

[34] *Essays: Theological and Literary* (Boston, 1901), p. 89.

[35] See Amer. Unit. Assoc., ed., *Christianity and Modern Thought* (Boston, 1872), p. 147; also Everett's *Psychological Elements of Religious Faith*, ed. Edward Hale (N.Y., 1902), esp. pp. 5, 15.

That Everett's neo-Hegelianism had its limitations was soon apparent. A student at the Harvard Divinity School from 1869 to 1872 wrote of his "disheartening experience of uninspiring study and retarded thought. The fresh breeze of modern thought rarely penetrated the lecture rooms, and a student found the intellectual atmosphere unexhilarating to breathe." [36] Everett's deanship nevertheless marked a new era. Of the school's six professors, Everett and four others had studied in Germany, and two held *Dr. phil.* degrees from Leipzig. Ephraim Emerton and Francis Greenwood Peabody both worked to make the study of theology scientific—Emerton by introducing the methods of the history seminar, and Peabody by applying those of the psychological laboratory.

Enough has already been said about the historical seminars to make a description of Emerton's work unnecessary. Peabody—who like H. B. Smith at Union before him had been a student of Tholuck at Halle and a firm disciple of Schleiermacher—regarded Ralph Waldo Emerson as one of America's greatest religious teachers.[37] The stimulus for his psychological study of religious phenomena came from Pfleiderer. On his return to the United States from Germany, Peabody informed his colleagues that "historically . . . the new theology is a child of almost pure German blood." Hegel and Schleiermacher had brought it into the world, yet "while the method of Hegel is rapidly passing into an historical curiosity," the spirit of Schleiermacher

[36] Francis G. Peabody, *Reminiscences of Present-Day Saints* (Boston, 1927), p. 65.

[37] In *Pioneers of Religious Liberty in America* (Boston, 1903), pp. 307–339.

had gone on revitalizing theological study.[38] From the religious feeling insisted upon by Schleiermacher came the "facts" of which theology was the scientific account. For in the "tendency in mankind to live religiously" Peabody saw "a fact capable of observation, ready for analysis, open to verification." [39]

The old conflict between the proponents of a theology of the intellect and a theology of the feelings now dwindled in importance. Facts called for investigation; investigation uncovered the needs and deficiencies in man's religious life; and for the theologian this discovery became a call to action. It was observed that the moral demands of religion addressed themselves to the will,[40] and that through the will piety and reason were synthesized and transformed into action. This action-minded theology led to the so-called Social Gospel, in whose preoccupation with conditions that could be observed, measured, and analyzed, the scientific character of the new theology once again came into play. Social experiments were conducted in the new university settlement houses, such as Hull House at Chicago and Andover House at Boston. Peabody's concern with social action led in 1883 to the first appearance in a divinity school curriculum of a course on social reform, and in 1906 to the founding of the social ethics department at Harvard. Here a museum collection of pictures, graphs, and statistics on social conditions was

[38] "The New Theology," *Unitarian Review,* XI (April, 1879), 352, 354.

[39] "The Method of the Psychology of Religion," *Unitarian Review,* XIX (March, 1883), 254.

[40] Peabody, *Jesus Christ and the Christian Character* (N.Y., 1905), p. 97.

the basis of a science of "inductive ethics." Peabody, who embodied the piety of Schleiermacher, Tholuck, and Emerson, combined with the Unitarian tradition of rational scholarship and German scientific practice, became *par excellence* the theologian of the Social Gospel.[41] For him that gospel was the natural result of the fusion of piety, science, and the reforming urge, and German *Wissenschaft* had made the "will to do good" intellectually respectable.

Faith and scholarship were thus the two dominant concepts in the history of American academic theology after the middle of the nineteenth century. To reconcile the experience of faith with the intellectual demands of the search after knowledge became the task of the theologians. When in the second half of the century the doctrine of evolution brought about the apparent schism between religion and science, Protestant theologians labored to bridge or obliterate this division—an effort in which Schleiermacher's *Vermittlungstheologie* gave them hope. His theology gave sanction to the acceptance in American scholarship of the historical method of the higher critics. It was the claim of professors of theology that their work was scientific when it was based on historical and psychological studies. American historians of church and dogma provided the bridge between theology and history —the first of the social sciences to outgrow the old moral philosophy and to establish itself as a scholarly discipline in its own right. Indeed, unless the work of the biblical critics is understood, we cannot fully understand the

[41] See my "Francis Greenwood Peabody: Harvard's Theologian of the Social Gospel," *Harvard Theological Review*, LIV (Jan., 1961), 45–69.

emergence of historical scholarship. And without first tracing the development of history as a scientific discipline, we cannot fully understand the emergence of the social sciences. Accordingly, from theology we must now turn to a consideration of historical science.

5

The Science of History and Politics

Historical work in America is mostly of the German type, solid, careful, exact, not at all the sort of work which theorists about democracy would have looked for, since it appeals rather to the learned few than to the so-called general reader.

—JAMES BRYCE, 1888

LORD BRYCE saw the "solid, careful, exact" work of American historians as a consequence of their belief that the United States "had fallen behind Europe in learning and science," and of their eagerness "to accumulate knowledge and spend their energy in minutely laborious special studies."[1] American historians no doubt desired to equal and to outdo their German teachers and colleagues. They found it a not insurmountable task to construct the whole apparatus of scientific research scholarship in America. They began to produce "scientific history" with a vengeance, addressing their works to their professional colleagues at home and abroad.[2] But they also sought to gain

[1] James Bryce, *The American Commonwealth*, 2nd rev. ed. (London, 1891), II, 648–649.

[2] Cf. W. Stull Holt, "The Idea of Scientific History in America," *Journal of the History of Ideas*, I (June, 1940), 352–362.

for themselves a prestige like that enjoyed by German historians; a prestige that gave them recognition as spokesmen for the aspirations of their country, and heralds of its destiny. Could their German colleagues serve as guides and models here as they had for scientific procedures? This was to be one of the crucial problems confronting the German-trained scholars who endeavored to establish the historical profession in America.

Lord Bryce was right in seeing the desire to make of history a strictly empirical discipline as a primary characteristic of American historical scholarship in the late 1870's and 1880's. He was right, too, in assigning the major role in this process to German-trained scholars. That "old German" [3] George Bancroft's multi-volume *History of the United States* was the first to receive acclaim from European historians. With Herbert Baxter Adams, Andrew D. White, Charles K. Adams, Moses Coit Tyler, Henry Adams, and many others—all men who had had firsthand experience in German universities—he worked to give history in America both professional status and scientific standards. These men made the seminar an integral part of American higher education. They established the Ph.D. degree as a certificate for teachers in all first-class colleges and universities. They originated the cult of the monograph and the research journal; and with the founding of the American Historical Association they formally constituted the historical profession. For better or for worse, graduate students flocked to their seminars and devoted themselves to developing an American science of history.

What distinguished the new, German-inspired history

[3] Quoted from Orie Long, *Literary Pioneers* (Cambridge, 1935), p. 158.

from the old? Fundamentally the distinction was one of method. According to Edward Channing,

> The true historical method consists in the examination of original records and other contemporaneous sources, and in generalizations based on such research. . . . It is preferable to the old historical method of copying the work of other historical students.[4]

The "true" historians saw themselves as empiricists, who —unlike the chronologists and literati of past generations—had brought the laboratory scientist's tools of observation and analysis to the investigation of past events. While the "true" American historians paid explicit respect to natural scientists, they also borrowed heavily from the methods and assumptions of biblical scholars in the seminaries and divinity schools. As the preceding chapter has shown, textual criticism in America was first practiced by theologians, and historical research found its first haven in denominational seminaries.

Bancroft himself, however, was a forerunner, rather than a full-fledged member of the "true" historical school. For all his praise of German scholarship, his generalizations were not "based on research," in accordance with Channing's criterion: they preceded rather than followed it. Bancroft began his *History* with the statement that his objective was "to follow the steps by which a favoring Providence, calling our institutions into being, has conducted the country to its present happiness and glory."[5] His account of the coming of the American Revolution

[4] In *Proceedings of the Massachusetts Historical Society,* 2nd ser., VII (Jan., 1892), 244.

[5] *History of the United States of America,* rev. ed. (Boston, 1876), I, 3.

invoked "a new messenger from the Infinite Spirit [who] moves over the waters";[6] and he asserted that "immutable laws of moral existence must pervade all time and all space, all ages and all worlds." [7] The "true" historians had reason to doubt whether "a new messenger from the Infinite Spirit" could have been discovered by induction; they suspected that its presence had been deduced from some speculative philosophical system, since they themselves had seen no incontestable evidence of either a guiding Providence or a spiritual messenger.

Bancroft's generalizations were in fact vestiges of the Hegelian philosophy of history, which was fast losing ground before the empirical idealism of the students of Ranke. The speculative philosophers had seen history as the gradual revelation of Reason, which for them was the ultimate reality, and of which observable phenomena were but physical manifestations. As we have already noted, the revolt of natural scientists and empirical philosophers and historians against both natural and speculative philosophy led to a new phase in European intellectual history. Bancroft, who had seen only its first glimmerings, may be pardoned for not casting his lot unreservedly with the new movement. The German historians themselves did not become thorough empiricists overnight. As late as 1842, for example, we read of the young Jacob Burckhardt's sense of the paltriness of his ambitions as measured against the lofty heights of speculative philosophy. He begged his tutor not to push him into speculative thinking, but to give him leave to collect and compare facts and make only

[6] *Ibid.*, III, 3–4.

[7] "Oration on . . . the Progress of Mankind," *Literary and Historical Miscellanies* (N.Y., 1855), p. 489.

the simplest generalizations: "For the moment let me remain at this low level. Let me sense and feel history, instead of understanding its first principles." [8]

It remained for Bancroft's American successors to reap the harvest of the German historians' revolt against speculative philosophy. For them Channing's "generalizations based on research." were the crucial mark of their craft, and their insistence on avoiding philosophical theory was typical of the followers of Ranke. The day of the all-inclusive *Wissenschaft* that equated science with philosophy, and that Bancroft had been exposed to, was over. When such later American scientific historians as Henry Adams dallied with the law-in-history school, they still insisted that the law be arrived at inductively from the facts, and also that history had nothing to do with metaphysics but was an empirical science.

Leopold von Ranke, the patron saint of German-trained American historians of the 1870's and 1880's, had said that speculation was anathema.[9] This his American students took to mean precisely that history as an empirical science was freed from any subordination to philosophy. He challenged them to devote themselves to "the bare truth, without embellishment," to "thorough investigation of concrete, individual cases. . . . The rest," he told them, "we leave to God. . . . Let us not fabricate, not even in the smallest detail; let us not follow phantasms." [10] Looking back on their German experience, the American students

[8] Letter to Karl Fresenius, June 19, 1842, in Burckhardt, *Briefe,* ed. Fritz Kaphahn (Leipzig, n.d.), pp. 58–59.
[9] In *Zur Kritik neuerer Geschichtsschreiber* (Leipzig, 1824), p. 28.
[10] *Ibid.*

could agree with Rudolf von Virchow: "In the measure in which philosophic systems were pushed in the background, sober observation and common sense asserted themselves." [11] Observation and common sense—these were the tools of empiricism, by means of which a "true historical science" would be constructed.

How was this belief in scientific historical work translated into practice? We have spoken, in the preceding chapter, of the historical criticism of the theologians. Textual criticism based on philological methods was not, however, a new development in the nineteenth century, but had been known as early as the fifteenth, when Laurentius Valla exposed the "Donations of the Emperor Constantine" as forgeries. Valla's was the first major critical examination of an official document,[12] and the beginning of diplomatics—the critical examination of diplomatic documents—as an auxiliary branch of historical science. Around the end of the eighteenth century, diplomatics was given new importance by the work of Johann Christoph Gatterer of the University of Göttingen.[13] It was there, too, that Gottfried Achenwall and August Ludwig Schlözer added statistics to the concerns of the historian. Statistics—which at Göttingen meant the careful assembling of all noteworthy facts concerning par-

[11] "The Founding of the Berlin University and the Transition from the Philosophic to the Scientific Age," *Annual Report of the Board of Regents of the Smithsonian Institution . . . to July, 1894* (Washington, 1896), p. 690.

[12] Eduard Fueter, *Geschichte der Neueren Historiographie* (München, 1911), p. 113.

[13] See Herbert Butterfield, *Man on His Past* (Cambridge, 1955), pp. 32–61.

ticular nations—in Schlözer's words, constituted history at rest, and history itself was statistics put in motion.[14]

In addition to diplomatics and statistics, a series of auxiliary disciplines were developed, in each of which the scientific historian had to achieve competency before he was ready to undertake the writing that was the culmination of his labors. Historical facts were not transmitted on paper or parchment alone; they were to be gathered from such inscribed artifacts as coins, seals, and coats of arms, and from works of art. Since paleography, epigraphy, numismatics, sphagistics, heraldry, art history, and archaeology all provided knowledge of the past, the historian had to be familiar with their methods. In the *Historische Vorseminarien* of German universities a student could work with scales, magnifying glass, yardstick, slide rule, and spectroscope, weighing, measuring, and assigning dates to his heart's content. In such seminars the apprentice historian carried out his work in exactly the same manner as the chemist among the test tubes of his laboratory. No wonder, then, that he not only thought of himself as a scientist, but carried the analogy between his discipline and that of the biologist or physicist past the laboratory and into his thinking about history.

The response of young American graduate students to the German gospel of science was enthusiastic. They were impressed, above all, to find that German historians were all specialists, who were historians first and teachers only secondarily. Their teaching thus had the prestige of *Wissenschaft* and an authority far superior to that of the

[14] Quoted in John T. Merz, *A History of European Thought in the Nineteenth Century* (Edinburgh, 1903), II, 555, n.1.

American moral philosopher, whose historical training was at best incidental. Although the whole specialized apparatus of seminars and source collections was awesome to American students, the appeal of scientific investigation was familiar enough from the Scottish common-sense philosophy, with its stress on the study of human behavior. In Germany the Rankean concern with the facts of history amounted to a demonstration of empirical philosophy put into practice. The lessons of Scotland and Germany thus neatly complemented each other.

Nevertheless, the early enthusiasm among American students for the German science of history was soon followed by a growing dissatisfaction in the American universities where German-trained professors had established historical seminars of their own. At Harvard Henry Adams found that "nothing is easier than to teach historical method, but, when learned, it has little use. . . . [The] wonderful method led nowhere." [15] At Baltimore Herbert B. Adams was apparently more successful in directing exercises in source criticism, but his students were skeptical and unenthusiastic. Woodrow Wilson, for example, refused to dig "into the dusty records of old settlements and colonial cities, . . . rehabilitating in authentic form the stories, now almost mythical, of the struggles, the ups and downs, of the first colonists here there and everywhere on this then interesting continent." [16] When Adams tried to overcome the dullness of his seminar with the introduction of "live" sources, he succeeded no better. John Franklin Jameson reported that "the men are not

[15] *The Education of Henry Adams* (N.Y., 1931), pp. 302–303.
[16] In Ray S. Baker, *Woodrow Wilson: Life and Letters* (Garden City, 1927), I, 174.

writing historical papers, even reviews of current historical literature are not systematically presented, and the staple of the meetings consists of outside 'attractions,' now a Confederate general to talk on a campaign, now an elderly party exhumed to 'reminisce' to us." Jameson confided to his father: "The seminary is a regular farce, and has been all the year. Adams knows that the time has passed when we could run it on the old plan, yet he won't spend the time to manage it on a new scheme." [17]

The shortcomings of the seminar were cogently diagnosed by Henry Adams. All too often, the history uncovered by research consisted of the facts and nothing more—"a tangled skein that one may take up at any point, and break when one has unravelled enough. . . . In essence incoherent and immoral, history had either to be taught as such—or falsified." If this was all that the seminar method could honestly produce, Adams concluded, it was not worth the effort; the students "might get their facts where they liked." [18] The presentation of the truth, the avoidance of falsification—that, to Henry Adams, was the historian's real problem; and it was a problem on which he concluded that the Germans were not very helpful. Although they were confident that they had found the royal road to "true" history, try as he might, Adams—and with him many of his colleagues—could find nothing in German historiography to substantiate such a claim. Rather, Adams held, the Germans had simply produced one of many historical interpretations. They based their belief that theirs was the "true" history

[17] In Elizabeth Donnan and Leo F. Stock, eds., *An Historian's World* (Philadelphia, 1956), pp. 23, 26.
[18] *The Education*, pp. 302, 301.

on their mastery of the historical method. Method, however, was but a tool to be used for the accomplishment of certain purposes—which in turn were simply certain human preferences based on a set of common assumptions. These assumptions, Adams thought, might be common to German historians but were not necessarily valid for all historians everywhere. Their so-called scientific history, in short, included elements that were not scientific after all.

For an insight into the nonscientific elements of scientific history as taught in Germany, we must once again go back to Leopold von Ranke. He saw historical scholarship as something more than "an immense aggregate of historical facts to be memorized." [19] Its final goal was the discovery and the presentation of historical truth, which was to be derived from empirically ascertainable facts but whose presentation involved the historian as organizer and interpreter. In fact, the moment the German scholars considered the function of the historian, they entered the realm of the higher criticism and its concern with human will and purpose. German historians of the school of Ranke here shared the assumptions of the philosophy of nineteenth-century empirical idealism.

The spokesman for this philosophy was Wilhelm von Humboldt, whose *Task of the Historian* was the manifesto of German idealist historiography. Historical truth, according to Humboldt, consisted not only of facts but of ideas—invisible elements of history "which relate the fragments to each other, put single phenomena in their proper perspective, give form to the whole," and which

[19] Quoted in Fritz Wagner, *Geschichtswissenschaft* (München, 1951), p. 207.

resided in the events of history as well as in the minds of men. The task of the historian was to fuse the visible facts with the invisible ideas; and since the ideas were invisible, the historian had to evoke them imaginatively. In so doing the historian resembled the poet, except that it was the historian's special duty to subordinate his imagination to an absolute fidelity to past actualities. Insofar as the historian drew past ideas out of past events he remained a scientist and avoided the unhistorical dicta of speculative philosophy. "Philosophy," warned Humboldt, "prescribes a goal for events. Its search for final causes . . . disturbs and falsifies the spontaneous insight into history's active forces (*alle freie Ansicht des eigenthümlichen Wirkens der Kräfte*)."[20] Here Humboldt was in agreement with Ranke's condemnation of speculative historiography, which "blithely deduces forced results from meager, superficial knowledge."[21] Historians, Humboldt added, knew ideas only in and from events.[22] From those ideas they could abstract history's leading tendencies and governing forces. Abstraction, to be sure, presupposed a philosophical mind, yet it shunned the speculations of philosophers who were contemptuous toward historical facts.[23]

Behind the *Ideengeschichte* of Humboldt and Ranke lay a belief that genuine historical knowledge was possible—that there was no unbridgeable chasm between the events of the past and the historian as knower in the

[20] "Ueber die Aufgabe des Geschichtsschreibers," *Abhandlungen der Historisch-Philologischen Klasse der Königlichen Preussischen Akademie der Wissenschaften aus den Jahren 1820–1821* (Berlin, 1822), pp. 305–307, 314.

[21] Wagner, *op. cit.*, p. 211.   [22] Humboldt, *op. cit.*, p. 322.

[23] Wagner, *op. cit.*, pp. 207–208.

present. The invisible element of the idea was inherent in the events themselves as well as in the mind of the historian; it existed in both object and subject, and it made true historical knowledge possible. In mathematics, Humboldt held, ideas appeared as concepts; in natural science they appeared as *Gestalt;* and in the humanistic sciences they were the expression of the soul of man, who was a spiritual being and a part of history. Through the medium of ideas he participated in the past as well as in the present, and was therefore capable of truthfully re-creating the past.

This enthusiastic belief in the possibility of attaining genuine historical knowledge acted as a magnet only less powerful than the gospel of science in attracting young Americans to Germany. Although few of them ever met Wilhelm von Humboldt, his faith was to be encountered in the works of Ranke and in the lectures of Gustav Droysen. The latter gave a systematic exposition of Humboldt's belief in historical thought as an epistemological category, distinct from those of the physical sciences and of speculative philosophy.[24] Whereas natural science dealt with concrete, measurable, nonhuman phenomena, and speculative thought with the realm of pure ideas, it was the function of historical science to explore the concrete and visible world that had been constructed by man and that was infused with ideas. Historical knowledge not only was true, but was also the most comprehensive knowledge of which man was capable, since by means of ideas it became the link between man and the world, between subject and object, between past and present.

Droysen gave as a motto for his students the state-

[24] *Ibid.,* p. 228.

ment, "Our method is to understand by means of investigation." [25] *Ideengeschichte* was to supply the tools by which the historian could understand past human actions in terms of the conditions under which they had taken place, and of the moral choices exercised by history-making individuals. The first task called for the apparatus of research, the second for what was called imaginative understanding.

The particular aspects of history that these German scholars urged upon their students' understanding differed with the historian. Ranke gave primacy to foreign policy, and concentrated his research on diplomatic history. Burckhardt's *Civilization of the Renaissance in Italy* became the first landmark of cultural history. Savigny and Mommsen applied themselves to jurisprudence, and Roscher to economic and social developments. Among young American historians there was a marked preference for political history as it was taught first by Ranke and later by Droysen, Sybel, and Treitschke. The Americans were especially impressed by the Prussian political historians' active engagement in the administrative and legislative affairs of their own day, and by the use they made of their political experience in understanding the past as well as of their knowledge of the past in helping to shape the events of the present. Droysen told his students that "politics is the history of the present, and history the politics of the past—at least in so far as history is concentrated in the realm of the state." [26] Treitschke later went to the extreme of declaring that "the further a

[25] In *Historik*, ed. Rudolf Hübner, 4th ed. (München, 1960), pp. 22, 328.
[26] Wagner, *op. cit.*, p. 230.

human activity is removed from the state, the less it belongs to history." [27] For the Prussian historians history became, in short, the science of the state. Many of the American students who listened attentively to these doctrines were ready to act upon them.

The political consciousness of the German professors also reminded American students of the moral philosophers at home, who had spoken of the citizen's obligation to participate in the politics of a democratic society. For the German professors, however, political activity was not so much the obligation of a free citizen as it was a duty imposed by official status. Their approach to politics and administration was in fact that of professional specialists. As a later chapter will bring out, this difference of attitude was to raise obstacles in the path of the American scholars at home; but during their student days they generally regarded the German scholars' engagement in politics with approval. They were the more impressed by the doctrines of German historians concerning the relation of history to politics in the years immediately following the crisis of the Civil War, when many American students saw in Prussia's rise to national leadership a parallel to the victory of the North in that conflict.

Among the German-trained scholars who embarked upon their careers in colleges and universities determined to introduce the science of history as the political science *par excellence* to America, the leaders were Herbert B. Adams of Johns Hopkins and John W. Burgess of Columbia University. Both men had attended the lectures and seminars of Droysen in Berlin, and their students— particularly those of Burgess—"went to Berlin in shoals.

[27] *Ibid.,* p. 276.

They all went to hear Droysen lecture, and came home with trunks full of Droysen's *Preussische Politik* and of the writings of Leopold von Ranke." [28] Droysen's *Grundriss der Historik,* Adams reported, became "a *Vade Mecum* of American teachers." [29] Adams himself rephrased Droysen and had inscribed on the walls of his seminar the words "History is past Politics and Politics present History." He also adopted this dictum as the leitmotiv for his Johns Hopkins University Studies in Historical and Political Science. Charles Kendall Adams of Cornell, likewise a student of Droysen, quoted his German professor that the historian's task was to change public opinion and "set it right." [30] But Droysen's most enthusiastic American disciple was Burgess, who in 1890 dedicated his two-volume *Political Science and Comparative Constitutional Law* to the memory of his "former friend and teacher." Before a meeting of the American Historical Association in December, 1896, Burgess reaffirmed Droysen's belief that "political science must be studied historically and history must be studied politically in order to [obtain] a correct comprehension of either. Separate them, and the one becomes a cripple, if not a corpse, the other a will-o'-the-wisp." [31]

[28] Herbert Adams, "History at Amherst and Columbia Colleges," *Education,* VII (Nov., 1886), 180.

[29] "Is History Past Politics?" *JHSt.,* XIII (March–April, 1895), 200. The *Grundriss* (1868) was translated by President E. B. Andrews of Brown University as *Outline of the Principles of History* (Boston, 1893).

[30] See "Recent Historical Work in Colleges and Universities of Europe and America," *Annual Report of the AHA for the Year 1889* (Washington, 1890), p. 36.

[31] "Political Science and History," *Annual Report of the AHA for the Year 1896* (Washington, 1897), I, 211.

Adams' and Burgess' views did not meet with universal approval from their colleagues, some of whom considered "history as past politics" too narrow a working definition. Adams himself later qualified it, protesting that he had "never taught that all history is past politics and that all politics are present history, but only that some history and some politics are thus defined." [32] After 1885 the Johns Hopkins Studies dropped the emphasis on political history. The second volume was published under the title *Institutions and Economics,* and in his foreword to the third Adams announced that he was going to promote "the cause of American Economic History." [33] Papers in this field, and on problems of modern municipalities and social movements, occupied the third volume. In 1890 Adams censured Justin Winsor's *magnum opus,* the eight-volume *Narrative and Critical History of America,* for its neglect of educational, social, and economic subjects "which form an important part of our history." [34] Eventually the dogma that "history is past politics" gave way to the New History of the social historians, typified by the frontier hypothesis of Frederick Jackson Turner— who, interestingly enough, had been a student in Adams' seminar—and by Beard's economic interpretation. While American historiography outgrew its political phase, Adams adjusted as gracefully as he could. Besides chafing under the restrictions imposed by a strict adherence to political history, many historians resented the pontifical

[32] "The Teaching of History," *Annual Report of the AHA* (Washington, 1897), I, 247.

[33] Vol. III (Jan., 1885), p. 5.

[34] In "Seminary Notes on Recent Historical Literature," *JHSt.,* VIII (Nov.–Dec., 1890), 532.

attitude of political scientists such as Burgess, who saw in history no more than the handmaid of political science. Burgess had told the historians that their task was exact scientific research into facts, whereas the political scientist made his distinctive contribution in the definition of principles, political creeds, laws, and institutions which aroused "a consciousness of political ideals not yet realized." [35] Such a view ended up making the study of history good only "for the purpose of justifying any particular theory of government"—a definition no historian would be willing to accept. They were glad to have the political scientist utilize their findings, but they did not concede that their only function was to provide data for others.[36]

Objections were also raised against the tendency to regard historical and political science as primarily an exercise in comparative institutional and constitutional analysis. Adams, Burgess, and many of their colleagues had met with this approach in the German seminars. After studying under Droysen and Treitschke in Berlin, Adams had attended the seminars of the historians Winkelmann and Erdmannsdörffer, the political scientist Bluntschli, and the economist Knies at Heidelberg. Burgess had studied in Göttingen under Waitz, an editor of the *Monumenta Germaniae Historica;* in Leipzig under Voigt and Wuttke; and in Berlin likewise under Droysen, Mommsen, and Treitschke. The outlook of these German professors was reflected in Adams' teaching and in Burgess' constitutional interpretation of American history. Adams sought to interest his students in tracing the evolution of democratic institutions. His pet theory was

[35] "Political Science and History," I, 205, 210.
[36] See remarks on Burgess' talk, *ibid.*, I, 211–213.

that these institutions had originated in the Teutonic forests of Central Europe and from there had been transmitted by Germanic peoples to England and the New World. This doctrine was set forth in monographs on the Germanic origin of the New England towns, on Saxon tithingmen and Norman constables in Massachusetts, on Teutonic village life on Cape Ann and in Salem, and on the Chautauqua meetings of Kentucky mountaineers, in which Adams thought he detected a resurgence of the ancient Teutonic folkmoots.[37] His first disappointment came when his students protested against the endless repetition of such comparisons. Franklin Jameson, while he was a member of Adams' seminar, declared that he had no "consuming zeal in the study of the Anglo-Saxon Origin of Policemen's Billies, the Historical Development of Pedlers' [sic] Licenses and other points of the hist. of Institutions (with a large I). . . ."[38] Burgess was likewise forced to recognize opposition to his narrow constitutional interpretation of history. He argued that the Civil War and the Reconstruction had both been "crimes" because they violated the Constitution. The crime of war must be condemned, he wrote, "even though we should ascribe to it the emancipation of the bondmen."[39] Concerning the Reconstruction he held that "from the point of view of a sound political science the imposition of

[37] See *JHSt.*, Vols. I, II; also "Higher Education of the People: The Work of Chautauqua," *The Independent*, Sept. 27 and Oct. 4, 1888.

[38] Donnan and Stock, eds., *op. cit.*, p. 22.

[39] In *The Civil War and the Constitution, 1859–1865* (N.Y., 1901), I, 44.

universal negro suffrage upon the Southern communities
. . . was one of the 'blunder-crimes' of the century." [40]
His readers and colleagues asked whether such dicta
could properly be termed the fruits of a scientific analyis
of history and politics.

The opposition to such studies lay not merely in the
unwillingness of scholars to force historical and political
science into an institutional or constitutional strait jacket.
Adams' notion of institutional history was intimately
bound up with the theory of evolution. He believed that
America's democratic institutions had sprung from Teutonic germs that had been carried by Aryan peoples—
in their blood, as it were—first across the English Channel
and then across the Atlantic, to come to fruition on the
shores of New England. Adams' friend the English historian Edward Augustus Freeman had written in the
Johns Hopkins Studies, "An eye accustomed to trace the
likenesses and unlikenesses of history will rejoice to see
the Germans of Tacitus live once more in the popular
gatherings of New England—to see in the strong life of
Rhode Island a new Appenzell beyond the Ocean—to
see the Great City of Arcadia rise again in the federal
capital by the Potomac." [41] Obviously, Adams and Freeman possessed just such an eye, which found evidence
of evolution everywhere. Other historians, and in particular students of America's colonial period, not only searched
in vain for Teutonic germs in New England, but also,
like Jameson, found the search a bit silly. Edward Chan-

[40] In *Reconstruction and the Constitution, 1866–1876* (N.Y.,
1902), pp. 244–245.
[41] In Vol. I (1883), p. 31.

ning, for one, declared in 1892 that he could not accept
"Prof. H. B. Adams' 'Germanic theory'" because he found
it "impossible to trace Germanic institutions through
English history from Germany to New England." [42]
Charles McLean Andrews, like Jameson a former student
of Adams, repeatedly expressed his dislike of the meticu-
lous and pedantic Germans and their theories, as well as
of the Whiggish and pamphleteering English.[43] He placed
Adams among the former, and Freeman among the latter.
Most historians agreed that evolution was a fruitful hypothesis to guide historical research. But when historical
research was reduced to cataloguing evidence in support
of the theory of evolution—particularly when that evidence was by no means unequivocal—Jameson, Wilson,
Channing, Henry Adams, Andrews, and Osgood, among
others, found it no longer acceptable.

The comparative study of developing institutions drew
its chief conceptual tools from the science of biology. In
addition to the theory of evolution, the institutional
historians relied heavily on biological metaphor and
analogy. Herbert Adams defended his hypothesis of the
evolution of the New England town out of a Teutonic
germ, on the grounds that biology "no longer favors the
theory of spontaneous generation." [44] He commended to
his students the research of Albert B. Hart of Harvard,

[42] In discussions on the "Genesis of the Massachusetts Town,"
Proceedings of the Massachusetts Historical Society, 2nd ser., VII
(Jan., 1892), 250.

[43] See A. S. Eisenstadt, *Charles McLean Andrews* (N.Y., 1956),
pp. 59–60.

[44] "The Germanic Origin of the New England Towns," *JHSt.,*
I (1882), 8.

who had "traced the course of the late River and Harbor Bill as a biologist would study the life-history of a chick, or a tad-pole, or of yellow-fever germs." [45] Institutional historians drew upon the vocabulary of biology when they spoke of growth, of germs, of the body politic, or of the state as organism. As historical development became historical evolution, the biological vocabulary expanded along with an optimistic evolutionary faith. Adams owed to Bluntschli his view of history as "the succession of states, empires, federations . . . slowly leading to such aggregations as the United States of America and the United States of Europe." [46] The historian studying the evolution of states soon came to see his metaphors as statements of fact. If the state was seen as a growing organism, the product of historical conditioning, Treit-schke's strictures against the "hollow abstractions of natural rights philosophy and its resultant revolutionary doctrines" gained new force.[47] Burgess quite logically concluded that "every student of political and legal science should divest himself, at the outset, of this pernicious doctrine of natural rights," [48] and Adams asserted that "political science no longer defends the Social Contract as the basis of government." [49] The use of biological

[45] "The American Historical Association," *The Independent* (June 2, 1887), p. 5.

[46] Adams, *The Study and Teaching of History* (Richmond, Va., 1898), pp. 8–9.

[47] Wagner, *op. cit.*, p. 275.

[48] "The American Commonwealth: Changes in Its Relation to the Nation," *PSQ*, I (March, 1886), 17.

[49] In *Maryland's Influence in Founding a National Commonwealth* (Baltimore, 1877), p. 64. Also in *JHSt.*, III (Jan., 1885), 49.

metaphor and analogy led the German-trained scholars of the historical school not only to confuse theory with fact, but also to repudiate the main stream of American political philosophy. Locke's theory of the contract and of the natural right to revolution could claim in its favor that it gave *ex post facto* recognition to what Americans already believed. The historians by means of their biological analogies sought to repudiate the natural rights philosophy; but they did so with the help of "facts" for which they never could gain undisputed acceptance. In retrospect, the attempt to base historical and political science on the concepts of biology appears to have been short-lived.[50]

Still more questionable than the theory of evolution or than the view of the state as an organism were the racial doctrines held by a number of biologically oriented historians in Germany, England, and America. That "the state as an historical person is the creation and expression of the racial community of the nation" was the view of Bluntschli,[51] who then proceeded to affirm the innate superiority of the Aryan peoples:

The Aryan spirit, most richly endowed by the creator and called to the highest degree of human independence, is destined to enlighten humanity with its ideas of law and the state. It will take over and wield the government of the world—which already has been placed into the hands of the Aryan peoples—in humanly-conscious and humanly-noble fashion by educating the remainder of humanity to civiliza-

[50] Cf. Albion Small, "The Organic Concept of Society," *Annals of the American Academy*, V (March, 1895), 745.

[51] *Politik als Wissenschaft* (Stuttgart, 1876), p. 120.

tion. History has assigned this task to the family of the Aryan peoples. With this duty she has also bestowed on them the corresponding right.[52]

In England Freeman was the spokesman for "the Anglo-Saxon militant, the Teuton rampant, and the Aryan eternally triumphant." [53] During the Franco-Prussian War of 1870–1871 the Aryans became "Dutch," and Freeman gratuitously included himself in their company. "We must have Elsass back again, if not Lothringen," he asserted, because the "whole Galwelshry" was "a standing menace to Dutchland and the world generally." [54] To H. B. Adams' credit we must say that his "Aryanism" never went further than to identify American democracy with the genius of the Teutonic peoples.

It was Burgess who propounded in America Bluntschli's theory of the innate political superiority of the Aryan race. In his *Political Science and Comparative Constitutional Law* he wrote, that the national state, the creation of Teutonic political genius, "stamps the Teutonic nations as the political nations *par excellence*, and authorizes them, in the economy of the world, to assume the leadership in the establishment and administration of states." [55] The "Teuton's burden" justified the use of force because "there is no right to the status of barbarism."

[52] In "Arische Völker und arische Rechte," *Deutsches Staatswörterbuch*, J. C. Bluntschli, ed. (Stuttgart, 1857), I, 331.

[53] William A. Dunning, "A Generation of American Historiography," *Annual Report of the AHA for 1917* (Washington, 1920), p. 350.

[54] Quoted in William R. W. Stephens, *Life and Letters of Edward A. Freeman* (London, 1895), II, 8.

[55] In Vol. I, p. 39.

Should a barbaric population resist "the exercise of force in imposing organization . . . the civilized state may clear the territory of their presence." [56] This was evidently Burgess' version of Bluntschli's "corresponding right." Applying the same theory to American politics, Burgess came out in favor of restricted immigration. "We must preserve our Aryan nationality in the state, and admit to its membership only such non-Aryan race-elements as shall have become Aryanized in spirit and in genius by contact with it." [57] In 1907, speaking at Berlin before the German Emperor, Burgess said of the Slavs, Czechs, Hungarians, and South Italians, "Uncle Sam does not want such rabble for citizens." [58]

The proponents of the Aryan race doctrine soon found themselves beset by contradictions. As historians they could scarcely have been unaware that Americans were not of pure Aryan, Teutonic, or Anglo-Saxon stock. Even Freeman could not but notice the racial heterogeneity of the American people when he visited his friend Adams in Baltimore. But he was quick to assert that America's social problems were the result of racial laissez-faire, and might be solved if only "every Irishman [were to] kill a Negro and be hanged for it." [59] The implications of Aryan racism were still more perplexing when it came to foreign policy. Germany, according to Burgess, was "the motherland of Great Britain, as Great Britain is the

[56] *Ibid.*, p. 46.

[57] "The Ideal of the American Commonwealth," *PSQ*, X (Sept., 1895), 407.

[58] "Uncle Sam!" in *Reminiscences of an American Scholar* (N.Y., 1934), p. 397.

[59] In "Some Impressions of the United States," *Fortnightly Review*, XXXII, n.s. (Sept., 1882), 327.

motherland of the United States. Moreover, Germany is . . . in some degree, racially, the immediate motherland of the United States." [60] But although Aryans could easily be equated with Teutons and Anglo-Saxons, the Irish and the Negroes did not fit the category—not to mention the "rabble" from southern and southeastern Europe. By 1914, Teutons and Anglo-Saxons were no longer observing familiar courtesies, and in 1917 "one grievous blow" brought Burgess' world down into "irretrievable ruin." [61] Burgess regarded the war as treason against the unity of the Aryan race. For him the traitor was Edward VII, who had banded together the "pan-Slavic program of Russia, the *revanche* of France, and Great Britain's commercial jealousy of Germany," [62] and had forced Wilhelm II, "the wisest, most intelligent, most warm hearted, most conscientious and most able and resourceful ruler of Europe," [63] to "defend the Teutonic civilization of continental Europe against the oriental Slavic quasi-civilization on the one side, and the decaying Latin civilization on the other." [64]

By 1914 German-trained professors of historical and political science found themselves involved in a paradox. When they evaluated their contribution to the institutional progress of American historical scholarship, they had every reason for satisfaction. They could point with pride to the graduate departments of historical and political

[60] In "Germany, Great Britain and the United States," *PSQ*, XIX (March, 1904), 2.

[61] Burgess, *Reminiscences*, p. 29.

[62] "On Behalf of Germany," *The Open Court*, XXVIII (Oct., 1914), 593.

[63] In *Germany and the United States* (N.Y., 1908), p. 30.

[64] "On Behalf of Germany," p. 588.

science, the research seminars, the American Historical Association, the whole apparatus of scholarly publication. They might dismiss the complaints of their students about the dullness of seminar research as the price to be paid for scientific progress. But they found matters more difficult when they proceeded to superimpose the German pattern of political and institutional development upon history as it was taught in America. The German belief in a universally applicable historical *Wissenschaft* had encouraged the attempt, which produced, as Lord Bryce saw it, "not at all the sort of work which theorists about democracy would have looked for," [65] and which aroused the antagonism of students and colleagues. Could it be, the German-trained historians began to ask, that German *Wissenschaft* did not thrive on American soil?

What, after all, was this German historical *Wissenschaft* that promised so much to its American devotees? Insofar as it was scientific it was not much more than training in the methods of empirical research and inductive generalization. As such it was not peculiarly German, but was known in England and France as well; moreover, as Henry Adams had observed, it conveyed no meaning, answered no ultimate question. It derived its particular German aura from the success of the nineteenth-century German universities in making historical scholarship into a specialized profession. The professor was no longer merely a "scholar and a gentleman," but a historian or a constitutional jurist. Although the Germans might agree that empirical historical science was but the application of common sense, they would have added that for common

[65] *The American Commonwealth*, 2nd rev. ed. (London, 1891), II, 648.

sense to be scientific it had to be rigorously trained and disciplined. Unlike common sense, the scientific method was not to be taken for granted.

Yet with the gradual elaboration of the interpretative framework of political and constitutional history and particularly that of the Prussian school of Droysen, Sybel, and Treitschke, German historical *Wissenschaft* acquired characteristics that were less universal than specifically Prussian. Prussia's political historians appealed to the ideas of Humboldt and Ranke that had become part of the fabric of German life in the nineteenth century. They addressed themselves to Germans caught up in the drama of Prussia's rise to power in Central Europe. Prussia's resurgence after the Napoleonic defeat, with the concomitant dependence of individual welfare upon the welfare of the body politic; the expansion of Prussia into a German empire that was the manifestation of social and racial energies—such ideas appeared to receive empirical verification in Prussian-German political history. Ranke's German history was Prussian history; his universal history was nineteenth-century German history writ large.

When American historical scholars like Herbert Adams and John Burgess accepted the German historiography as "true" history they were guilty of too simple an identification of disparate national histories. Adams was mistaken in seeing the United States as a purely Teutonic civilization, and Burgess in equating the North with Prussia and proceeding to champion United States dominance in the Western Hemisphere.[66] In fact, both Adams and Burgess identified the United States with

[66] In "Present Problems of Constitutional Law," *PSQ*, XIX (Dec., 1904), 575.

Prussia and their own position with that of the German historians. To treat the American Civil War as a stage in an evolving American nationalism was to disregard the earlier nationalism of Manifest Destiny, and amounted to viewing secession as an act of consolidation. Small wonder that Burgess finally took refuge in the Hegelian dialectic! To speak of America's Teutonic civilization was to close one's eyes to the facts of American immigration. To import the concept of the German scholar-aristocrat to America was in effect to deprive the historian of the "imaginative understanding" of his democratic society that was, according to Droysen, the *sine qua non* of historical work. It is no wonder, then, that before Turner and the social historians could do any original work they had to declare their break with the institutional history of Adams and his school.

Adams himself sensed the basic incompatibility of his theories with the traditions and conditions of American history. He knew that his German masters did not easily communicate their thoughts to his countrymen. After his return to Baltimore Adams failed to maintain his connections with German scholars, but instead corresponded extensively with his colleagues in England. This fact has led Professor Holt to suggest that "the orthodox account of the dominant influence of German scholarship in America during this period [1876–1901] may need revision." [67] Adams came to realize that England's democratic social system was more congenial to Americans than the aristocratic one of Germany. In Chapter 7 we shall give more detailed attention to Adams' changing views.

[67] "Historical Scholarship in the United States, 1876–1901," *JHSt.*, LVI (1938), 403.

Suffice it to say here that slowly but steadily Adams forsook his German masters for the "democratic" scholars and schoolmen of England. With Burgess the case was different. He lacked Adams' willingness to consider new facts and ideas, and his basic beliefs and assumptions after 1890 did not change. He continued to defend the principle that the state "can do no wrong." [68] As a disciple of Hegel he absolved both the German and the American "state" from responsibility for the corruption of politics, and blamed instead the ever increasing power of the governments. In Germany, he argued, individual liberty was threatened by the notion "that some government must be able to regulate and control everything." [69] In the United States the threat to liberty came from trust-busting presidents and progressive legislation.[70] What he thought both countries needed to preserve the state was more educated leadership on the one hand, and both less government interference and less direct democracy on the other. As he saw it, Germany's hope lay in Wilhelm II, and America's in her lawyers and scholars. Thus Burgess had nothing but scorn for American progressives and advocates of European parliamentarianism,[71] and he turned a deaf ear to Wilson's call to make the world safe for democracy. Gradually he lost his students and his readers, and withdrew to the woods of New England. His aversion to "purely" historical work eventually became a

[68] *Political Science and Comparative Constitutional Law*, I, 57.
[69] *Ibid.*, II, 183.
[70] In *The Reconciliation of Government with Liberty* (N.Y., 1915), pp. 358ff., 370.
[71] In "Tendencies of the Present in the Development of Constitutional Government in Europe," *Columbia Law Times*, I (Dec., 1887), 65–75.

disregard for the actual workings of political institutions. His infatuation with the ideal state and his narrow constitutional interpretation of history not only destroyed the usefulness of his political theory for his contemporaries but also closed his mind to the influence of economic and social forces on history, law, and politics. Finally his emulation of the German academic elite cut him off from an understanding of his native land and its people. He unwittingly signaled the end of his influence as a scholar and as a citizen when in 1914 he hailed the German scholars as "the salt of the earth." [72] Burgess' science of politics had had its day.

Triumph in the reform of American higher education, failure in the attempt to transfer a German science of history and politics to America—this must be our verdict on the German-trained Americans of the historical school. It is of interest to note that this failure was entirely their own doing. Had they really grasped the *Ideengeschichte* of Humboldt and Ranke, they would have realized that not only the facts but the ideas of American history had to come from American sources. When they mixed American facts with German ideas, they could not but founder upon the shoals of cultural diversity.

[72] *The Truth about Germany and the Facts about the War,* broadside (Newport, R.I., Sept. 17, 1914).

6

The Sciences of Society:
Political Economy and Sociology

> The authority of English economy is
> shattered beyond recovery; can a truer
> system of economic thought gain control
> over the American mind?
> —HENRY CARTER ADAMS, 1887

HENRY CARTER ADAMS accurately identified the central problem for America's political economists of the 1880's: the passing of the laissez-faire dogma of classical economics and the uncertainty of what was to take its place. To be sure, economists of the old school were to put up a determined fight, and Social Darwinians such as William Graham Sumner were to assert once again that the natural laws of economic science were those of the biological struggle for survival. Yet economics as a science of immutable natural laws had seen its day. The body of economic and social thought that now emerged was, in Morton White's phrase, "anti-formalistic." American scholars had become convinced that "logic, abstraction, deduction, mathematics, and mechanics were inadequate to social research and incapable of containing the rich, moving, living current of social life." [1] This social life, as the German historians would have said, was part of the realm of man rather than of nature. Its study would require a "true" social science, not merely the application of the procedures of natural science to social phenomena. The present chapter is concerned with the coming of a historical social science to America, and with its gradual incorporation into the social thought of the American pragmatists.

The American economists and sociologists who had been trained in Germany were all too ready to make the teachings of the German empirical idealists of the historical school the foundation of their labors in America. As it turned out, they had in fact been better served by their German teachers than had their colleagues in historical and political science. In economics and sociology, society rather than the state was the main object of inquiry, and the investigation of the ceaselessly changing facets of society satisfied the empirical bent of the historical school better than the contemplation of either the relatively stable institutions of the state or the theoretical concepts of politics.[2] The extent of the influence of the historical school on the German-trained social scientists may be seen in the results of an inquiry conducted by Professor Farnam of Yale shortly after the turn of the century. Of the 116 economists and sociologists responding to Professor Farnam's queries, 59 had studied in Germany between 1873 and 1905, and 20 had returned

[1] Morton White, *Social Thought in America: The Revolt against Formalism* (Boston, 1957), p. 11.

[2] Cf. Joseph Dorfman, "The Role of the German Historical School in American Economic Growth," *American Economic Review: Papers and Proceedings*, XLV (May, 1955), 28.

with the *Dr. phil.* degree. Of the more than 80 who specified what they regarded the most important influence on their thinking, 30 listed the historical school, 23 the scientific and historical method, 15 the "point of view," and 8 the theory of state intervention. Fourteen referred to Professor Böhm-Bawerk's Vienna school of marginal utility economics; most of these stressed its resemblances rather than its contrast to the German school. Among the teachers most often cited as influential were Wagner, Schmoller, Conrad, Roscher, and Knies.[3]

With the exception of Adolph Wagner all of these men represented the German historical school of *Volkswirtschaftslehre*, the science of the national economy. As taught by these scholars, it dealt with the economic thought and action of entire peoples throughout the whole course of their existence. Just as a nation was the sum total of all its individual members, past and present, so the national economy was a social organism whose life transcended that of individuals, interest groups, or single generations. To the German scholars the analogy with a biological organism suggested a rejection, both implicit and explicit, of laissez-faire economics as well as a warning against the hasty subordination of economic thought to theoretical models of a fugitive present. A social body had its own history, German scholars told their students, and no *a priori* theory—whether individualistic or collectivistic—could do it full justice.

The national economists thus deliberately aligned them-

---

[3] In Henry W. Farnam, "Deutsch-amerikanische Beziehungen in der Volkswirtschaftslehre," in *Die Entwicklung der deutschen Volkswirtschaftslehre im 19. Jahrhundert, Festschrift für Gustav Schmoller* (Leipzig, 1908), Vol. I, Ch. 18, pp. 25–29.

selves with the idealism of the higher critics in philology, theology, history, and jurisprudence. In 1843 Wilhelm Roscher declared that national economists were to present "that which nations have thought, willed, and sensed concerning economic affairs, that which they strove for and which they attained, and the whys of their endeavors and their attainments." In their investigations of national thought, will, sensibility, aspiration, and attainment, the national economists freely acknowledged the bond that united them with the higher critics in other fields. Roscher professed that he wanted to achieve "something similar" to the labors of Savigny's historical school of jurisprudence.[4] Bruno Hildebrand wanted to deal with the economic aspects of national life in the same manner as the historical philologists dealt with its literary aspects.[5]

These two men were the founders of what has been called the older historical school of national economy. For both of them, evolution, flux, growth, and process were key concepts. "We do not hesitate," wrote Roscher, "to declare economic science a pure empirical science. For us history therefore is not a means, but the object of our investigations." [6] Such theoretical statements as they might make were to be firmly anchored in time and space. In the words of Karl Knies, general economic laws were to be nothing but "historical explications and progressive

[4] Wilhelm Roscher, *Grundriss zu Vorlesungen über die Staatswirtschaft nach geschichtlicher Methode* (Göttingen, 1843), pp. iv, v.

[5] Bruno Hildebrand, *Die Nationalökonomie der Gegenwart und Zukunft* (Frankfurt am Main, 1848), pp. v, 4–5.

[6] "Der gegenwärtige Zustand der wissenschaftlichen Nationalökonomie und die nothwendige Reform desselben," *Deutsche Vierteljahres Schrift*, XLV (1849), 182.

manifestations of truths." [7] Roscher summarized this view by saying that

in our theory we refrain from the elaboration of ideals. Instead we try our hand at simple description, first of the nature and needs of a people, secondly of the laws and institutions of the latter, and finally of the greater or smaller success enjoyed through these laws and institutions. These are things firmly based on reality. They can be proved or refuted with the usual operations of science. They are either false or true, and if true, they can therefore never be really outmoded.[8]

The nature of the "generalized descriptions" of the historical process that were ultimately to be yielded by the science of national economy may be understood by contrast with the laws of classical economics, against which the historical school of national economists were in protest. They wanted to be factual above all: this was their primary understanding of the term "scientific." Thus they leaned towards philosophical nominalism; but they also acknowledged that science became impossible if that nominalism became a total refusal to employ concepts or generalizations. Since these were unavoidable, care had to be taken that they were merely descriptive—that they did not extend beyond the data they summarized.

The data thus assembled concerning one national economy could then be compared with those of another. In this application of the comparative method their science reached a second level: the similarities it showed became rules; the dissimilarities were the exceptions. And in these

[7] *Die politische Ökonomie vom Standpunkt der geschichtlichen Methode* (Braunschweig, 1853), p. 19.

[8] "Der gegenwärtige Zustand . . . ," p. 186.

rules, Roscher believed, economic science would find the natural laws governing human needs and their satisfaction by the state.

From these German national economists their American students received an intellectual framework that was practically identical with that of the historians. The concept of the social organism, the rejection of speculative theories, the reliance on empirical data, the practice of the higher criticism, the search for limited generalizations, the use of the comparative method—all these characteristics of the German historical science were to mark the work of the "new" economists in America, and were to be the cause of conflict with those of the old school.

The founding of the American Economic Association in 1885 brought the conflict to a head, and the next year witnessed the publication of a debate in the weekly journal *Science*.[9] Edwin R. A. Seligman and Richmond Mayo-Smith of Columbia, Edmund J. James of the University of Pennsylvania, Richard T. Ely of Johns Hopkins, Henry Carter Adams of Michigan and Cornell—all charter members of the Association—confronted F. W. Taussig of Harvard, the Johns Hopkins astronomer Simon Newcomb, and Arthur T. Hadley of Yale. The new economists made five essential points: that the historical approach was fundamental to the study of political economy; that economic activities constituted but one aspect of a developing social organism and were intimately related to its religious, political, and social activities; that because of the relatedness of all human activities, a concern with

[9] Vols. VII and VIII, April, 23–July 30. Reprinted as *Science Economic Discussion* (N.Y., 1886).

ethics was indispensable; that this concern, in turn, demanded a consideration of the role of the state in economic affairs; that the historical approach, stressing the unique features of each social body, argued against a slavish imitation of German models, and particularly of their socialistic tendencies.[10]

Against all this, the natural scientist Simon Newcomb held that science was concerned with things as they were, not as they ought to be, but at the same time that science was not to be content with factual enumeration but must lead to deductive theory. Taussig and Hadley both rejected the concern with any but strictly economic factors as premature, since what they saw as merely "a wide speculation in sociology" was "for the present likely to check scientific progress." Their main contention was that in the hands of the scholars of the historical school, political economy ceased to be wholly science.[11] The new economists argued in their turn that the subject matter of political economy could not be treated like that of natural science, which dealt with immutable nature, since economic science was concerned not with nature but with men. It therefore neither could nor should be theoretical, deductive, or mathematical, but must of necessity be descriptive and historical, yielding contingent and relative truths. As a science its method was historical, comparative, and statistical. In any discussion of the question that had already been raised in Germany, as to the nature

[10] Seligman, April 23, p. 375; Ely, June 11, p. 529; Adams, July 2, p. 15; Ely, *ibid.;* James, May 28, pp. 485–486; Seligman, *ibid.,* p. 382.

[11] Newcomb, June 18, p. 541, and July 9, p. 26; Taussig, May 28, p. 489; Hadley, July 16, p. 48.

of historical and social science,[12] it is well to remember the distinction made by the German empirical idealists between the sciences of man, the *Geisteswissenschaften,* and the sciences of nature, the *Naturwissenschaften.* These men had pointed out that nature was governed by a strict determinism of cause and effect, whereas human affairs were characterized by freedom of choice. The function of the sciences of man was to inquire into the laws of social development—laws that were historically conditioned and that made allowance for man's freedom to will and choose. The German empirical idealists thus rejected both the *a priori* strait jacket of speculative reason and the positivists' denial of laws. The sciences of man, they held, occupied a category distinct from the nonhistorical realms of both reason and nature.

The "new" economists in America took exactly the same position, rejecting the mathematical-deductive approach to economic science defended by Newcomb in favor of description and generalization, and relying on comparative and statistical methods. The latter term, however, might well give us pause—for is not statistics a tool of mathematics? And should it not therefore have been regarded by the new economists as inappropriate for historical scholarship?

The new economists did, by and large, reject statistics because it was a tool of a deductive science. They repeated Karl Knies' warning that economists using the methods of statistics were obliged to reject analogies and inductive generalizations, and to speak solely in terms of causal relations, averages, and comprehensive quantitative generalizations—and hence to move away from the

[12] Adams, July 30, p. 104; Smith, July 23, p. 87.

concrete data of history.[13] Like Knies, and later Schmoller, the new economists maintained that if statistics were to be used at all then it should be used only as an auxiliary way of handling historical materials.[14]

Strictly speaking, Knies would have argued, generalizations based on statistical inquiries were but frequency functions of observed economic phenomena, which in themselves could be "true" only for a given time and place. Roscher made the same statement, and Hildebrand emphasized that what the comparative method disclosed were evolutionary laws. Knies expressed the same view when in 1853 he declared that economic science could discover laws of analogy only, not laws of strict and invariable causality.[15] Gustav Schmoller again underscored this opinion when in 1893 he asserted that a lifetime's experience had convinced him "beyond all doubt" that "exclusively mathematical-scientific studies usually disable the scholar to judge matters political and economic." [16]

Yet despite these reiterations that the tools of natural and mathematical science were inadequate to deal with the materials of human history, not all German economists were of the same mind. Gustav Schmoller himself declared in 1874 that "the flow of time made manifest

[13] *Die Statistik als selbstständige Wissenschaft* (Kassel, 1850), p. 152.

[14] Knies, *Die politische Ökonomie*, p. 319, and Schmoller, "Die Volkswirtschaft, die Volkswirtschaftslehre und ihre Methode (1893)," in *Über einige Grundfragen* (Leipzig, 1898), pp. 266–674. See also Roscher's remark in *Geschichte der National-Ökonomik in Deutschland* (München, 1874), p. 1035.

[15] Knies, *Die politische Ökonomie*, p. 346.

[16] "Die Volkswirtschaft . . . ," p. 298.

nothing but laws of causality," and he had clearly reverted to the belief in strict scientific laws in 1898, when he wrote that "German [economic] science only attempted to find causal explanations and the strong proof of truth for ancient ethical-religious and legal-political imperatives." [17] On the issue of statistics Ernst Engel and Adolph Wagner dissented from Knies and Roscher. Dr. Engel, the director of the Royal Prussian Statistical Bureau, told his American students that the "search for and the discovery of natural laws in the lives of states and peoples and of human society is the task of modern statistics based on natural science." [18] Adolph Wagner, professor of political science at the University of Berlin, added that statistics were to be applied to "*all* phenomena . . . which as functions of constant and accidental . . . causes do not show absolutely uniform behavior patterns, but which in the large number of cases possess a regular character determined by the constant causes." [19] Statistics, then, dealt with social *and* natural phenomena in a uniform quantitative manner, and constituted both a method and a science that yielded laws explaining causal relationships.

In both Germany and the United States, the deterministic overtones of Wagner's statement were disturbing to historical scholars. His views brought economics too

[17] "Offenes Sendschreiben an Herrn Professor Dr. Heinrich von Treitschke . . . ," *Jahrbücher für Nationalökonomie und Statistik,* XXIII (1874), 251, and "Wechselnde Theorien und feststehende Wahrheiten . . . (1897)," in *Über einige Grundfragen,* p. 343.

[18] "Das statistische Seminar und das Studium der Statistik überhaupt," *Zeitschrift des Königl. Preussischen Statistischen Bureaus,* XI (July–Dec., 1871), 195.

[19] "Statistik," in J. C. Bluntschli and K. Brater, eds., *Deutsches Staatswörterbuch,* X (1867), 464.

close to the universalism of natural science. In addition, historical scholars took exception to the ahistorical rigidity of Wagner's state socialism. By and large, the American representatives of the new economics accepted the opinion of Knies and Schmoller that to seek causal relations in history that were based on numerical averages and generalizations meant to assume that men were but so many atoms, each replaceable by another. To most Americans, the sacrifice of human uniqueness and free will required by the statistical science of Engel and Wagner amounted to sacrilege.

Yet statistics had uses which even the new economists were unwilling to forego, if only they could be adapted to social science. The two men regarded by their contemporaries as America's foremost statisticians set out to do just that. General Francis Amasa Walker, president of the Massachusetts Institute of Technology, had also become president of the American Economic Association as a result of his efforts to mediate between the old and new schools. It is thus hardly surprising to find him silent on the theoretical problems of his research. His fame as a statistician was due to his work with the United States Census. In his popular college text, *Political Economy* (N.Y., 1883), Walker defined the statistician's work as fact-finding, whereas it was the economist who put "the facts into their place in the industrial system." In 1890 Walker recommended the study of statistics on purely utilitarian grounds, as a means of detecting fallacies and of settling arguments. His final conclusion was that statistics was but a method, and that as such it qualified "the student of history, of sociology, or of political economy confidently and surely to reduce from thousands of pages closely packed with figures some hitherto unsuspected law of human life or conduct." [20] Just what the nature of these "unsuspected laws of human life and conduct" might turn out to be—whether they would resemble the invariable laws of nature or the contingent evolutionary laws of history—Walker refrained from speculating.

While Walker cautiously refrained from exploring the relationship of statistics to social laws, Professor Richmond Mayo-Smith of Columbia courageously took the stand that social laws were found as the proper results of statistical science. Taking his cue from the German scholar Georg Mayr, Mayo-Smith differentiated the statistical method used in the natural and the social sciences from what he called statistical science. The former, he said, was universally applicable, whereas the latter belonged only among the social sciences. In natural science, according to the view held by Mayr and Mayo-Smith, the statistical method was useful when applied to certain phenomena, but was not indispensable. They argued that the validity of a natural law could be tested by a single experiment, as in the freezing of water at 0° C., or established by observing one instance, as in the botanical description of the species *Anemone nemorosa*. But in social science, they went on, a single observation proved nothing. The endless complexity and variety of social phenomena demanded a long series of observations, which then had to be evaluated statistically. This curious—and, it may be added, spurious—definition of natural science

[20] *Political Economy*, p. 24, and "The Study of Statistics in Colleges and Technical Schools," *Discussions in Education*, J. P. Munroe, ed. (N.Y., 1899), p. 302.

allowed Mayr and Mayo-Smith to identify the statistician with the sociologist, and to declare that statistics was a social science.[21] The weakness of their argument was in their unawareness that for natural scientists the concept of a mechanistic, strictly deterministic causality was already giving way to one defined in terms of mathematical probability.

The motivation behind Mayo-Smith's argument is easy to understand. The German scholars of the historical school, and with them Mayo-Smith as their disciple, were eager to make historical and social studies scientific without capitulating to what they thought was the determinism of natural science. Mayo-Smith himself put the case plainly:

The tendency of every social science is to reduce the phenomena of human life to the position of actions controlled by law,—that is, to limit the province which in former times was allowed to the freedom of the human will. . . . If however we admit freedom of the will, what becomes of statistics as a science?[22]

It became, Mayo-Smith said, a social rather than a natural science, a social science that observed irregularities as well as regularities, and that had as its objective not the establishment of natural laws but the scientific direction of social reform.

Walker and Mayo-Smith demonstrated that the historical economists could in fact refuse to accept Simon

[21] See Mayr, *Die Gesetzmässigkeit im Gesellschaftsleben* (München, 1877), pp. 1–21, and Mayo-Smith, "Statistics and Economics," *Publications of the AEA*, III (Sept.–Nov., 1888), 237–363. See also Mayo-Smith, *Statistics and Sociology* (N.Y., 1895), *passim*.

[22] "Statistics and Economics," pp. 355, 357.

Newcomb's view of economics as a deductive science, while nonetheless using statistical data as raw materials of the purest kind. Such data were precisely the "facts" that scientific historians were forever pursuing. Furthermore, the new economists found quantitative information eminently useful in the formulation of economic and social policies and reforms. For the American graduate students at Engel's bureau in Berlin,[23] this was confirmed by the diverse uses to which the data of the United States Federal Census had been put at home. During the 1880's the belief that statistics could be useful in bringing about social reforms prompted many German-trained scholars to support enthusiastically the efforts of Carroll D. Wright, United States Commissioner of Labor after 1885, to introduce the study of statistics in American colleges.[24]

For the new economists the usefulness of statistics only bolstered their devotion to social reforms. They endorsed Wagner's and Engel's commitment to legislative efforts, made their own adaptation of the Germans' advocacy of state socialism, and proceeded to give these doctrines concrete application through the American Economic Association.[25] The new economists hoped to wean away their profession from the traditional laissez-faire theories of American political economists. In support of this project they drew upon the heritage of college moral philosophy and upon the imperatives of Christian charity, as well as upon the Reform Darwinians and their own mentors in

[23] See W. Lexis, "Statistik," and "Die staatswissenschaftlichen Seminare," in Lexis, ed., Die deutschen Universitäten (Berlin, 1893), I, 598–606.

[24] See Carroll D. Wright, "The Study of Statistics in Colleges," Publications of the AEA, III (March, 1888), 12ff.

[25] See supra, Ch. 2, n. 35.

Germany. The science proposed by the new economists was to present clear and constructive solutions to the problems raised by the industrial revolution; and with the support of religion it intended to prove that what was moral was also scientific.

In Germany the reform movement among the national economists had been bound inextricably to the scholarship of the historical school. In 1848 Hildebrand, one of the rebels against laissez-faire economics, had asked his students to consider "what social reforms were demanded by the growing rift between poor and rich, and what duties were imposed by the right to private property." [26] In 1874 Roscher noted with approval that economists had returned to the old question, What is permitted? [27] Schmoller believed that institutions were shaped by ethical ideals, and rejected the view that economic conditions were solely the product of natural forces; accordingly, he called for the help of economics as an ethical science in molding institutions. Economic scholarship was to deny the dominance of nature over culture and to refute the Social Darwinians, for whom man, an animal like any other, was a product of nature alone. Above all, such scholarship was to make sure that its ethical pronouncements had a truly scientific basis.[28]

A scientific description of existing conditions and a scientific elucidation of ethical imperatives—these made up the *Volkswirtschaftslehre* of the German historical school. The factual and empirical aspect, and that con-

[26] *Op. cit.*, p. 3. [27] *Geschichte*, p. 1034.
[28] "Die soziale Frage und der preussische Staat," *Preussische Jahrbücher*, XXXIII (1874), 337, and "Offenes Sendschreiben," p. 246.

cerned with ideals and moral obligations, were both held to be indispensable, and economic science was somehow to bring them together in a unified whole. The attempt undertaken in 1872 led to the formation of the *Verein für Sozialpolitik*. Perhaps because German scholars tended to take their scholarship for granted, from the very outset they emphasized their desire to make the *Verein* an instrument for putting their prescriptions into effect. Professor Conrad stated the purposes of its founders thus:

The *Verein* wanted to counteract the free-trade activities of the Congress of National Economy, founded in 1858; to help clarify opinions through thorough, strictly scientific investigations and publication of economic conditions; to resist laissez-faire views through public discussion of German legislative tasks. It saw as its special mandate the proof of the necessity of state activity, particularly for the protection of the lower classes, and an investigation into the extent of requisite state interference in practical affairs.[29]

In 1873 the founders spelled out their convictions concerning the active role of the state in social and economic affairs:

We are convinced that the unrestricted play of contrary and unequally strong private interests does not guarantee the common welfare, that the demands of the common interest and of humanity must be safeguarded in economic affairs, and that the well-considered interference of the state has to be called upon early in order to protect the legitimate interests of all. We do not regard state welfare as an emergency measure or as an unavoidable evil, but as the fulfillment of one of

[29] *Grundriss zum Studium der Politischen Oekonomie*, Vol. I, *National Oekonomie*, 7th rev. ed. (Jena, 1910), p. 430.

the highest tasks of our time and nation. In the serious execution of this task the egotism of individuals and the narrow interest of classes will be subordinated to the lasting and higher destiny of the whole.[30]

The *Verein*'s stand on state intervention in the economy was its chief reform proposal, emerging in the summation of all its debates, and calling forth most of the attacks of its enemies.

The *Verein's* original members were all economists of the historical school, among them Roscher, Hildebrand, Knies, and Schmoller, in addition to Wagner and Engel. These men were united in their opposition on moral grounds to the natural-law doctrines of classical economics. It is less easy to specify the points on which they were positively agreed. They all emphasized historical laws and ethics, and they all believed in organized interference with economic processes for the sake of individual or social welfare. They were believers in evolution rather than revolution, vociferously condemning "bomb-throwers, dynamiters, and anarchists." Toward socialism their attitude was ambiguous. Of those who looked to religion as an aid to reform, some were drawn to the English and German Christian Socialists, others to the French and German Catholic solidarists, who held that little was gained by the substitution of collectivism for individualism. The solidarists proposed, instead, a synthesis of laissez-faire individualism and socialism, since they regarded society as an organism each of whose members both contributed to and were dependent on the welfare

[30] In *Jahrbücher für Nationalökonomie und Statistik,* XXI (1873), 123.

of the whole.[31] The majority of the *Verein's* members, however, rejected any association with the socialists, preferring to base their reforms entirely on science— which, they believed, held no brief for socialist doctrine. Still others, notably Adolph Wagner, were more interested in economic theory. They worked at developing a theory of state intervention, and did not hesitate to call themselves state socialists. For them the state was the guardian of the public weal, the protector of the weak, and the chastiser of the ruthless. In the social legislation of Bismarck they saw their theory put into practice.[32]

The members of the *Verein* as a whole were close enough to the socialist program to be tagged *Katheder-sozialisten*—professorial socialists—by friend and foe alike. They were attacked by economists of the classical school for being radical and by Social Democrats for not being radical enough. From among scholars of other disciplines came accusations of unscientific behavior, culminating in the 1874–1875 debate carried on between Treitschke and Schmoller in the pages of the *Preussische Jahrbücher* and *Hildebrands Jahrbücher für National-ökonomie und Statistik*. Treitschke's target was "socialism and its supporters." He began by exempting from attack the economists of the early historical school—i.e., Roscher and Knies, whom he certified to be free from "socialistic influences." But, he wrote, "in the heat of battle the enthusiasts of professorial socialism . . . proposed many a vague ideal which looked very much like the phantasms

[31] See Gerhard Stavenhagen, *Geschichte der Wirtschaftstheorie,* 2nd ed. (Göttingen, 1957), pp. 172–176.

[32] See Adolph Wagner, *Grundlegung der Politischen Oekonomie,* 3rd ed., 2nd part (Leipzig, 1894), p. 14.

of crude socialism and which, if carried out, would destroy any social order. . . . The most dangerous weakness of the professorial socialists, however, is that they so frequently *den Ton verfehlt haben*"—that is to say, did not conform to Treitschke's idea of academic respectability.[33] Schmoller replied that socialism was not a cause but a result of social tensions, and that the *Verein* "did not intend to teach or to propose a new economic or political theory, but rather to win over a recalcitrant public opinion to those social reforms . . . which had been long demanded by scholars." He accused Treitschke of viewing human inequalities as solely the result of natural forces and thus always present, whereas Schmoller himself believed them to be culturally produced as well, and therefore amenable to reform. "Your point of view is aristocratic or oligarchic; mine is democratic," Schmoller told Treitschke.[34]

The tenor of the Treitschke-Schmoller debate clearly indicates that by the mid-seventies the activities and concerns of the reform-conscious historical economists were social and political rather than methodological. To the facetious question asked by their detractors—"Economics, what is that?"—came the answer, "Oh, yes, I know. . . . You are an economist if you measure workmen's dwellings and say that they are too small." [35] Professor Conrad was quite right in saying that "the historical school had done more for economic policy than for

[33] "Der Socialismus und seine Gönner," *Preussische Jahrbücher,* XXXIV (1874), 286–288, *passim.*

[34] "Offenes Sendschreiben," XXIV (1875), 118; XXIII (1874), 348.

[35] Quoted in Joseph A. Schumpeter, *History of Economic Analysis* (N.Y., 1954), p. 803, n. 6.

economic science, and that its chief justification lay in the indispensability of historical study for the development of legislation." [36]

Professor Conrad might have said the same had be been asked to evaluate the work of his American students, since the new economists in the American Economic Association echoed the pronouncements of the *Verein für Sozialpolitik*. But they had always to reckon with the opposition of the old school, and were forced to tone down many of their assertions. On the question of government intervention in the economy, for example, the new economists pointed to Schmoller's pronouncement that "monarch and civil servants, these pre-eminent representatives of the idea of the state . . . must seize the initiative for a great legislative program of social reform." [37] Thus they proposed to open a statement of principles by the American Economic Association with the thesis, "We regard the state as an agency whose positive assistance is one of the indispensable conditions of human progress." This was mild enough, one might have supposed; but the softening of "interference" or "regulation" to the blander "positive assistance" was still offensive to members of the old school, on whose account a footnote was added, to the effect that the principles were "not to be regarded as binding upon individual members." [38] But despite such concessions, the economists of the old school boycotted the Association until 1888, when the statement of principles was dropped. Thereupon men like Simon Newcomb felt able to join the Association.

[36] *Op. cit.*, p. 430.
[37] "Die soziale Frage und der preussische Staat," p. 342.
[38] See *Publications of the AEA*, I (1887), 35–36.

But even though the German-trained new economists showed a willingness to compromise in tactical matters, they were not deterred from continuing to advocate state interference. For a while they were notably ineffectual in promoting their beliefs, erring now on the side of bluntness and again in being too vague. Edmund James and Simon Patten declared, for example, that the state was to curb "the greed of the capitalist and the shortsightedness of the laborer" and to promote "the symmetrical development of [the nation's] material resources." [39] Ely acclaimed the state as "the starting-point of modern industrial as well as social life . . . , the only agency through which the energy of civilization can be maintained." He pronounced the state divine, and predicted that "when men come to look upon their duty to the state as something as holy as their duty to the church . . . it will be easy for government to perform all its functions." [40] Such declarations were neither really scientific nor particularly constructive, and it is possible to sympathize with Newcomb's complaint that he was "unable to form any clear conception of the ground taken" by the new economists on the issue of state interference in economic affairs. [41]

To this objection Henry Carter Adams provided an answer with his essay, "The Relation of the State to Industrial Action." Adams' argument was that economic freedom was the result, not the enemy, of state action, and that it was the function of the state through govern-

[39] *Ibid.*, 3rd series, XI (1910), 52–53.
[40] "Co-operation in Literature and the State," in William E. Barns, ed., *The Labor Problem* (N.Y., 1886), pp. 9–10, and "Recent American Socialism," *JHSt.*, III (April, 1885), 303.
[41] In *Science*, VII (June 18, 1886), 538.

ment "to maintain the beneficent results of competitive action while guarding society from the evil consequences of unrestrained competition." The Germans, Adams observed, viewed the state as the all-encompassing organism; the English regarded it as a necessary evil; whereas the true position, as Adams saw it, was that society was "the organic entity about which all our reasoning should center." Both state action and individual economic activity were functions of society, and a consideration of social purpose should govern the influences allotted to each.[42]

Henry Carter Adams had unquestionably struck the keynote for the accommodations of the German *Kathedersozialismus,* with its dutiful recognition of the state, to the individualistic tradition of American political economy. Society was this theme. Although American economists had habitually viewed the state as antagonistic to the individual, they still did not postulate an irremediable antagonism between the two. Man, after all, was a social being. And whereas for many German-trained political scientists—such as Burgess—political theory became what amounted to a science of the state and its government, the economists trained in Germany found it easy to transform their discipline from a division of moral philosophy into a branch of social science. Ely wrote that economics was "a branch of sociology"—which he regarded as the all-embracing science of human association.[43]

It is clear by now that the new economists did not restrict their scholarly objectives to "pure" research,

[42] "The Relation of the State to Industrial Action," *Publications of the AEA,* I (Jan., 1887), 499, 494.

[43] *Outlines of Economics,* 3rd ed. (N.Y., 1920), p. 13.

analysis, and description, but were committed to reforming the economic system of society. It was their particular
concern to make sure that their reform proposals were
truly scientific—in other words, to establish a science
of reform. Like their German masters and colleagues,
they found it well-nigh impossible to win undisputed
acceptance for what they proposed. In the eyes of their
adversaries, their involvement in politics and legislation
branded them as unscientific. Moreover, political activity
and controversy left little time for a much needed examination of the assumptions and methodological problems
of the historical school. Although they reiterated that
scholarship and reform were inseparable, they did not
succeed in showing how and why this inseparability
could avoid violating the demand for scientific objectivity.

Among the economists Henry Carter Adams tried to
show that the problem could be solved by discarding the
concept of economics as an independent science. Rather,
he argued, economics dealt with the problems of society,
and such problems could be attacked only by a comprehensive social science. As reform scientists, economists
could not afford to consider economic institutions, beliefs, and practices alone. They had to open the way for an
"all-embracing science of human association," be it called
the science of society, social sciene, or sociology.

This move had likewise been undertaken in Germany,
where during the 1880's historians had striven to escape
from the narrow confines of the political school into the
broader fields of social and cultural history. Inevitably
this change of course brought them into close contact
with sociologists—a contact which led in turn to a revived interest in theoretical discussions of the functions

of history and sociology. Among the national economists Roscher had stressed that as a disciple of the historical method the economist had "to transpose himself into the soul of the man whose activities or sufferings he wants to describe or evaluate." [44] The scholars found that individual men bore little resemblance to the "economic man" of the classical school. The range of their needs, wishes, and activities was far wider. If economic science were to do justice to men, it had to consider the place of custom, law, politics, art, and society, and—according to Schmoller—to treat these data as "partial ingredients of an interrelated whole." [45]

Among the academic historians Karl Lamprecht sounded the call for this more comprehensive approach. "History," he declared, "is primarily a socio-psychological science." After 1870 "description alone was no longer the watchword [of German historians], but an intelligent comprehension." To comprehend culture the historian had to understand what Lamprecht called "socio-psychic movements." Their investigation was "nothing but the application of greater intensity of observation to historical material." History in effect became "nothing but applied psychology." Using the psychological approach, historians were obliged to study the phenomena of religion, law, economics, politics, language, literature, and the arts. Lamprecht's impatience with the narrowness of a predominantly political history thus corresponded to the historical economists' discarding of a "purely economic" science of national economy. The modern science of history, Lamprecht concluded, "has opened up for itself a vastly greater field of endeavor and conflict and . . . will

[44] *Geschichte,* p. 1036.   [45] "Die Volkswirtschaft," p. 268.

require thousands of diligent workers and creative minds to open up its rich and in many respects unknown regions, and to cultivate them successfully." [46]

Historians and economists alike had begun to explore the possibilities of a more comprehensive social science. Auguste Comte in France and Herbert Spencer in England advanced the claims of sociology. In Germany Albert Schäffle moved from economic studies to the biologically and psychologically oriented concept of the *Bau und Leben des socialen Körpers* (1875). Seeking to analyze "the interconnections of human phenomena in general," Schäffle was brought face to face with the qualitative difference of material and psychic factors influencing human behavior. [47] Sociology dealt, just as economics did, with material wants and their fulfillment, and also with human volition and sentiment—with phenomena that were inorganic, organic, and social. If it were to be scientific it had to apply to the objects of its study a consistent methodology, which was to be taken from the natural sciences, and was to eschew metaphysical speculation in favor of a strict empiricism. [48]

A similar conclusion was reached by Paul Barth in his *Die Philosophie der Geschichte als Soziologie* (1897), where he agreed with Lamprecht that history properly written had as its object "human societies and their changes" through time. But Barth went on to propose that this history be given the name of sociology—which

[46] *What Is History?* trans. E. A. Andrews (N.Y., 1905), pp. 33–35, *passim.*

[47] See Albion Small, "Some Contributions to the History of Sociology," *AJS*, XXX (Sept., 1924), 179–180.

[48] Schäffle, *Bau und Leben des socialen Körpers*, Vol. I (Tübingen, 1875), pp. 7–8.

in his view was "nothing but history arrived at a consciousness of its task." It was to be a science and therefore strictly empirical; thus the comparative method, the biological analogy, and the standard social theories of the time would no longer serve, because "it is the task of science to rise from the mass of detailed facts to universally valid truths." Science, however, had only one means of arriving at such truths—namely, the application to empirically verified facts of the law of causality. Barth thus affirmed that a common methodology could unite all science—whether natural or social—even though its branches differed in the objects under investigation. The subject matter of social science was man—a part of nature, but endowed with a will that affected his own history. A science of society had therefore to accept the historical approach as the royal road to all knowledge concerning social phenomena. A developing subject matter whose transformations were to be explained in terms of historical causality was the field of social science. According to Barth, "There is only *one* science of the history of the human race. One may call it sociology or the philosophy of society, or, as we prefer, the philosophy of history." [49]

In America it was Albion Small who carried on the crusade for social science begun by Lamprecht, Schäffle, and Barth.[50] A historian by training, Small moved from institutional history, as taught by Herbert B. Adams, into

[49] *Die Philosophie der Geschichte als Sociologie*, 1st part (Leipzig, 1897), pp. 1–13, *passim*.

[50] See the author's "From Moral Philosophy to Sociology: Albion Woodbury Small," *Harvard Educational Review*, XXIX (Summer, 1959), 237–238, 244.

social history,[51] and from there into sociology proper. For several years he recommended Schäffle's theory of the social organism, and then found support, in Barth and the Austrian sociologist Ratzenhofer, for his concept of the social process. This concept began by acknowledging the basic contention of the historical school, that society was ever in flux, and could not be caught, as it were, in static formulae. But science, either social or natural, nonetheless could not exist without a fixed logic which made possible meaningful communication among scholars; and finally, empiricism was the scientist's one acceptable road to knowledge.

The implications of this concept for scholars of the ethical school were significant, to say the least. Social science, dealing with the ever changing social process, promised to yield reform proposals that need not claim universal validity, but could be scientifically derived from and directed toward a particular, clearly defined stage of the process. As Small saw it, sociology dealt with the processes of human association. Since men have wills and make choices, sociology had to include in its descriptive purview not only the physical facts of the human environment and constitution but also the psychical facts of the human consciousness. An analysis of both kinds of fact would yield "concrete social ideals" as well as "precise ethical precepts." Values, for Small, were psychical facts which could be scientifically observed, described, and analyzed by the sociologist. The task of sociology, however, did not end with description and analysis, but included evaluation and constructive action as well; it was,

[51] See Small's review, "Von Holst on American Politics," *Civil Service Reformer*, IV (Dec., 1888), 141.

Small wrote, "to find a coherent meaning for that part of experience which is within human power of observation." When that meaning was found, it demanded expression in conduct. "The last phase of social science is the transmuting of valuations into life." [52] A more concise rationale for social science as the wellspring of social reform could scarcely be found.

Small's achievement lay in his demonstration of a logical connection between the empiricism of the historical school and the reform activities of the *Verein für Sozialpolitik*. The German scholars of the historical school, and their American students likewise, had embraced reform activities simply as moral imperatives, naively asserting that they were also scientific. Their opponents had not failed to point out the missing link between scientific description and ethical prescription. Small circumvented the problem by introducing the "social process" concept into American sociology. The concept was, of course, a direct descendant of the historical approach. Since the end of the process must lie hidden in the future, Small firmly rejected the Aristotelian teleology of the idealists, maintaining rather that the universe was open-ended, and that it proceeded according to the Darwinian mechanism of evolution.[53] If for a system of sociological ethics "we represent to ourselves any good whatever as a complete and closed finality," he wrote "we do so by suspending the thought-process." [54]

[52] *The Meaning of Social Science* (Chicago, 1910), pp. 143, 261.
[53] Cf. John Dewey, *The Influence of Darwin on Philosophy* (N.Y., 1910), pp. 1–19.
[54] "The Significance of Sociology for Ethics," *University of Chicago Decennial Publications* (Chicago, 1903), IV, 124.

The judgments of a sociological ethics would be relative, as the term was used by scholars of the historical school—that is, valid only in reference to the conditions of a given time and place. Since the conditions were known to be temporary, reform programs based on ethical evaluations had to be continually re-evaluated. Thus the social process, or history, was accompanied by a process of moral evaluation and practical reforms, and "progressive improvement" or "more of the process" emerged as the ultimate discoverable social end.[55] As Small put it,

The human situation being always and everywhere, either actually or potentially, a becoming, human conduct is always good or bad according to the demands of the particular stage of the process to which it is referred, or in which it must function. In finite conditions, and for finite intelligence, there is hardly more possibility of discovering an absolute good or bad in concrete acts, than there is in determining an absolute up or down in space. Our acts are all relative to a process which, so far as we know, may be infinite in all its dimensions. Our judgments have to be relative to so much of the process as we can make out. So soon as we clearly understand this condition, we realize the vanity of all the absolute or categorical system of ethics.[56]

Small's statement is significant in that it documents the transition between the historical relativism of nineteenth-century German social science scholarship and the ethical relativism of the American pragmatists. The parallel between the formulations of Small and John Dewey is striking and undoubtedly resulted from their close work-

[55] *Ibid.*, p. 141.
[56] *General Sociology* (Chicago, 1905), p. 677.

ing relationship at the University of Chicago.[57] Small wrote that "the indicated end of the process is *more of the process,*" Dewey that "growth itself . . . [is] the only moral 'end.'" Small held that "there can be no generally recognized ethical standards until we have a generally accepted sociology," Dewey that "morals based upon concern with facts and deriving guidance from knowledge of them would at least locate the point of effective endeavor." [58] Their ethical relativism, based on social, historical, and psychological facts, led Small and Dewey to give up the quest for absolute certainty, and thus reminds us of Charles Sanders Peirce's dictum that "people cannot attain absolute certainty concerning questions of fact." [59] Both Small and Dewey emphasize not only the possibility of but the demand for social action based on relative, finite, factual knowledge, and guided by intelligence. Small's sociological ethics and Dewey's instrumentalism are both consistent theories relating thought to action and knowledge to conduct, such as had been lacking to the historical school. With Small the heritage of the German historical school was absorbed into the main stream of American pragmatism and ceased to be identified with the country of its origin.

The American pragmatists in the social sciences succeeded where the German historicists had failed. They

[57] Dewey's *My Pedagogical Creed* (Chicago, 1897) contained Small's essay, "Some Demands of Sociology upon Pedagogy."

[58] Small, "The Scope of Sociology: IX," *AJS,* X (July, 1904), 32; Dewey, *Reconstruction in Philosophy* (N.Y., 1920), p. 177; Small, "The Significance," 113; Dewey, *Human Nature and Conduct* (N.Y., 1922), p. 12.

[59] In Charles Hartshorne and Paul Weiss, eds., *Collected Papers of Charles Sanders Peirce* (Cambridge, 1931–1935), I, 61.

supplied a logical connection between scholarship and reform, between thought and action. As either Small or Dewey might have said, thought *was* action—or, to put the matter another way, in the process of experience thought and action were inseparable because experience, life, and the "social process" were all one. For Americans this was no new doctrine. The Northampton philosopher Jonathan Edwards had proclaimed it, and ever afterward the moral philosophers had more or less articulately preached it. Those of their students who went to Germany had found the professors there vastly more articulate, and they naively regarded the latter's specialized philosophical language as the token of a profounder truth. That "truth," however, was simply a renewed affirmation of the historical nature of knowledge in the social sciences. In their conflict with the moral philosophers and the deductive scientists, the German-trained scholars stripped away much that was shallow and insubstantial, forcing their opponents to modernize their arsenal and to strengthen their own position. When the smoke of battle cleared a new philosophy had been born. It asked for a social science that viewed man's experience as a developing whole; that was based on history, incorporating facts and values alike as the elements of experience; and that concerned itself with the whole, not merely with its parts.

7

Scholarship and Social Action

> I would have American scholars, espe-
> cially in the social sciences, declare their
> independence of do-nothing traditions. I
> would have them repeal the law of custom
> which bars marriage of thought with ac-
> tion.   —ALBION W. SMALL, 1896

THOUGHT and action, scholarship and reform—such
were the polar opposites that for the German scholars of
the historical school defined their field of activity. Most of
their American students adopted the same view, and in so
doing encountered the same difficulties, for lack of what
one might call a unified field theory of social science. The
systems proposed by Schäffle and Barth offered a partial
solution, but were weakened by too great a reliance on
biological and physical analogies and models. In America
Small and Dewey succeeded in modifying Schäffle's and
Barth's rigidly naturalistic frameworks by substituting
for the Germans' "scientific" analogies the concept of the
social process, believing that a scientific methodology
could thus do justice to the phenomena of society.

Small and Dewey, however, were not representative of
the German-trained social scientists, most of whom—this
is especially true of the new economists and of Ely in
particular—did not move beyond the position they had

inherited from their teachers. The problem of adapting the methodology and the assumptions of the historical school to American conditions demanded imagination and boldness, as well as a willingness to re-examine one's assumptions in the light of new circumstances. The very aggressiveness and conviction displayed by the new economists in the struggle with their colleagues of the old school proved their severest liability. Against the force of the opposition the new economics quickly hardened into an orthodoxy that had to be propagated and defended at the same time.

This crusade took its inspiration from the supreme confidence displayed by the German scholars of the Wilhelmian *Gründerjahre*—an attitude that in America frequently made its exponents appear to be spokesmen for the complacency of what Mark Twain called the Gilded Age, as well as for Theodore Roosevelt's progressivism. Like their German colleagues, the American professors not only believed in action but exulted in it, and as in Germany, they were at home in the new universities that had been founded at the centers of economic, social, and political life. Just as the universities at Berlin, Leipzig, München, Halle, Heidelberg, and Freiburg outranked those in the more provincial cities of Bonn, Königsberg, Tübingen, Münster, Erlangen, Rostock, Greifswald, Marburg, Jena, Würzburg, Giessen, Kiel, Göttingen, Breslau, and Strassburg, the graduate schools in Baltimore, Washington, Boston, Chicago, and New York challenged the colleges of the hinterland for leadership in American education. Under these conditions active participation and leadership in politics, economics, and social reform became a professorial hallmark.

162

The urge to become identified with events led inevitably to the surrender of scholarly objectivity before the demands of the hour. In Germany, where social science was virtually identical with the historical school, the compromise proved fatal to scholarship at the climactic juncture of World War I. In the United States, where social scientists were already losing confidence in the historical school, the Teutonic mystique of intuition was quickly discarded. If social action was to be related to academic thought, it was argued, that relation ought to be demonstrable in exact terms. Historicism as an explanatory hypothesis was vague and equivocal. Its romantic adumbrations must be cleared away in favor of the more rigorously analytical concepts of process and operation, and its language must become that of empirical social science. Germany's aggressive posture in international politics during the first decade of the twentieth century helped persuade American progressives to disavow collectivistic theories and to identify themselves once more with the ideals of Jeffersonian democracy —a change symbolized in 1912 by the rejection of Theodore Roosevelt's New Nationalism for the New Freedom of Woodrow Wilson.

Within the German universities the problem of thought and action first became acute over the issue of academic freedom, and more specifically of *Lehrfreiheit*—that freedom to teach the results of their investigations unimpeded by supervision or interference from outside which American students in Germany had been encouraged to regard as the very cornerstone of higher education. According to the German theory, that freedom was to be jealously guarded not only by professors and students but also by the state, as creator, sponsor, and protector of the universities, against the threat of censorship and suppression of thought by religious authorities.

In return, the professors freely gave their services to the state. The catalogue of those who did so was impressive. Among the German scholars best known to Americans, Bluntschli, Droysen, Gneist, Mommsen, Sybel, Knies, Wagner, and Schmoller had served in the parliaments of their respective states. Waitz and Droysen had taken leading roles in the Frankfurt National Convention of 1848. Niebuhr, Ranke, Gneist, and Schmoller had been members of the Prussian Council of State. Gneist, Mommsen, and Treitschke had been elected to the Imperial Diet; Wilhelm von Humboldt had been Prussia's minister of education; Niebuhr had represented Prussia at the Vatican; Wagner and Conrad had advised Bismarck and Caprivi on economic policy. Such scholars, entering the main stream of Germany's scientific, cultural, and political life, had given their nation new direction and purpose, and had functioned first as the harbingers and later as the guardians of a united Germany. They made no complaint that their freedom to teach had been violated.

To understand this apparently happy accommodation between the scholars and the state, American students had but to glance at the history of the German states and especially of Prussia. After the French armies had shattered its military and political power, early in the nineteenth century, the state authorities turned to scholars and scientists for help in the task of reconstruction. Under the guidance of Wilhelm von Humboldt the University of Berlin had been founded in 1809. In 1811 came Breslau, in 1818 Bonn; and Bavaria followed Prussia's example in 1826 with the opening of the University of München. These universities were expected to become centers of national revival, and their establishment was in direct contrast to the centralization of the Napoleonic system of higher education. They were envisioned as free academic republics set up within and by the political state. Their founders anticipated the future gradual withdrawal of the state to strictly political functions, and the complete independence of the academic republics from nonacademic direction.

But so long as the universities remained not only the creation but also the organ of the state, the latter inevitably had interests and purposes of its own which the universities were expected to serve. This was particularly true of the philosophical faculty, which was expected to train teachers for the public secondary schools, along with civil servants and natural scientists. Its professors were thus not only investigators, free citizens of the autonomous world of science, but also teachers in daily contact with the problems and aspirations of their country's youth. Most contemporary observers saw in this twofold role a unique opportunity for imbuing future teachers and civil servants with the ideals of the disinterested search for truth. As the century progressed, however, more and more voices were raised in warning against the increasing subordination of scholarly objectives to the requirements of professional training. By 1913 Eduard Spranger was to speak of Humboldt's hope that the state, once having created the universities, would gradually withdraw its supervision over academic matters as "the most erroneous prognosis ever attempted." [1] It was not the demands of science but the requirements of civil service examinations that dictated the content of academic lectures.

In addition to this pressure by the state on the internal affairs of the universities, there was also the influence upon the professors of their own extramural political activities. Their involvement in politics frequently made it difficult if not impossible, to maintain scientific objectivity. All but imperceptibly, advisers to statesmen became apologists for national policies. By 1914 this unfortunate situation became manifest when a group of influential German scholars stated, in a formal declaration, that they were "enraged over the intent of Germany's enemies, England foremost among them, to make a difference, professedly in our favor, between the spirit of German science and of what they call Prussian militarism." There was, they asserted, no such difference; rather, they went on, "We believe that the welfare of all European culture depends on the victory which German 'militarism' will win." [2] When the war began the signers of the document had, in short, come to identify Germany's policy with the ideals of *Wissenschaft*.

Americans in Germany also learned that the professor's freedom to teach was limited by his status as a *Staatsbeamter*. With the exception of the *Privatdozenten*, all German professors were civil servants, bound by their

[1] *Wandlungen im Wesen der Universität seit 100 Jahren* (Leipzig, 1913), pp. 14–15.

[2] *Erklärung der Hochschullehrer des Deutschen Reiches* (Berlin, Oct. 16, 1914).

oath of office to support the state and its government. More often than not they viewed this as a merely theoretical and therefore negligible restraint upon their freedom. Even the farsighted and liberal-minded Friedrich Paulsen could demand of his colleagues "a positive relationship to the nation and to the state" as a prerequisite for their positions, going on to argue that "so long as the Social Democrats glory in their being a party of intransigent revolutionaries . . . no professor, no matter what field he represents, can join this party without resigning his office." [3] Although as a scholar he was to be guided by the ideals and standards of the scientific method, as a teacher he was to be mindful of his status as a civil servant. If he criticized the government officials who were his superiors, he had to be certain that his criticism was "positive." It may easily be seen that the phrase "positive criticism" is open to varied interpretations, not all of them likely to strengthen the scholar's freedom in the classroom.

Even the *Privatdozenten* were subject to restrictions. As academic apprentices and aspirants to a professor's chair, they were not classified as civil servants, did not receive a salary out of the public treasury, and were not bound by oath to serve the state. They were responsible only to the faculty they served, and were theoretically free to teach whatever social or political doctrine they could defend scientifically. But at Berlin Leo Arons, *Privatdozent,* was suspended from his post in 1899 for having refused to give up his membership in the Social Democratic Party, and a colleague of his, one Dr. Preuss,

[3] *Die deutschen Universitäten und das Universitätsstudium* (Berlin, 1902), pp. 313, 316.

was reprimanded for parodying in the classroom a verse from the Book of Job.[4] The Prussian government, through its Ministry of Education, kept a watchful eye on its university teachers, and did not tolerate either political or religious indiscretions.

Thus the celebrated privilege of *Lehrfreiheit* applied, strictly speaking, only when a professor spoke *ex cathedra*. It did not extend to his utterances as a citizen or a civil servant outside the classroom. Although this did not mean that he was forbidden to speak on political subjects outside the university, it did mean that he was not supposed to engage in partisan politics. He was to speak as a scholar, not as a politician. In the words of Friedrich Paulsen, "The professors, the representatives of scholarship, cannot and shall not make politics."[5] Nevertheless many German scholars, disregarding Paulsen's admonition, did engage in politics. In so doing they both claimed the privilege of academic freedom and profited from the esteem in which they were held as members of the social aristocracy. Theirs was a prerogative sanctioned by custom yet revocable at any time by their administrative superiors in the civil service bureaucracy. It may be asked whether the American admirers of *Lehrfreiheit* recognized the implications it held for their own future careers in the United States. Did they give heed to the discrepancy between German academic ideals and political and administrative practice? For an answer, we shall

[4] See *Die Aktenstücke des Disciplinarverfahrens gegen den Privatdozenten Dr. Arons* (Berlin, 1900), and William C. Dreher, "A Letter from Germany," *Atlantic Monthly* (March, 1900), p. 305.

[5] *Op. cit.*, pp. 314, 325.

follow some of the American graduate students in Germany to their later posts in the United States.

Among German-trained scholars John W. Burgess was perhaps the least critical. He had almost no fault to find with the German theory of academic freedom and training, since through Hegelian glasses he saw an identity of purpose in the academic and political worlds. The one object of his scorn was the state socialism of Wagner and the *Kathedersozialisten;* apart from this "aberration," he saw German scholarship as the nearest imaginable approximation to the ideal. Albion Small, on the other hand, gradually lost his first enchantment with both social thought and academic practice in Germany. By 1915 he had unequivocally condemned the militarism of Treitschke and Bernhardi, which the Germans themselves had embraced. He wrote that the conduct of German scholars, "some of them my own intimate friends," was "disgraceful and humiliating." In 1917 he also condemned the *Verein für Sozialpolitik*, which in 1910 he had seen as an "instructive precedent for American academic men," for having "always counted toward increase of the prestige of the Prussian monarchy." [6]

But even those who later disavowed much of German university thought and practice tended to accept the theory of academic freedom as set forth by Paulsen. Both Burgess and Small, together with Ely, "that excellent

[6] See "Germany and American Opinion," *Sociological Review,* VIII (April, 1915), 110; *Origins of Sociology* (Chicago, 1924), p. 31; *The Meaning of Social Science* (Chicago, 1910), p. 270; and "Americans and the World Crisis," *AJS,* XXIII (Sept., 1917), 159.

German professor in an American skin," [7] and many others, saw academic freedom primarily as a responsibility. Concern with it merely as a right, Small contended, led to "mechanically manufactured alarm," whereas an American professor "whose digestion is good and who has escaped brain-fag has all the freedom he wants." [8] Both their professional status and the obligations of scientific objectivity imposed upon scholars a self-discipline which—or so Small optimistically believed— would justify their prerogatives and forestall any attacks on them. The implication here—and Small was not alone in it—was that such attacks were needlessly brought on by some scholar's ill-considered flaunting of his "rights."

The circumstances under which the issue of academic freedom was raised in Germany and in the United States were obviously different. In Germany that freedom could be limited only by the state, whereas in the United States any infringement generally originated with boards of trustees or individual founders. Small assured his colleagues that the danger was slight: at Chicago, he pointed out, Rockefeller wealth had never been used to muzzle the professors, and he urged scholars who were inclined to be unduly sensitive to note "the generosity of rich men toward all the academic work, of the ultimate value of which they must often be very incredulous." The best way of strengthening the case for freedom was to improve the standards of research. Still, Small was not blind to actual violations of academic freedom. When Professor E. A.

[7] Quoted from Joseph A. Schumpeter, *History of Economic Analysis* (N.Y., 1954), p. 874n.

[8] "Academic Freedom—Limits Imposed by Responsibilities," *Arena*, XXII (Oct., 1899), 471.

Ross was dismissed from Stanford under pressure from Mrs. Stanford, the founder's widow, Small wrote of his "hope that the wrong-headed old lady may be brought to her senses after all." [9] In this instance the hope was ill founded, and the state of Professor Ross' digestion, and whether or not he had escaped brain-fag, were both irrelevant to the outcome.

In Germany, when pressure was exerted from outside the universities, the state could act as the guardian of academic freedom. The same thing could also happen at an American state university. Thus when Oliver E. Wells attacked Ely as a socialist in the pages of *The Nation*, the State of Wisconsin came to Ely's aid through the university's Board of Trustees, and affirmed in ringing words the scholar's freedom to investigate and to teach.[10] Although many American scholars saw in this official defense of academic freedom an affirmation of the professor's right to free speech, there is reason to believe that Ely's victory was mainly due to his own status among his colleagues, to his influential friends, and to the bad name his accuser had made for himself. Ely was neither willing nor in a position to rest his case on the citizen's right to free speech. Other scholars who had claimed their right to free speech in the market place of ideas exposed themselves to the derision of uneducated, prejudiced, and ill-mannered men who did not hesitate to make personal attacks or to demand a scholar's removal. When this

[9] *Ibid.*, 470; "Immoral Morality," *The Independent*, LV (March 26, 1903), 710–714; and in B. J. Stern, ed., "The Letters of Albion W. Small to Lester F. Ward," *Social Forces*, XV (Dec., 1936), 184.

[10] See Merle Curti and Vernon Carstensen, *The University of Wisconsin* (Madison, 1949), I, 508–527, and Ely's *Ground under Our Feet* (N.Y., 1938), pp. 218–233.

happened, the good professor would often shift his ground to seek refuge behind his supposed right to academic freedom. Usually his adversaries would spurn the argument, denouncing the "undemocratic arrogance" of a self-appointed academic aristocracy. It was not usual for Americans to recognize the claims of privilege and status, or to acknowledge the social prerogatives that professors often expected.[11]

Through all the varied situations and individual idiosyncrasies there persisted one common factor, namely the insistence of the German-trained professors that their case for the freedom to teach was based on a sense of social responsibility. Ely spoke for many of them when he wrote of his social philosophy:

I am . . . an aristocrat rather than a democrat; but when I use the word "aristocrat," I have in mind of course not a legal aristocracy, but a natural aristocracy; not an aristocracy born for the enjoyment of special privilege, but an aristocracy which lives for the fulfillment of special service.[12]

Assuming that their philosophy was shared by the individual founders and the boards of trustees who controlled the universities, men like Burgess, Small, and Ely tended to attribute the attacks that did take place to the shortsightedness of particular individuals, and held to the conviction that truth wins out in the end. In this they took the position of academic noblemen, unprepared and unwilling to meet the enemy on its own ground—an at-

[11] Cf. Richard Hofstadter and Walter P. Metzger, *The Development of Academic Freedom in the United States* (N.Y., 1955), pp. 367–412.

[12] "Fundamental Beliefs in My Social Philosophy," *Forum*, XVIII (Oct., 1894), 183.

titude to which their familiarity with German conditions contributed its share. It was only in 1915 with the establishment of the American Association of University Professors and the report of its committee on Academic Freedom and Tenure that American scholars directly and effectively addressed themselves to the problem of how to defend the freedom to teach in a society largely unfamiliar with the ideals of objective scholarship, and unimpressed by either social status or the canons of professional ethics. Of the committee's thirteen members eight had studied in Germany. One of them was Richard T. Ely.

Given the differences in their position, the role of American professors in public affairs naturally could not correspond to that of the German academicians. The former made their mark primarily in the fields of education, religion, and social legislation, rather than in political administration. One reason for the difference was no doubt that in democratic America politics was everybody's business, whereas in Germany it was the business of experts. When a German-trained professor returned to his native shores, eager to contribute his knowledge and skill to the shaping and guidance of American domestic and foreign policy, he met with deaf ears on the part of statesmen and politicians. Instead of citizens eager for sage counsel and specialized information he encountered Americans preoccupied with their own selfish advancement and cynical toward scholarly disinterestedness.

The scholar who mounted the pulpit or platform of the reformer had, on the other hand, the problem of maintaining his professional objectivity. For even though coolly dispassionate words were ineffectual with popular audiences, scholars continued to maintain that they must be used. The university, after all, was the scholar's real home, and specialized research came before agitation for reform. For this reason Francis G. Peabody, Harvard's exponent of the Social Gospel, ranked theology ahead of sociology. The latter, he said, had become "a passion for inventive minds," and its "passion for service had supplanted the passion for truth." [13] Richard T. Ely, although he had been deeply involved in the labor reforms of the 1890's, reported while his academic freedom was on trial that he had spoken before a labor group only twice in his life.[14] Albion Small, who early in his career was lavish in his praise of the *Verein für Sozialpolitik,* found it necessary to castigate the founders of the American Economic Association for neglecting scholarship in favor of agitation for reform.[15] These were no ivory-tower academicians. Envisioning the professor as one who could serve his countrymen in a specialized capacity, even though their success as reformers depended on an appeal to popular audiences, they continued to regard academic status as the cornerstone for whatever they might achieve.

In one way or another the German-trained scholars were all educational reformers. Earlier chapters have dealt with their influence, both direct and indirect, in bringing about institutional changes in American college education, especially in the social science curriculum.

[13] *The Approach to the Social Question* (N.Y., 1909), p. 51.

[14] See Hofstadter and Metzger, *op. cit.,* p. 433.

[15] "Scholarship and Social Agitation," and "Fifty Years of Sociology in the United States," *AJS,* I (March, 1896), 567; XXI (May, 1916), 768.

Here we shall examine their views on the political and social influence of higher education.

For Burgess, who decided to devote his life to teaching "men how to live by reason and compromise instead of by bloodshed and destruction," [16] the founding in 1880 of Columbia's Graduate Faculty of Political Science provided the setting he required. Burgess modeled the school after the Ecole Libre des Sciences Politiques in Paris and the Cameralistic Faculty of the German university in Strassburg—both institutions devoted to the training of civil servants. Through the education of lawyers and civil servants Burgess hoped to instill American politics with the ideal of scholarship, since, as he said, "the lawyers are the rulers of the country," and the American governmental system an "aristocracy of the robe." [17] Richard T. Ely wrote that the new graduate "schools of economics and politics ought to be, above anything else, civil academies." [18] Herbert B. Adams called for "a civic West Point" to be established in Washington by the federal government after the example of the Ecole Libre and of Doctor Engel's Statistical Bureau in Berlin. Its training of civil service interns—the equivalent of the German *Verwaltungsreferendare*—would narrow the gap between academic theory and administrative practice. Adams hoped thereby both to fight the corruption of the spoils system

[16] *Reminiscences of an American Scholar* (N.Y., 1934), p. 29.

[17] As quoted by Munroe Smith in *A History of Columbia University, 1754–1904* (N.Y., 1904), p. 225, and *Political Science and Comparative Constitutional Law* (Boston, 1891), II, 365.

[18] "The Proper Aims of Schools of Economics and Politics," *Independent*, XLIV (May 19, 1892), 682.

and to enlist the universities in the cause of civil service reform.[19]

This blueprint, however, was never fully realized. In 1880 the Columbia trustees warned, "It is not to be assumed that as political affairs are now managed, the possession of superior qualifications will necessarily afford . . . [a graduate of Burgess' school] any very substantial preliminary advantage." The prediction proved sadly correct. By 1890 the enrollment in Burgess' school was not appreciably more than in 1884.[20] In order to attract students Burgess began in 1887 to train teachers of political science as well as civil servants. In American political life during the 1880's and 1890's, rotation in office and the spoils system were both too deeply entrenched to allow the reform proposals of Burgess, Ely, and Adams to succeed. Direct influence by the universities on national politics proved to be far too ambitious a goal.

But although the national reform proposals of Burgess, Ely, and Adams aroused no effective response, Ely did succeed with similar innovations on the state level. He became a devoted exponent of the Wisconsin Idea— namely, the use of the university's resources in preparing state legislation. The extent to which he and other Wisconsin reformers copied the German pattern becomes clear from casually leafing through Charles McCarthy's treatise on the subject. Here are some excerpts:

When one sees Germany, once a country of poor peasants,

[19] "Defense of a Civil Academy," *Science*, IX (May 20, 1887), 484–485, and "The Promotion of Higher Political Education," USBE, *Report of the Commissioner for 1885–1886* (Washington, 1887), Appendix XI, pp. 743–747.

[20] Munroe Smith, *op. cit.*, pp. 227, 272.

shot over by every conquering swashbuckler, transformed by the might of intelligence, noble philosophy and keen foresight into a shining example for the rest of the world, we feel certain that our own country cannot long remain indifferent. . . . German professors have come repeatedly to Wisconsin and have been surprised by the German spirit in the university. Therefore it is only natural that the legislation of Wisconsin should receive an impetus from men who believe that laws can be so constructed as to lead to progress and at the same time preserve to the fullest all human betterment; that the advice of scholars may be sought; that what has made Germany happy and prosperous may be duplicated in America. . . . If Wisconsin is a prosperous state to-day, there is no doubt that it is largely because of German ideas and ideals, early instituted in the state.[21]

The chief argument put forward for the utilization of scholarship in drafting legislation was simply that the university was a state institution, and "should not be blamed for having men upon whom the legislature may call for advice. They are paid from public funds; why should the public not avail itself of their services?" This reasoning could be applied as well in Wisconsin as in Germany; and so could the arguments for a state civil service system based on merit. McCarthy quotes an assemblyman from Milwaukee as saying, "We Germans believe in civil service; we believe in merit and fitness; we believe that men should be educated for administrative duties; we do not like 'pull' in state business." [22] John R. Commons, the Wisconsin economist and historian of labor, pointed to the state civil service law of 1905 as

[21] *The Wisconsin Idea* (N.Y., 1912), pp. 10, 30–31.
[22] *Ibid.*, pp. 138, 175.

177

"the greatest service [Governor Robert M.] La Follette rendered to the people of the state." [23] It is no exaggeration to say that during the first decade of the twentieth century the University of Wisconsin became a truly statewide laboratory for testing a German-style union between academic theory and legislative practice.

The fame of the Wisconsin idea, which came to fruition only in the first decade of the twentieth century, and in a state with a sizable German population, is indicative of its uniqueness. A more common experience was that of Herbert B. Adams at Johns Hopkins. During his student days in Europe Adams had admired the systems in Germany, France, and Italy for state-supervised professional education: the state-administered examinations and the nationwide uniformity of standards that served to counteract provincialism and to foster a spirit of national unity. Adams believed that if such a system could be adopted in America, it would constitute an effective counterforce to academic parochialism and political sectionalism.[24] In 1887 Adams decided that to go directly to the public with the gospel of "higher education for the people" was the only means of political reform and social and cultural advance at all suited to American democracy. Through his favorite projects—university extension, the Chautauqua movement, summer schools, public libraries, philanthropy, and labor reform—he believed the scholar could influence his nation's history.

[23] *Myself* (N.Y., 1934), p. 105.
[24] "Cooperation in University Work," *JHSt.*, I (1882), 47, and memorandum to Daniel C. Gilman, reprinted in W. Stull Holt, "Historical Scholarship in the United States, 1876–1901," *ibid.*, LVI (1938), 474–479.

In this new campaign Adams could no longer rely on his German experience. The German universities were not concerned with the spread of knowledge among the people. German professors did not customarily leave their lecture halls and laboratories to teach farmers and factory workers. They might occasionally wonder what went on in the minds of those who built their houses and produced their food, but mainly they were content, with Treitschke, to quote Aristotle: "Who is engaged day by day in material work can only rarely raise his thoughts above his own personal interests; material needs claim most of his attention." [25] Adams, his Christian conscience repelled by such doctrines, looked for support to French and British scholars whose outlook seemed to him more democratic.

The French legislator Jules Siegfried had inspired Adams to place the words "Education of the People is the first duty of Democracy" on the masthead of the educational numbers of the Johns Hopkins Studies. Adams also revived the germ theory of Teutonic institutions when he maintained that the spread of university extension in Great Britain, and of the Chautauqua movement in the United States, were manifestations of the Germanic spirit of democracy. He overlooked the relative absence of popular education in Germany, since what really mattered, he felt, was the spread of "the spirit of Germanic self-government and of ancient civic freedom." Adams likened British university extension to the extension of the franchise, and called it "humanism in a new form." It brought the tools and materials of science to farmers

[25] "Der Socialismus und seine Gönner," *Preussische Jahrbücher,* XXXIV (1874), 86.

and laborers, to schoolmasters and laymen; it raised the general level of intelligence, and made the nation stronger and better. In Britain, Adams wrote, "the middle wall of partition between the . . . universities and the . . . people, has now been completely broken down." [26] Why could not the same results be achieved in democratic America?

Adams likewise saw promise in the Chautauqua movement, which he described as an "unconscious educational adaptation of the old Frankish idea of the folkmoot," demonstrating anew the democratic affinities between the United States and Great Britain. In England its example had encouraged the organization of home reading circles. In America it was supplemented by summer schools, which Adams described as "laboratories for discussing solutions for the educational problems of democracy." Similarly, Adams gave high praise to the public library movement—which like "the Bessemer process . . . transforming molten iron into steel" converted private wealth into public improvement—as well as to college settlement houses, the support of popular education by private charities, and the cooperation of religious and educational institutions in social reform. What all these movements had in common was their reliance on the principle of voluntary, cooperative self-help under competent guidance. Adams considered this combination of democratic self-help and academic leadership especially well suited

[26] "University Extension in Great Britain," *Report of the Commissioner of Education for the Year 1898–1899* (Washington, 1900), I, 966; "University Extension in England," *Report of the Commissioner of Education for the Year 1885–1886* (Washington, 1887), pp. 748–749; and "The Higher Education of the People," Appendix, *Report of the 38th Annual Meeting of the State Historical Society of Wisconsin* (Madison, 1891), p. 84.

to American conditions, finding the working relationship among the "free common schools, free libraries, and the true university spirit of teaching and research" [27] superior even to its British counterpart.

Yet disappointment awaited Adams and his colleagues even in the area of popular education. After Adams and his colleagues had introduced university extension at Baltimore in 1887, university men followed his lead in New York, Pennsylvania, Indiana, Wisconsin, Minnesota, and Michigan. But the experiment did not prosper.[28] Its chief disadvantages were its unattractiveness to serious students and its drain on the professor's time and energy.[29] The much-praised Chautauqua movement suffered from the same faults. Adams and Ely were once told that they did not bring in enough money to pay their salaries: "It is men like [the Methodist evangelist] Sam Jones who make it possible to engage you." [30] Adams, unwilling to give up hope, attributed his own failure to the lack at Johns Hopkins, a private university, of the backing of a state university system such as had been developed in New York and in the West—where according to Adams' student Frederick Jackson Turner, there was "the steady

[27] "Summer Schools and University Extension," in N. M. Butler, ed., *Education in the United States* (Albany, 1900), II, 826, 843; "Educational Extension in the United States," *Report of the Commissioner of Education for the Year 1899–1900* (Washington, 1901), I, 302; and "Public Libraries and Popular Education," Univ. of State of N.Y., *Home Education Bulletin No. 31* (May, 1900), p. 56.

[28] See Adams, "University Extension in America," *Forum*, XI (July, 1891), 510, and "University Extension and Its Leaders," *Review of Reviews*, III (July, 1891), 593–609.

[29] Curti and Carstensen, *op. cit.*, I, 729.

[30] Told by Ely in *Ground under Our Feet* (N.Y., 1938), p. 80.

pressure of democracy upon its universities to adapt them to the requirements of all the people." Adams likewise concurred with Charles McCarthy's observation that in the East "such have been the aristocratic influences of education . . . that [university extension] has died down . . . until it has become simply a name." [31] In his writings Adams nonetheless continued to promote "the higher education for the people" as the perfect synthesis of democratic aspirations and aristocratic leadership, of Anglo-American democracy and German scholarship, even though in practice it had not altogether succeeded.

The German-trained scholars who sought to reconcile academic standards with the democratic idea of equality fared best when they joined their efforts with those of organized religion toward educational and social reform, most notably in the Social Gospel movement. Audiences of businessmen retained the practical man's suspicion of the theorist, and it is doubtful whether those made up of workers were disposed to accept Ely's counsel of continence, patience, and self-discipline except when it was given a religious tone. "There is no atom of help to you in drink," Ely exhorted his audiences. "Beware of demagoguery. . . . Cast off the slavery of party politics. . . . Imitate no violence. . . . Cast aside envy, one of your most treacherous foes. . . . Elevate, organize, wait. Christ and all Christly people are with you for the right." [32] The academician could afford such patronizing language only when he exchanged the scholar's gown for the robe of the

[31] Turner, *The Frontier in American History* (N.Y., 1920), p. 283, and McCarthy, *op. cit.*, pp. 131–132.

[32] "Preface to Workingmen," *The Labor Movement in America* (N.Y., 1886), pp. ix–xiii.

clergyman. Americans who refused to attend a scholar's lecture meekly accepted his sermonizing.

As with university extension, the academic social gospelers found their main examples in England rather than in Germany. Adams, in calling for the support of such private and church-sponsored agencies as the YWCA and the Helping Hand Society, wrote that "in the United States, as in the mother country and in United Christendom, the school was the daughter of the church." This was certainly not true of the nineteenth-century German universities. Adams' study of the literature of charities is noteworthy for an almost total absence of German references. Page after page deals with the work of such English reformers as Thomas Arnold, Charles Kingsley, Arnold Toynbee, and F. D. Maurice, and such matters as workingmen's clubs, popular amusements, summer gardens, housing conditions, and poor laws, in England. The four citations of Germany deal with housing, saving banks, poor relief, and pauperism.[33] Ely's *Social Aspects of Christianity* (N.Y., 1889) and *Introduction to Political Economy* (N.Y., 1889), which established him as the first university scholar who brought the support of social science to the Social Gospel,[34] were read, according to a historian of the Social Gospel,

by every young minister who entered a Conference of the Methodist Episcopal Church. . . . [They] were also on the

---

[33] "Work among Workingwomen in Baltimore," *Notes Supplementary to the JHSt.*, Nr. 6 (June, 1889); "The Church and Popular Education," *JHSt.*, XVIII (Aug., 1900), 406; and "Notes on the Literature of Charities," *ibid.*, V (Aug., 1887), 283–324.

[34] See Charles H. Hopkins, *The Rise of the Social Gospel in American Protestantism, 1865–1915* (New Haven, 1914), p. 106.

required reading list of theological students in the church of the United Brethren in Christ and were used as texts in theological seminaries. . . . [They] were read so widely that they tended to become the norm for all endeavor in the field of Social Christianity.[35]

Although Ely's ideas bore a marked resemblance to the program of the German ethical school, his suggestions for action were derived from English examples. As a co-founder in 1891 of the Christian Social Union of the Protestant Episcopal Church and in 1893 of Chautauqua's American Institute of Christian Sociology, he was consciously following the examples of the English Christian Socialists and of England's Christian Cooperatives; Canon Fremantle's *The World as the Subject of Redemption* was also a major inspiration.[36] Even Francis G. Peabody, who imported so much of German "exact science" into Harvard's department of social ethics, resorted to English patterns when he moved outside the Yard. The Cambridge Prospect Union—"the last and best method of philanthropy"—was organized as an evening college for workingmen along the lines of English university settlements and extension lectures.[37]

This predilection for English examples indicates the difficulty of adapting German examples to American con-

[35] James Dombrowski, *The Early Days of Christian Socialism in America* (N.Y., 1936), pp. 50–53, *passim*.

[36] See Ely's introduction to "The History of Cooperation in the United States," *JHSt.*, VI (1888), 5–9, and his introduction to the American edition of Fremantle's work (N.Y., 1892), pp. i–iii.

[37] "The University and the Workingman," *The Prospect Union Review*, Nov. 6, 1895, p. 3. See also David B. Potts, "The Prospect Union: A Conservative Quest for Social Justice," *New England Quarterly*, XXXV (Sept., 1962), 347–366.

ditions. That German churches were state supported would, many Americans felt, necessarily vitiate their efforts toward social reform—which, as Peabody put the matter, must on the one hand be "met by the emperor's dictum that the clergy should leave politics alone," and on the other "by the Socialist belief that religion is a superstition maintained in the interest of the confiscating class." [38] Small felt that the German concepts of "the church" and of "the state" were both inapplicable to America. An orthodox Baptist, he objected to the Social Gospel's invocation of "the church" as though anything like the state church of Prussia existed in America. He saw in this only an "impotent institutional ambition," adding that "a good deal of our trouble is from disappointed professional pique." In his opinion, the churches ought to encourage their members to work for reform as individuals, but they were not to promote it directly.[39] Ely likewise disparaged the social reforms of German churches, especially when German Protestant reformers defended the "Christian state" and the alliance of "throne and altar." He had in mind men like Court Chaplain Adolf Stoecker, founder of the Christian Social Labor Party, who was orthodox in religion and conservative in politics, with pronounced aristocratic and monarchical leanings. A notorious anti-Semite, who was also outspoken in his attacks on constitutionalism, liberalism, and Marxist socialism, he drew his main support from the Prussian middle class—artisans, merchants, army officers, civil servants, and students—and was, in the words of his

[38] *Jesus Christ and the Social Question* (N.Y., 1900), p. 51.
[39] "The Church and the Social Problem," *Independent,* LIII (Feb. 28 and March 7, 1901), 480–484, 537–539.

biographer, "the greatest agitator ever produced by conservative Protestant Prussia." [40] For Ely, Stoecker's anti-Semitism showed "how little nobility there is in his nature." On the other hand, Ely professed admiration for Bishop Baron von Ketteler, to whom he attributed the relatively greater sympathy shown by German Catholics for the needs of the lower classes.[41]

The attitude of most German-trained scholars toward the German Protestant churches was summed up by Peabody. "State churches with their dignitaries and diplomacy," he wrote, "are as foreign to the American mind as are autocratic and military systems of government." The war, he believed, had borne out his contention: "Then, in an instant, this umbrageous beauty of an external, governmental, and superimposed religion crashes to the ground like a tree smitten by a tornado, and at its heart there is laid bare an interior rottenness and decay." [42] The example set by democratic England was far more acceptable.

Participation in the Social Gospel movement and in other religiously inspired reforms brought the American students of German scholars face to face with economic questions. Their chief confrontation was with socialism, which may be regarded as the nineteenth-century protest against the free market economy and the laissez-faire theory of classical economics. It represented "the ten-

[40] Walter Frank, *Hofprediger Adolf Stoecker und die Christlichsoziale Bewegung* (Berlin, 1928), p. 67.

[41] *French and German Socialism in Modern Times* (N.Y., 1883), pp. 256–257.

[42] "The Religious Education of an American Child," *Religious Education*, X (April, 1915), 113, and "Americans Abroad," *North American Review*, CCI (March, 1915), 370.

dency inherent in an industrial civilization to transcend the self-regulating market by consciously subordinating it to a democratic society," and the "endeavor to make society a distinctively human relationship of persons which in Western Europe was always associated with Christian traditions." [43] Among the forms taken by this heterogeneous movement were the utopian programs of Robert Owen and Charles Fourier, the agitation of the Chartists, the *Communist Manifesto* of Karl Marx and Friedrich Engels, the declarations of trade unions and labor parties, the lectures of the Christian Socialists, the academic teaching of the French solidarists and German professorial socialists, the American Social Gospel, the single-tax proposal of Henry George, and the nationalism of Edward Bellamy.

All these movements had in common the protest against an economic order which sacrificed the individual in the name of immutable law. Among believers in organized interference with the self-regulating market in the interest of individual and social welfare, there were inevitable differences concerning method. Some advocated revolution, others reform. Some attacked the existing order on the economic and political plane, others on the moral and intellectual. Other divergencies stemmed from differences of philosophy, ranging from historical determinism to a belief in man's ability to control his own collective destiny against the forces of nature.

The American students of German social science tended to accept the latter view, and to regard the humanitarian motives of socialist reformers with approval. Although

[43] Karl Polanyi, *The Great Transformation* (N.Y., 1944), p. 234.

they might look down upon what they saw as the unscientific naiveté of Henry George's single-tax movement and similar utopian proposals, they contrasted the humane impulse upon which the reformers acted with the indifference to human suffering which they attributed to the "soulless" captains of business and industry, and to the economic and social theorists who defended them.

As a result of their strictures upon the latter, many professors were soon under attack as socialists. Particularly painful to them were the broadsides fired by their colleagues of the "old" school. William Graham Sumner condemned "nine-tenths of the socialistic and semi-socialistic, and sentimental or ethical, suggestions" for engaging in what he called "the absurd effort to make the world over." Simon Newcomb, believing that "labor discontent is perennial in human nature," accused Ely of the same bias and bitterness commonly found "in the ravings of an Anarchist or the dreams of a Socialist," and concluded that Ely was "seriously out of place in a university chair." [44] Most of the German-trained scholars took a position midway between individualism and collectivism, thus drawing barbs from both the right and the left. During the 1880's and 1890's, an attack from the right might have endangered one's professional status, while one from the left might actually have enhanced one's standing with trustees and donors.

In fact, the German-trained scholars were mainly middle-class and middle-of-the-road, not at all inclined to endorse Marxist socialism, anarchism, or any of the radical doctrines of which they were periodically accused.

[44] Sumner in *Forum*, XVII (March, 1894), 93; Newcomb in *The Nation*, Oct. 7, 1886, pp. 293–294.

Burgess saw in socialism the "height of folly and moral turpitude," whose insidious danger had been manifested in Germany, where a government "so true and capable and successful as that of the Hohenzollerns" had had to rely on "the influence of a foreign church prince" (the Pope) to maintain the public order against the machinations of the Social Democrats.[45] Ely denounced "rebels against society" who stood for "common property; socialist production and distribution; the grossest materialism, . . . free love . . . and . . . anarchy." What he found most despicable in their doctrine, was that "in the name of 'fraternity,' hate is deified! In the name of liberty, dynamite is prescribed for the rebel, and the rope for the enemy; while equality is made the corner-stone, if not the very essence, of morality!" [46] Small sought to clear himself from the taint of socialism by emphasizing the "sociologist's point of view." Peabody preferred to speak of "social ethics" rather than socialism, and Ely dubbed himself a "progressive conservative."

These men who regarded socialism in its secular, Marxist form as both dangerous and damnable, were ready to endorse a socialism defined as voluntary cooperation in the cause of economic and political reform. Cooperative self-help, which they especially valued in Christian socialism, was the topic of the sixth volume of Adams' Johns Hopkins Studies. In it Ely's foreword struck an often-

[45] "The Ideal of the American Commonwealth," *PSQ*, X (Sept., 1895), 411, and "The 'Culturconflict' in Prussia," *ibid.*, II (June, 1887), 340.

[46] "Recent Phases of Socialism in the United States," *Christian Union*, XXIX (April 24, 1884), 389–390, and "The Celebration of Thanksgiving Day by the Socialists of Chicago," *ibid.*, XXX (Dec. 18, 1884), 594.

repeated note: "One of the prime conditions of success of cooperation is moral integrity of the cooperators." When that integrity failed, according to Ely, it was time for the state—which he defined as a "coercive cooperative commonwealth"—to interfere for the restraint of selfish individuals and groups. Taking a leaf from the book of his teacher Adolph Wagner, Ely advocated nationalization of the railroads and public ownership of monopolies, insisting that voluntary cooperation and the nationalization of public service industries were both compatible with individual initiative and responsibility. Ely called his readers' attention to Bismarck's policy, which made the state "a benefactor and protector of the weak and needy." He defended the "leadership of wise and strong men" over "those who are virtually children," and asserted the right of the government to exclude Negroes, paupers, vagabonds, and dependents from the suffrage, so long as "every honest industrious laborer has his vote." As long as the program of the state socialists recognized the "divine element in the state," Ely was ready to endorse their benevolent paternalism; otherwise he condemned their doctrines as incompatible with human dignity and wise leadership,[47] and his colleagues generally agreed.

[47] See *JHSt.*, VI (1888), 9; Ely's *Introduction to Political Economy* (N.Y., 1889), p. 89; "A Brief Sketch of the Railway History of Germany," *Papers Relating to the Foreign Relations of the United States* (Washington, 1880), p. 420; "Competition: Its Nature, Its Permanency, and Its Beneficence," *Papers and Proceedings of the AEA*, 3rd series, II (Feb., 1901), 69; "Bismarck's Plan for Insuring German Laborers," *International Review*, XII (May, 1882), 509; "Fraternalism vs. Paternalism in Government," *Century Magazine*, LV (March, 1898), 781; "Administration of the City of Berlin," *The Nation*, March 23, 1882, p. 246; and "Land, Labor, and Taxation," *Independent*, XXXIX (Dec. 22, 1887), 7.

For Peabody, voluntary industrial cooperation was a moral movement that contrasted favorably with the revolutionary spirit of the socialists. He looked for a scientific philanthropy to eliminate vagrancy by organizing labor colonies for tramps. In municipal reform Peabody likewise originally shunned government action as tending "to weaken the self-confidence and self-respect of the people." By 1894, however, he had become convinced that only a state-controlled system of labor colonies could remedy what he termed the "fearful downdraft" of the city upon its "inefficient citizens." Everyone was to contribute to the common good. "If that is socialism," Peabody wrote, "let us make the most of it. It is also the hope of stable civilization and the secret of judicious charity." [48]

In the social and political theory taught by the German academic aristocrats, German-trained scholars believed they saw a remedy for the defects of American social and political life. They bitterly decried the predominance in America of sectional and group interest, the neglect of the public weal in favor of private gain, the rampant individualism of the captains of business and industry, the graft and corruption of the spoils system, and all the other foibles and extravagances of the Gilded Age. For them, the example of Bismarck's Germany, with its fervent nationalistic spirit, was the one to follow. Burgess, who

[48] "Industrial Co-operation in England," *Forum,* VIII (Nov., 1889), 274–285; "The German Labor Colonies for Tramps," *ibid.,* XII (Feb., 1892), 751–761; "A Case for Good City Government," *ibid.,* XIII (March, 1892), 53; "Colonization as a Remedy for City Poverty," *ibid.,* XVII (March, 1894), 59–61, *passim;* and "Developing the Social Up-Draught," *Charities Review,* VI (July and Aug., 1897), 413–419.

in 1888 called for "a new baptism of nationalism all around,"[49] believed that the army, the civil service, and the universities ought all to be rebuilt after the German model. Ely, H. B. Adams, and Peabody called for a like reform in municipal administration. They advocated university training in public affairs and administration on a nationwide scale; or the cooperation of church and state in social reforms; or an executive comparable in strength and authority to the Kaiser's; or the view of the state as a fraternal commonwealth and of government as its paternalistic supervisor; or the nationalization of public service monopolies; or the founding of postal savings banks and of a social security system; or stress on the duties rather than the rights of citizenship—all as German examples adaptable to American conditions. It was the opinion of German-trained scholars as a whole that such measures had proved their worth in Germany, and that when tempered with the more democratic reforms of Victorian England they could minister to the social and political ills of America.

The fruits of Albion Small's scholarly investigation of possible German contributions to American political thought appeared in *The Cameralists* (1909) and *The Origins of Sociology* (1924). As a true disciple of the historical school, Small adopted from Bluntschli the concept of the organic state as the moral arbiter of social life, and from Adolph Wagner and the *Kathedersozialisten* his denunciation of laissez-faire as a bankrupt policy. On the basis of these attitudes he subscribed to Henry Carter

[49] "The Law of the Electoral Court," *PSQ*, III (Dec., 1888), 653.

Adams' thesis, as set forth in *The Relation of the State to Industrial Action,*[50] of the interdependence of the individual and the state. It was his conclusion concerning German political thought that

there was no more virile political thinking in Europe in the seventeenth and eighteenth centuries than that of the German cameralists. . . . Their works contain in embryo everything which has made the German system today the most effective economizer of national energy in the world.

These "pioneers of German social polity" had developed their theory within the framework of the multifarious German states and principalities—which, though "ignoble and obstructive enough," Small wrote,

each with its minute cameralistic organization, functioned like the drill sergeants with the raw levies. The incapable masses of the German people were divided into squads, and disciplined for civic duties, and after the dull drill of centuries were delivered over to the united nation as the most completely socialized citizens in modern European history.[51]

But the brilliance of the cameralistic period declined, and after 1765 there was a movement in Germany to protect the individual against the state, whose members became "willing or unwilling pupils of the British classical economic school." This "departure from the ways of German impulse" was not overcome until 1850, when it became the prevailing conclusion that "human relations in connection with wealth cannot be truly stated in terms of individuals," and that only a renewal of the social approach to economics could protect the majority against

[50] Cf. *supra,* ch. 8, n. 52.
[51] *The Cameralists* (Chicago, 1909), pp. xv, 17.

an economically dominant minority. After 1871, with Bismarck's establishment of a strongly centralized state, Small believed that Germany had committed herself "to a permanent policy of promoting human improvement"— a policy that had the support of Karl Knies and Adolph Wagner. Now that the Germans had come "back to themselves," Small wrote, they were "likely long to remain collectivists." [52]

The collectivist social theory was for Small the greatest gift of German political genius to modern Western thought. The attitude of the cameralists, and later of the professors of the historical school, who "saw in the welfare of the state the source of all other welfare," was in sharp contrast to the Anglo-American tradition of individual liberty and laissez-faire. Small, while protesting that he did not wish "to glorify German bureaucracy at the expense of American republicanism," believed that Americans stood to gain from an understanding of German institutions, since they had been productive of results "which democracies thus far have not attained"; and although he cautioned that German practices and methods must not be blindly imitated, he believed they could be adapted to American circumstances.[53]

Small, who unlike Burgess never lost sight of his own reservations concerning things German, did not fail to censure what he considered the aberrations of German scholarship. In 1913 he described Paul Rohrbach's *Der Deutsche Gedanke in der Welt* as an unbelievable exam-

[52] *Origins of Sociology* (Chicago, 1924), pp. 133, 238, and "The Present Outlook of Social Science," *AJS*, XVIII (Jan., 1913), 442.

[53] *Cameralists*, pp. viii, xvi–xvii, 16.

ple of muddle-headed thinking, which "would belong in a museum of pathological exhibits, if there were not thousands of otherwise sane and intelligent Germans whose ideas on the manifest destiny of Germany, and the reason for it, are in a way reflected in its pages." He also noted that "the Germans have always been conspicuously lacking in the larger morality," and compared them unfavorably to the English, who had always been distinguished for "constructive social virtues." The war of 1914, which revealed the sinister implications of German collectivism, was, for Small, the most vicious fruit of the Hegelian doctrine that the state was the ultimate manifestation of reason. In Germany the historical school had regarded as their arch-enemy this philosophy whose triumph represented, for Small, the victory of speculation over science.[54]

The fatal flaw of German scholarship, Small concluded, lay in its disregard for practical political morality. During the war German social scientists had demonstrated that expert knowledge and skill did not ensure a healthy attitude toward current affairs—"in spite of the fact," as Small pointed out, "that so large a proportion of German social scientists . . . have been in close touch with actual politics." Small's explanation of this paradox was that although the Germans had laid the groundwork for sociology, the methodology of the new science had been developed in America, whereas in Germany sociology as an applied science had remained subservient to an outdated educational theory. This was what had been known in America as faculty psychology, and had been rejected by Small and Dewey when they placed philosophy, edu-

[54] In *AJS*, XVIII (Sept., 1912, Jan., 1913), 200–214, 574–575; XXVI (March and May, 1921), 624, 787–788.

cation, and ethics on a sociological foundation. Small's conclusion, as given in a paper, "Some Demands of Sociology upon Pedagogy," was as follows: "The collapse of German social science as a guide to political righteousness, or even to farsighted political expediency, during the late war, is an exhibition on a large scale of the falsity of the vicarious conceptions of intellectual training." He ended by calling for a reconstruction in philosophy and a reformulation of ethics in harmony with modern scientific concepts and sociological reality.[55]

Small's analysis excels by virtue of its author's insight and the force of his reasoning. But although it illuminated so well the strength and the weakness of German collectivistic social and political theory, it did not make specific suggestions about how in America a collectivistic theory could be translated into a program of political action. That task was undertaken in the writings of Herbert Croly, who as a youth had fallen under the spell of the social theories of Auguste Comte, and had studied at Harvard under George Herbert Palmer, Josiah Royce, William James, and George Santayana.[56] The strongest influences on his thought were those of Comte, James, and the new economists and other scholars of the ethical school, whose pronouncements are paralleled by his own to a remarkable degree.

Thus Croly trained his guns on "the automatic harmony of the individual and the public interest which is the essence of the Jeffersonian democratic creed." Taking his

[55] Small in *Origins*, p. 32, and in John Dewey, *My Pedagogical Creed* (Chicago, 1897), pp. 19–36.
[56] Cf. Charles Forcey, *The Crossroads of Liberalism* (N.Y., 1961), pp. 16–21.

text from Albion Small, he urged that the "live-and-let-live" philosophy, based on an "ultimate individualism," be replaced with a philosophy of "live-and-help-live"—a philosophy based on "an ultimate collectivism, which conceived different human beings as part of the same striving conscious material, and which makes the individual fulfillment depend upon the fulfillment of other lives and upon that of society as a whole." Cooperation among individuals urged by "the principle of human brotherhood" was to harmonize liberty and egality, the "one representing the individual and the other the social interest." Wherever cooperation could prove its efficiency, "it should be the effort of all civilized societies to substitute cooperative for competitive methods." Thus corporations and labor unions were to be encouraged and recognized, provided they were also regulated by the government. Cooperation, moreover, was a highly complex affair, for which scientific training had to be provided; and through widespread higher education people had to be taught "to consider highly educated officials as representative." Croly contended that what threatened America was not European feudalism, social classification, technical methods, or intellectual standards, but rather "a sterile and demoralizing . . . Americanism of national irresponsibility and indiscriminate individualism." Did not the superiority of America's new scholars consist precisely in the specialized skills they had acquired in the universities of Germany?[57]

When it came to socialism, Croly asserted that

---

[57] *The Promise of American Life* (N.Y., 1909), pp. 152, 208, 359; *Progressive Democracy* (N.Y., 1914), pp. 426–427, 377.

the proposed definition of democracy is socialistic, if it is socialistic to consider democracy inseparable from a candid, patient, and courageous attempt to advance the social problem towards a satisfactory solution. It is also socialistic, in case socialism cannot be divorced from the use, wherever necessary, of the political organization in all its forms to realize the proposed democratic purpose.

Thus the state must take a hand in improving the distribution of wealth. Croly denied, however, that such a theory was entirely socialistic. Rather, it was "unscrupulously and loyally nationalistic"—a Hamiltonian rather than a Jeffersonian program whose spokesman was not Eugene Debs but Theodore Roosevelt. Unlike the latter's New Nationalism, which implied "a democracy of individual and social improvement," but like many programs of reform, socialism, Croly maintained, amounted simply to "a new system of special privilege intended for the benefit of a wage-earning rather than a property-owning class." Croly's nationalism, on the other hand, looked toward the abolition of all special privilege in favor of social justice on a national scale.[58]

Croly thus allied himself with the scholars of the ethical school in calling for a new knowledge of individual and social life that would have "an essentially moral character." To gain this knowledge the tools of the German historical school—description, analysis, comparison—were necessary but in themselves insufficient. Before his *Progressive Democracy* appeared in 1914, Croly had immersed himself in the sociology of Small and of Charles H. Cooley, in the social psychology of James Mark

[58] *The Promise*, pp. 209, 173–174; *Progressive Democracy*, p. 119.

Baldwin, and in the philosophy of John Dewey.[59] Croly held with Small and Dewey that "raw knowledge must be born of morally and socially creative purposes," and that individuals and societies were not natural facts, but "willful processes—moral creations" which were "going on and must continue to go on." He echoed the language of Small in referring to society as "the power of socializing," and that of Ely and Peabody when he concluded, "Thus the progressive democratic faith, like the faith of St. Paul, finds its consummation in a love which is partly expressed in sympathetic feeling, but which is at bottom a spiritual expression of the mystical unity of human nature."[60]

Theodore Roosevelt, champion of the New Nationalism, found in the ideas expounded by Croly a blend of individualism with nationalism, of democratic enthusiasm with a predilection for aristocratic leadership, that appealed to his own tastes and temperament. The New Nationalism was certainly not a coherent system of political theory, but an amalgam of diverse elements that had all the theoretical defects and the practical advantages characteristic of such political hybrids. Along with his concern for what was workable and popular, Roosevelt had an interest in the historic process that predisposed him to favor the thought not only of Croly but of the German-trained professors generally.[61] Roosevelt said that Ely had introduced him to radicalism in economics "and

[59] Cf. David W. Noble, *The Paradox of Progressive Thought* (Minneapolis, 1958), p. 125.

[60] *Progressive Democracy*, pp. 194–195, 427.

[61] Cf. John Morton Blum, *The Republican Roosevelt* (Cambridge, 1954), p. 86.

then made me sane in my radicalism." [62] This sequence—
"first you do, then you don't"—was equally typical of
Roosevelt and of the German-trained scholars, and arose
out of a middle-of-the-road position, a continual tension
between theory and direct involvement in action. This
amounted in effect to viewing the world of affairs from
a historian's perspective. Roosevelt not only took pride
in his own historical writings but frequently praised the
historian's contribution to the shaping of American minds;
and his appreciation of the continuous and transitory
elements that were combined in the flow of history was
a quality he shared with scholars.

The best way of illustrating Roosevelt's affinity for the
German-trained scholars' historical point of view is to
contrast his program and outlook with those of his 1912
rival, Woodrow Wilson. Although the New Freedom and
the New Nationalism were both progressive programs,
they were based on fundamentally different theories of
government. The Wilson of 1912 "was still a progressive
of the Jeffersonian persuasion, undisturbed by Croly's
challenge," [63] philosophically an individualist in the traditional American pattern. Roosevelt denounced this as a
"rural toryism" insensitive to the course of history. In an
era of triumphant industrialism Roosevelt saw business
combines and collective bargaining as equally inevitable,
to be acknowledged and at the same time regulated by
the government. Wilson retorted that this amounted to
the legalization of special privilege for the economically
prosperous and of government paternalism toward labor—

[62] Quoted by Ely, *Ground under Our Feet,* p. 279.
[63] Arthur Link, *Woodrow Wilson and the Progressive Era, 1910–1917* (N.Y., 1954), p. 20.

a program abhorrent to the American heritage of liberty and democracy. Thus Wilson claimed the role of the traditionalist committed to uphold an ideal, while Roosevelt, although no less wedded to tradition, was led by his awareness of historical forces to call for an adjustment of inherited ideals to new and changing circumstances. Ely's statement, "The truth is that the world has changed and I have endeavored to keep an open mind," [64] might have been made by Roosevelt himself. Thus many of the old-line progressives in 1912 gave their support to Wilson, while the nationalist progressives represented by Croly and the *New Republic* gave theirs to Roosevelt.

In the New Nationalism of 1912, the historical school of social science had its moment of triumph. In Roosevelt's progressivism scholars saw the long-awaited synthesis of American individualism and German collectivism, and of democratic and aristocratic tendencies. The German elements in this mixture were precisely what Wilson and the La Follette progressives found unpalatable, and what led later historians to speak of Roosevelt's "pseudo-progressivism." [65] It is impossible to determine the precise extent of the German contribution to the matrix of Roosevelt's complex ideas, but it may well have been greater than historians commonly suppose. If the recommendations of men like Burgess, Ely, and Small ever had any visible and measurable effect on national politics it came through their incorporation in the New Nationalism of Theodore Roosevelt.

I have already quoted Professor Conrad's statement

[64] Ely, *op. cit.*, p. 251

[65] Cf. Daniel Aaron, *Men of Good Hope* (N.Y., 1961), pp. 245–280.

that German scholars had done more for their country's legislation than for its science. Their American students might have said the same for themselves. That their legislative impact, though small, was on the whole more durable than their influence on the course of American scholarship, is profoundly ironic. The irony is not only that men so intensely committed to scholarship should have enjoyed so fleeting a reputation as scholars, or that after declaring themselves so passionately and impressively on the sanctity of science, they should have rushed from their classrooms to sponsor reforms, only to return to the lectern to deprecate the reformers. It is also that they were content to bask in whatever acclaim they received as men of action. Insisting that action must originate in thought, that reform must emerge out of learning, all too often they used reforms to justify that learning. Of the American scholars of the historical school discussed in this chapter, Small alone may be said to have liberated himself from the empty formulae of his German masters. The scholars' failure stems from the eventual bankruptcy of the German historical school, and was but another aspect of the crisis of historicism—a theme that will be treated in the next chapter.

8

The German Influence and American Social Science

> The historical or genetic, temporal aspect of all observable phenomena and ideas dominated the foreground of the whole evolutionary and early pragmatic approach to nature and man.
>
> —PHILIP P. WIENER, 1949

WITH the opening of The Johns Hopkins University in 1876, the massive influence of the German historical school on American social science began. Thirty-eight years later, with the outbreak of World War I, it came to an end. The four decades between saw the establishment of an American social science. From Germany its founders brought home their program for the empirical study of human behavior, and their belief in the indispensability of the historical approach. Perhaps it would be better to terminate the discussion at this point. Previous chapters have depicted the German-trained scholars as institution-builders of prime importance, and have indicated their failure to make a successful accommodation of the credo of the historical school to American scholarship. Having presented the "facts" as he sees them, the historian might be advised to leave well enough alone.

But it is also a fact that the story did not end in 1914. The war and its aftermath forced scholars in both Germany and the United States to review the bequest of the historical school in the light of new developments. For American scholars, this review could not stop with the German influence on American social science, but had to go on to deal with the state of American social science in the 1920's and 1930's. In re-evaluating the German bequest, American scholars were able finally to free themselves from its dominance and to move on into new fields.

I should begin by saying that this chapter is not history in the strictest factual sense—that is, it will add no new data concerning the German influence on American social science. Rather it seizes upon the problematical bequest of the German historical school, touches upon some of the problems as they appeared in the work of later German and American scholars, and draws a sketch of the American response to these problems in the writings of Beard, Becker, and Dewey. It will not attempt to chronicle or to analyze the "crisis of historicism"—a subject yet to be adequately dealt with by an American scholar—but will give, rather, the author's estimate of the significance of the German historical school for American scholarship.

The American disciples of the German historical school saw history as alone possessing the tools that could do justice to a scientific study of man. For them, man was distinct from all other natural phenomena because he alone had a history; he alone could remember and anticipate. Since for man it was history that gave meaning to existence, the province of a science of man, if there were to be such a thing, could only be history—the main stem, of which the separate social sciences were but specialized branches.

Pushed to its logical extreme, this became an assertion that social science was not only distinct but unique—an assertion that ran counter to the original emulation of natural science by the scholars of the historical school, and to their desire to establish a discipline comparable to that of natural science. Although biologists were indeed obliged to recognize the historical approach, it was by no means appropriate to all of their investigations; and for physical science it had no meaning at all. Thus social scientists ultimately had to choose between affirming the autonomy of historical studies and adopting a naturalistic positivism or behaviorism.

For them the choice was not quite so simple or clear-cut as it appears with the benefit of hindsight. Nevertheless, the problem was real. For those who did not opt for positivism, idealist historicism offered an alternative; but it also thrust upon them the problem of value: how could norms of behavior be scientifically prescribed? For idealist historicists there could never be a universally valid answer, since ethics was to a large extent a matter of historical conditioning, folkways, and tradition. The increasing upheaval of world politics in the years just before and during World War I led to a historical relativism and plunged German scholars into what became known as the Crisis of Historicism—a crisis from which German historiography and social science never completely recovered.

A similar though not identical crisis beset historical scholarship in America. Among historians relativism, presentism, and subjectivism were all variants of the prevailing uncertainty of historical knowledge. Here as in Germany, those social scientists who did not opt for positivism, naturalism, or behaviorism joined the historians' rebellion against the ideal of scientific objectivity, deliberately setting themselves adrift on the raft of subjective knowledge. At Cambridge, however, a group who met under the unlikely name of the Metaphysical Club worked out a novel approach to scientific knowledge. Men as diverse in temperament and interests as Charles Sanders Peirce, William James, Chauncey Wright, Nicholas St. John Green, Justice Holmes, Joseph Warner, and John Fiske agreed that a refinement of method could make possible a valid single approach to the problems of both the natural and the social sciences. This method, which was to be celebrated under the name of pragmatism, called for the clarification of all ideas, the testing of all concepts, both scientific and ethical, and the checking of all prior assumptions concerning any investigation against their expected consequences. It was the intention of these men, and subsequently of John Dewey, to approach values no less empirically than they did facts. For them the question of meaning was one whose answer lay in the future. Nevertheless, they believed it was possible to "expect" a particular kind of answer. Such an "expectation" was to be treated as a hypothesis, and was to be constructed just as rigorously as those by which natural scientists "expected" the "facts" yet to be discovered. Although the pragmatic method could not yield certain knowledge either of the future or of the meaning of the past—any more than could the empirical-hypothetical method of scientific investigation—it was the pragmatists' contention that the reliability of the empirical methods of natural and social science was a matter of degree only, not a categorical difference. A strengthened empiricism, aware of its limitations, thus reaffirmed and redefined the possibilities of scientific knowledge. The response of the pragmatists to the crisis of historicism gave hope of ending old debates and of opening new vistas.

The Historical School at High Tide

Neither the crisis of historicism nor the pragmatists' answer really dominated the debates among American scholars until the beginning of the 1920's. On the contrary, the early years of the new century were characterized by a confidence and assurance quite unlike the soul-searching of the twenties and thirties. Nowhere did the self-satisfaction of scholarship find better expression than at the International Congress of Arts and Science, held at the 1904 World's Fair in St. Louis, with Simon Newcomb as president. He was assisted by Albion Small and by Hugo Münsterberg, a German who was professor of psychology at Harvard, and for whom the central purpose of the Congress was to promote the "unification of knowledge." Explaining what he meant by this, Münsterberg declared that a Hegelian synthesis was out of the question because of Hegel's "absurd neglect of hard solid facts." He found positivism, naturalism, and realism equally inadequate because they did not account "for those tendencies which are aiming at an interpretative as well as a descriptive account of civilization." Accordingly, Münsterberg declared, they were giving way to a new idealism—which turned out to be nothing other than the *Weltanschauung* of the historical school:

Historical thinking begins again to take the leadership which for half a century belonged to naturalistic thinking. . . . The world of phenomena must be supplemented by the world of values, . . . description must yield to interpretation, and . . . explanation must be harmonized with appreciation. . . . The ideal of truth is thus not to gain by reason or by observation ideas in ourselves which correspond as well as possible to absolute things, but to reconstruct the given experience in the service of certain purposes.

Here, in the opening address, was the credo of the historical school. Throughout the meetings of the Congress ran as a leitmotiv the assertion that the "unification of knowledge" was to come through a merger of empirical studies and idealistic interpretation. The number of addresses on the histories of various sciences makes it clear how highly the organizers of the Congress valued the historical approach.[1]

A classification devised by the planners of the Congress divided the "sciences of man" into three main groups: general history, including the history of law, religion, language, literature, and art; the social sciences, including anthropology, psychology, and sociology; and the "practical" studies of economics, politics, jurisprudence, education, and religion. The view that history was concerned not with individual men but with collective man was forcefully presented by such "new" social historians as

[1] See Münsterberg, "The Scientific Plan of the Congress," in Howard J. Rogers, ed., *Congress of Arts and Science, Universal Exposition, St. Louis, 1904* (Boston, 1905), I, 93, 101–104, and in *Science*, XVIII (Oct. 30, 1903), 562.

Woodrow Wilson, James Harvey Robinson, and Frederick Jackson Turner. All would have agreed with Robinson's statement that "history is and must always remain . . . a highly inexact and fragmentary science." For Simon Patten, as for the German economist Johannes Conrad, who had been his mentor, the inexactness of history only underscored "man's great independence of nature"; and although historical studies helped "to make good conduct," they were "not a safe basis for prediction." Even if history were a social science, its lack of precision would forever prevent a comparison with natural science.[2]

The social scientists proper, whose concern was with practical application, appeared a trifle less willing to admit that social science could never be exact. The Columbia psychologist James McKeen Cattell foresaw an increase in quantitative psychological studies; his Johns Hopkins colleague James Mark Baldwin foresaw the flowering of naturalism, positivism, and experimentalism; the Columbia sociologist F. H. Giddings looked for the universal acceptance of the science of statistics, and the Austrian general Ratzenhofer for a scientific sociology in which what he regarded as a "naive empiricism" would be transcended by "conscious and purposeful action." The expectations of these men obscured what had already been realized by the historians—that social science relied on an idealist philosophy with which naturalism could not possibly be reconciled. A statement by George Vincent of Chicago is typical of the ambiguity that characterized the

[2] Robinson, "The Conception and Methods of History," in Rogers, ed., *op. cit.*, II, 48; Conrad, "Economic History in Relation to Kindred Sciences," *ibid.*, II, 207; Patten, "The Present Problems in the Economic Interpretation of History," *ibid.*, II, 221.

social science of his day: "To put social philosophy into the language of a natural science is not to make it a science. But as a philosophy it [this language] . . . has preserved the unity of social theory." [3]

The "practical" social scientists, who were in need of a theory of social action, retorted with a denunciation of social scientism. The Cornell economist F. A. Fetter called the analogy of economics with natural science misleading. John Bates Clark, a Columbia economist, and Elisha Andrews, a Nebraska political scientist, asserted that it was only in practical tasks, not in its theory, that social science had truly progressed. According to the Johns Hopkins political scientist W. Willoughby, analytical studies had become scientific by the rejection of old absolutes and the affirmation of relative standards. Felix Adler of Columbia said bluntly that "in the strict sense there are no social laws, and, therefore . . . there cannot be prediction of the future, or ethical imperatives." Educators and theologians finally clinched the argument by declaring that social science dealt with men collectively, and could not predict the future choices of men. "Pedagogy," said Professor Rein of Jena, "must avoid claiming to be a branch of natural science." The impression given by the addresses of the assembled social scientists is that in 1904 the empirical idealism of the historical school still

[3] Cattell, "The Conceptions and Methods of Psychology," *ibid.*, V, 601; Baldwin, "The History of Psychology," *ibid.*, V, 612; Giddings, "The Concepts and Methods of Sociology," *ibid.*, V, 798; Ratzenhofer, "The Problems of Sociology," *ibid.*, V, 815–819, *passim;* Vincent, "The Development of Sociology," *ibid.*, V, 811.

dominated among both European and American social scientists.[4]

The natural scientists at the Congress were ready to admit that a positivistic empiricism was no longer tenable; for even though all science rested on observation and experiment, man himself was a part of the nature with which it dealt. Robert Simpson Woodward of the Carnegie Institute regarded the scientific study of man as the means of bringing about the final unification of science. Physics was described by Professor E. L. Nichols of Cornell as both mechanical and speculative, and Professor A. L. Kimball of Amherst added that "every science is an intellectual structure" and therefore had man at its center. William A. Noyes of the National Bureau of Standards, in asserting that "human knowledge is not bounded by the limits of sense-perception," and the Harvard geographer William Morris Davis, in counseling his colleagues to "see and think" rather than just "go and see," indicated a consciousness that the scientist's role in the process of scientific investigation was not to be ignored, and that a philosophical analysis of the scientist's work was needed. Here Münsterberg had made sure that the philosophy of idealism would receive a hearing. Professors Bowne of Boston University, Howison of California, Woodbridge of Columbia, and Royce of Harvard proclaimed the vic-

[4] Fetter, "The Fundamental Conceptions and Methods of Economics," *ibid.*, VII, 19; Clark, "Economic Theory in a New Character and Relation," *ibid.*, VII 47–56; Andrews, "The Tendencies of the World's Politics during the Nineteenth Century," *ibid.*, VII, 312; Adler, "The Relation of Ethics to Social Science," *ibid.* VII, 674; Rein, "The Place and Office of Pedagogy in the University," *ibid.*, VIII, 57.

tory of idealism over naturalism. Otto Pfleiderer of Berlin found the root of religion in the individual's "emotional consciousness of God," and Ernst Troeltsch of Heidelberg asserted that this consciousness must be studied psychologically, critically, and with a concern for normative values. The Leipzig scientist Ostwald attempted to identify all certainty with subjective experience, the law of causality with mere expediency, and the so-called historical laws with "laws of collective psychology." He contended that scientists must concern themselves with ethics, and with the realm of values, even though, as the Cambridge philosopher Sorley had said, "ethics involves a point of view to which science must always remain a stranger." This was the uncomfortable contradiction to which the attempted unification of science and philosophy led. In a cautiously hopeful attempt to resolve this dilemma, the Austrian physicist Ludwig Boltzmann pointed out that science dealt with facts through the medium of human thought, whose laws were not infallible. "On the one hand we shall start from facts only, and on the other we shall take nothing into consideration except the effort to attain to the most adequate expression of these facts." In order to do so, the scientist, who dealt with facts, and the philosopher, who dealt with the laws of human thought, must pool their labors. Each must leave behind his own dogma of absolute truth, and acknowledge the contingency of phenomena in the realms both of nature and of man.[5]

[5] Woodward, "The Unity of Physical Science," *ibid.*, IV, 14; Nichols, "The Fundamental Concepts of Physical Science," *ibid.*, IV, 27; Kimball, "The Relations of the Science of Physics of Matter to Other Branches of Learning," *ibid.*, IV, 71; Noyes, "Present

Although there were at St. Louis perceptive scholars who envisioned science as a construct of the human intellect, which could and should be applied to any set of phenomena, the great majority could not free themselves from the narrower conceptions of their own fields. Philosophy was dominated by personalist idealism, social science by the historical school; the natural scientists remained committed to observation and experiment; and in the applied social sciences the psychological approach prevailed. Münsterberg had planned the program in such a way as to emphasize the historical school's rejection of positivism. The keynote was sounded by the German and German-trained American scholars attending the Congress. Out of 308 scholars who presented major papers 202 were American, 41 were German, 21 were English, and 17 were French. A total of 106 of the non-Germans present had received training in Germany; together with the 41 Germans they gave nearly half of the addresses. Of the chemistry professors at the Congress, 80 per cent were German or trained in Germany; in the historical division the figure came to 53 per cent, and in the social sciences to 50 per cent. Besides those already mentioned, the scholars at the Congress included the historian Lamprecht; the economists Hadley, Ross, H. C. Adams, Seligman, Ely, Max Weber, and Sombart; the political scientists

---

Problems of Organic Chemistry," *ibid.*, IV, 285; Davis, "The Relations of the Earth-Sciences in View of Their Progress in the Nineteenth Century," *ibid.*, IV., 489; Pfleiderer, "The Relation of the Philosophy of Religion to the Other Sciences," *ibid.*, I, 272; Troeltsch, "Main Problems of the Philosophy of Religion," *ibid.*, I, 288; Ostwald, "On the Theory of Science," *ibid.*, I, 351; Sorley, "The Relations of Ethics," *ibid.*, I, 402; Boltzmann, "The Relations of Applied Mathematics," *ibid.*, I, 599.

Lowell, Dunning, and Lord Bryce; the sociologists Ward, Small, and Tönnies; the geographer Penck; the anthropologist Boas; the psychologist Hall, the pedagogues Bishop Spalding and Sadler, and the physical scientists Poincaré and Rutherford. This was indeed an illustrious gathering of spokesmen for nineteenth-century scholarship —although Münsterberg, rather than encouraging them to speak of their present work or their expectations for the future, assigned them the task of looking backward over the nineteenth century.

As a result, the representatives of the social sciences, in particular, eulogized an era that had passed its zenith—as no one saw more clearly than a young Chicago philosopher named John Dewey. In a vigorous protest Dewey called Münsterberg's program "a scheme characteristic of one limited school of philosophical thought." He was seconded by R. S. Woodward, who scorned "philosophers and literary folks who indulge in such extravagances . . . [that] tend only to make science and scientific men ridiculous." Dewey contended that the place to look for a unity of science was in the current investigations of scholars, and that Münsterberg had made up his mind beforehand to look for that unity nowhere but in the philosophy of idealism.[6] Münsterberg and his organizing committee, on the other hand, genuinely believed that the triumph of idealism over materialism, naturalism, and positivism was the culmination of scientific progress in the nineteenth century. The proceedings of the 1904 Congress thus breathe an air of confident satisfaction with past achieve-

[6] Dewey in *Science*, n.s., XVIII (Aug. 28, 1903), 277; Woodward, *ibid.*, (Sept. 4, 1903), 303.

ments but are for the most part silent on the problems and tensions within late-nineteenth-century *Wissenschaft*.

The Crisis of Historicism

This confident assertion of the unity of all science was soon belied by rising doubts, as the nineteenth-century belief that a strictly mechanistic determinism governed natural events gave way to the insight that the laws of nature were not inherent in the natural world but were superimposed upon it by human thought. Since, as Boltzmann had declared at St. Louis, the laws of human thought "were not infallible," historical scholars were obliged to recognize that the historical understanding was itself part of the historical process, inextricably bound up with the historians as subjective individuals, and was thus deprived of the sovereign objectivity to which it had once laid claim. With this realization the crisis of historicism became acute.

"Historicism" is in itself a slippery term, whose meaning varies from one writer to another with disconcerting frequency.[7] For some it denotes the belief that an objective historiography is possible; for others it represents the exact opposite. Thus Karl Popper and F. A. Hayek have condemned it as a deterministic philosophy, whereas Walther Hofer has seen it as a recognition of the indeterminate aspects of history.[8] In the present context, "historicism" refers to the *Weltanschauung* of the historical

[7] See Dwight E. Lee and Robert N. Beck, "The Meaning of Historicism," *AHR*, LIX (April, 1954), 568–577.

[8] Karl Popper, *The Poverty of Historicism* (London, 1957); F. A. Hayek, *The Counter-Revolution of Science* (Glencoe, 1952), also partially in *Economica*, n.s., VIII (1941), and Walther Hofer, *Geschichtsschreibung und Weltanschauung* (München, 1950).

school—that is, the body of beliefs concerning the nature of history and of historical scholarship held in common by the men discussed in this book—and thus to methodology as well as ideology. It was both the methodological tool with which scientific historians approached Ranke's question of the *wie es eigentlich gewesen,* and the idealistic framework within which history was to be interpreted.

Whether scholars derived that framework from the literature of the romantic movement or from the preoccupation of early-nineteenth-century historians with the individual,[9] the crucial concern of the idealists was with man's uniqueness as a being capable of choice, and with the resulting flux and multiplicity of the affairs of men. The historian lived in a world different from the orderly and constant realm of natural science.

Although in Germany the crisis of historicism broke into the open only around 1910, and in America not until the depression of the 1930's, the roots of the crisis reach deep into the past. The events of the twentieth century merely brought to the surface the *problematik* of the historical school: namely that as idealists they asserted the autonomy of their discipline and of all *Geisteswissenschaft,* while as empiricists they proposed to use the tools of natural science. Of these tools induction had been used by logicians since Aristotle, and after Newton had postulated a strictly mechanical causality it had become the basis of the naturalistic determinism with whose aid the historicists eventually sought to explain the very change they had also attributed to man's capacity for choice.

[9] Cf. Friedrich Meinecke, *Die Entstehung des Historismus* (München, 1936), I, 2–5.

As the preceding chapters have indicated, this was the dilemma of nineteenth-century scholars wedded to the Newtonian view of nature.

As they groped for a new synthesis of causality and human freedom, the historicists were aided by certain developments in natural science. One of these was thermodynamics, which had apparently begun to replace the concept of a mechanically determined chain of events with that of statistical probability.[10] The historicists in the social sciences welcomed statistical studies of social phenomena as a new way of maintaining "scientific" accuracy without denying the possibility of free choice to individual men. The new experimental psychology permitted historicists to replace vaguely conceived historical "laws" with those of what they regarded as the true sciences of genetics and psychology.[11] By such means the historicists at the St. Louis Congress shored up the foundation of their *Weltanschauung*—the argument that history was a science in its own right, with its own independent existence— against the onslaught of positivism, naturalism, and materialism.

Twenty years later, the picture was drastically changed. The crushing blow dealt by war, defeat, and revolution seemed to prove Henry Adams right in saying that history, and German history above all, revealed nothing but chaos. What was its meaning? What were the laws, if any, that governed chaos? For the German historians, challenged

---

[10] Cf. J. Bronowski, *The Common Sense of Science* (Cambridge, 1943), pp. 76–87, *passim*.

[11] Cf. Wilhelm Dilthey, *Einleitung in die Geisteswissenschaften* (Leipzig, 1892), pp. 80ff.; Karl Lamprecht, *What Is History?* (N.Y., 1905), *passim*.

to prove that scientific history could deal with the problem of meaning, not only their own status as professional
scholars but also the German concept of national destiny
was at stake. Among the German historians who figured
in the ensuing desperate search for their history's meaning, Friedrich Meinecke believed that historical understanding was possible to the participant who exercised
conscience, sensitivity (*Takt*), and self-discipline.[12] Even
though the door might indeed be opened to "anarchy of
thought," Meinecke argued that only subjective action
could reaffirm individual selfhood and permit man to discover his own humanity.[13] Meinecke thus saw the search
for meaning as a gamble based on the faith that humanity
would win out over anarchy. Max Weber came to believe
that the value and meaning of scholarly work must accord
with "our ultimate position towards life"—a position that
could not be given a scientific basis.[14] Karl Mannheim,
who remained closer to the relativism of the historical
school, would have limited the province of scientific analysis to the framework of a given "perspective," and spoke,
with the fervor of one who hopes against hope, of the
collective insight of scholarship as the universal perspective.[15] Ernst Troeltsch, on the other hand, sought the
universal perspective in the values of the Christian faith
—which at least offered "a compromise between natural-

[12] *Vom geschichtlichen Sinn und vom Sinn der Geschichte*
(Leipzig, 1939), pp. 22, 24.

[13] *Aphorismen und Skizzen zur Geschichte* (Leipzig, 1942), p.
126.

[14] "Science as Vocation," reprinted in H. H. Gerth and C.
Wright Mills, eds., *From Max Weber* (N.Y., 1946), pp. 134–156.

[15] *Ideology and Utopia* (N.Y., 1936), pp. 136–138.

ism and idealism, between the practical necessities of man's earthly life and of the ideal goals of his spiritual life."[16] In Troeltsch's view the problem of historicism could be solved only by transcending the limits of history and science.

These twentieth-century scholars caught up in the crisis of historicism were no more able to resolve the issue than their predecessors in the historical school had been. Although they recognized that the one way out of their dilemma was the rejection of either science or history, they were unable to make the choice. Their commitment to sympathetic understanding precluded them from performing the act of rejection. They thus fell victim to the history they studied, and their work is a commentary on nineteenth-century German history that contrasts sharply and tragically with the popular view of the Age of Greatness. When Meinecke wrote in 1942, "The historicism which analyzes itself and seeks understanding from a study of its genesis is a snake that bites its tail,"[17] he not only summed up the crisis of historicism but also composed its epitaph.

The American Attack upon the Science of History

A crisis in historical thought came into the open in the United States during the 1930's, and for nearly a decade was a major topic of debate. It began with the heated denial that the idea of objectivity cherished by scientific historians could be realized. Carl Becker's "Everyman

[16] Der Historismus und seine Überwindung (Berlin, 1924), p. 104.

[17] Aphorismen, p. 11.

His Own Historian" and Charles A. Beard's "Written History as an Act of Faith" and "That Noble Dream" became the manifestoes of the new iconoclasm.[18]

Becker's work consisted of an analysis of the way historians worked. Two decades earlier, he had anticipated the debate in "Detachment and the Writing of History"— perhaps the most radical critique ever written by an American historian, notwithstanding its matter-of-fact tone and gently ironic charm and wit. When Becker wrote that "the 'facts' of history do not exist for any historian until he creates them, and [that] into every fact that he creates some part of his individual experience must enter," he struck at the very heart of the scientific credo. He neither belittled the historiography of the past nor made any philosophical or methodological pronouncements. Even his suggestion that the "new" social historians might not be as "scientific" as they thought they were—that there was a difference between the sociologist who simplified by generalizing and the historian who did it by selection —took the form of a simple description of what went on as a historian studied, wrote, or taught history. The closest Becker came anywhere in his article to pressing his views upon his colleagues was in the statement that "the time may come—there have been such times in the past—when it is most important that every one should care greatly what happens," and that at such a time the "objective man" might be ill adapted to survive.[19] What

[18] "Everyman His Own Historian," in *AHR*, XXXVII (Jan., 1932), 221–236; "Written History as an Act of Faith," *ibid.*, XXXIX (Jan., 1934), 219–229, and "That Noble Dream," *ibid.*, XLI (Oct., 1935), 74–87.

[19] *Atlantic Monthly*, CVI (Oct., 1910), 524–536, *passim*.

the historian cared about would depend upon his understanding of the past, just as it would inevitably be influenced by the conditions of his present existence and his expectations for the future. Forever trapped between past and future in the specious present, the historian was called upon to exercise all the scholarship, imaginative sympathy, and literary craftmanship he could command.

Although Becker's definition of the historian's task did not differ essentially from that of the German scholars of the historical school, he was less inclined to brood over paradox and incongruity; and in the America of the early decades of the twentieth century, history did not yet appear as a chaos devoid of meaning. During the 1930's, when "Everyman His Own Historian" was written, the faith in reason, though weakened, was still alive. Becker observed of Benjamin Franklin that he found politics "an interesting, alas even a necessary, game; but men being what they are it is perhaps best not to inquire too curiously what its ultimate significance may be." [20] In the end he believed that it was necessary to stake one's faith on human rationality, even though the historian's involvement in the present made an absolute objectivity impossible.

Beard carried Becker's analysis a step further, into a discussion of its implications. He began with an attempt to acquaint his colleagues with the issues of German historiography—in which, unfortunately, he got off to a false start. He made a vigorous attack on the late-nineteenth-century American scientific historians, whom he identified with Ranke's famous *wie es eigentlich*

[20] Becker, "Benjamin Franklin," *Dictionary of American Biography*, VI (N.Y., 1931), 597.

gewesen, with the intention of exposing the falsity of their notion of objectivity. He declared that the crisis in American thought was the same as that experienced by contemporary European thinkers—among whom he cited Croce, Riezler, Karl Mannheim, Mueller-Armack, and Heussi.[21] In so doing, however, Beard had not only misread Heussi and the rest, but had also misunderstood the entire development of the German historical school. Again and again these German scholars had affirmed the inseparability of empirical research from idealistic interpretation, and had refused, in their quest for a theory of *Geisteswissenschaft,* to endorse either a consistently "objective" positivism or a purely speculative historiography. The example of the American scientific historians who had been unable to adapt the idealistic philosophy of their German masters to the circumstances of their own country, caused Beard to regard the historical school as the seedbed of positivism.

Just why Beard refused to deal with Ranke as the great proponent of *Ideengeschichte,* and thus ignored half of the historicists' message, can only be surmised. His earlier economic interpretation of history suggests that he was really attacking a view that had once been his own. His economic interpretation must be seen against the background of the belief of the "new" historians that social science would come to the aid of historiography in realizing the hope for a truly historical science. In the two articles published in 1934 and 1935—"Written History as an Act of Faith" and "That Noble Dream"—Beard demolished both the old and the new faith in scientific

---

[21] See "Written History," 220, and *passim.*

history, producing a crisis that was consequently all the more acute. In succumbing to the temptation, ever present in such circumstances, to strike out blindly, he gave a poignant demonstration of the intellectual dilemma faced by many of his colleagues. His error was in asserting that what Heussi and other German scholars meant by the Crisis of Historicism was simply the substitution of faith for scientific objectivity. What was actually at stake for them was the preservation of a social science that would be worthy of the name without excluding a consideration of the realm of human values or the search for meaning.

In his subsequent writings Beard came closer to the problem of the historicists. Asserting the necessity of free choice, he sought to harmonize this admittedly subjective act with the requirements of an objective social science. It must be admitted that Beard's proposals are not convincing. Like the philosopher John Dewey, Beard placed his hopes in the refinement of the scientific method. But quite unlike Dewey, he went on to suggest the use by social scientists of "the method of realistic dialectics."

Under this conception [Beard wrote] history is viewed as assertion of ideas and interests, antagonism to ideas and interests thus asserted, and resolution of the conflict by victory and adjustment. Hence the formula: thesis, antithesis, and synthesis.

Thus the sworn enemy of Rankean empiricism allied himself with the dialectic of Ranke's arch-antagonist, Hegel! For Beard that dialectic was "scientific" because it avoided value judgments, restricting itself to "taking in all relevances and giving order to them," and was "realistic" in its striving "for conformity to known facts and situations." [22] It would seem, then, that despite the shattering of the historian's "noble dream" it was still possible to "know facts and situations," that despite the "act of faith" required of the historian, it was still possible for him to be "scientific," and that the ordering of relevances was still possible—even though value judgments lay outside the historian's realm! Beard's answer to such an objection, presumably, would have been to assert that it was the dialectic that did the ordering, while the historian with his value judgments stood outside what he had merely recorded. But this brings us back to the claims of the scientific historians. So far as Beard as a historical thinker is concerned, I find it impossible to come to his defense. One can easily recognize and sympathize with the crisis in his thinking, but it cannot be granted that he resolved it, or that he was a truly representative spokesman for the crisis of historicism. That spokesman is to be found, if at all, among the philosophers.

The Response of an American Philosopher

John Dewey in his treatise on *Logic* attacked the problems raised by Becker and Beard, as well as by the German historicists. He agreed with the former that the historian inevitably chose what was to be included in or excluded from his narrative. For Dewey a historical topic could be defined as a problem in need of solution. It was the scholar's desire to solve such problems, and his search for new knowledge, that gave unity to all scientific work, whether it dealt with the natural world, with human

[22] *The Discussion of Human Affairs* (N.Y., 1936), pp. 114–120, *passim.*

224

society, with history, or with philosophy. The act of choosing a topic, however, was inseparable from the historian's involvement in the present, and was thus conditioned by what Becker called "the climate of opinion" at that time, as well as by the historian's own experience, character, and interests. Since the data were chosen for their relevance to the problem that was to be solved, Dewey asserted, "we are committed to the conclusion that all history is necessarily written from the standpoint of the present, and is, in an inescapable sense, the history not only of the present, but of that which is contemporaneously judged to be important in the present." In thus restating the argument of the presentists, Dewey conceded the impossibility of an objective scientific history just as Becker and Beard had done.[23]

Dewey went on to compare the solution of problems in historical writing with that in the natural sciences. According to him historians concerned with a problematical situation resolved it by describing and analyzing its outcome. Yet they had to acknowledge the disconcerting fact that different historians assigned different "outcomes" to the French Revolution, for example. The "outcome," moreover, to a large extent determined the historians' choice of data. Since both "outcome" and data were colored by the historians' view of the present and their hopes for the future, the writing of history was bound to change along with the changes of history itself. "The selection of the end or outcome," Dewey wrote, "marks an interest and the interest reaches into the future. It is a sign that the issue is not closed . . . History cannot escape

[23] John Dewey, *Logic: The Theory of Inquiry* (N.Y., 1938), pp. 232–237, *passim*.

its own process. It will, therefore, always be rewritten." [24]
Could the same thing be said of science? It was at this
point that Dewey parted company with Becker, Beard,
and the German historicists. His position, which had been
foreshadowed by his criticism of the planners of the
St. Louis Congress, was that any insight into the unity of
science must come from observing the scientist at work,
and that the crucial problem of the historicists was the
nature not of their subject matter but of scientific inquiry
in itself.

Dewey held that for all scientists the "outcome" of a
problem invariably lay hidden in the future, since the
unexpected was always taking place, and new events or
new knowledge were continually forcing men to revise
their hypotheses. The necessity for revising previously
accepted scientific concepts made certain knowledge in
any field of inquiry impossible; nevertheless, the limitations of human knowledge did not deter the scientist from
his work. The "outcomes" he assigned to past events, or
that he predicted for his research in the natural or social
sciences, were alike subject to revision from the moment
they proved inadequate. In the field of historical and
social studies these hypothetical outcomes—referred to
by Dewey as "ends-in-view"—although informed by
knowledge of the past and by considerations of logic,
because of their nature as hypotheses could have no
absolute normative force. "Only recognition in both theory
and practice that ends to be attained (ends-in-view) are
of the nature of hypotheses and that hypotheses have to
be formed and tested in strict correlativity with existential

<hr>

[24] *Ibid.*, pp. 238–239, *passim.*

conditions as means, can alter current habits of dealing with social issues." [25] In thus demonstrating the possibility of a common methodological basis for investigations in history, the social studies, and the natural sciences, Dewey gave new strength to the assertion by historical scholars that their work need be no less scientific than that of natural scientists.

There remains the question of how he dealt with value and meaning, and with the belief in the uniqueness of man. He maintained that ends-in-view were hypotheses, without normative force, and that the "ought" could never be derived from the "is." But, echoing the German historians, Dewey went on to note that men did ask for values to live by, and that their demand for moral guidance tended to remove ends from the realm of inquiry, and to posit them as an "act of faith" entirely cut off from science. What in *The Quest for Certainty* he called "the deepest problem of modern life" was precisely this divorce between man's empirical knowledge of the world and his beliefs about the values that should guide his conduct. Dewey's answer to the question at the heart of the crisis of historicism—that of the meaning of history— was to call for an "experimental empiricism in the field of ideas of good and bad." [26] Although for scientists and historians the highest values would only be manifested by the entire course of history, of which they knew only part, Dewey maintained that the experimental methods of science might at least yield "outcomes" for both the present and the near future. He thus called on social scientists,

[25] *Ibid.*, p. 497.
[26] *The Quest for Certainty: A Study of the Relation of Knowledge and Action* (N.Y., 1929), pp. 255–258.

not to base value judgments on past experience alone (the "ideological" values of Karl Mannheim) or on absolutist desires for the future (Mannheim's Utopias), but rather to construct "enjoyable objects" (ends-in-view) out of the controlled recollection of past experience. "Reflection upon what we have liked and have enjoyed . . . tells us nothing about the *value* of these things until enjoyments are themselves reflectively controlled." [27] Even then we can have neither certainty of the highest values nor absolute answers to ultimate questions, since the process of history is incomplete and our knowledge of consequences uncertain. But although the inability of scientists to obtain certain knowledge of the future means that the quest for certainty is unending, Dewey argued that the methodology of inquiry he had set forth did at least allow for "an adjustment between the conclusions of natural science and the beliefs and values that have authority in the direction of life." [28] Dewey agreed with Weber that science cannot give us answers to ultimate questions, and cannot solve the riddle of meaning; he disagreed with Beard's conclusion that neither historiography nor science had anything at all to say about questions of value and meaning. He went beyond Weber, however, in suggesting how science might approach the solution of social problems despite the limits imposed by the nature of knowledge and of history.

Dewey's entire philosophy thus hinges on what he found the nature of knowledge and of history to be. He defined knowledge as the outcome of the process of human inquiry into the phenomenal world—the process and its

[27] *Ibid.*, p. 272.　　[28] *Ibid.*, p. 284.

objects both existing within the stream of history. Knowledge in itself, and the world as known, were thus likewise historical—that is, they existed in the present as temporary states moving from the past into the future. The values men cherished, and the meaning they ascribed to history, were likewise historical, and changed with the passage of time. Absolute, unchanging values did not exist within history, even though the yearning for certain knowledge and unchanging values that stemmed from a deep-rooted psychological need, were also facts of that history. Man as a historical being could not hope to raise himself by means of science to a perception of eternal truth. For Dewey the acknowledgment that the knowable universe and the realm of history were open-ended, and that there could be no scientific guide to conduct other than what empirical methods made available, did not lead to an arbitrary act of faith, nor was it the prologue to pessimism and despair. He was quite unlike either Beard on the one hand or Weber and Mannheim on the other, resembling rather the confident yet modest Becker in his acceptance of the limits of human knowledge and his stress on what the resources of science could actually provide.

In retrospect Dewey, the philosopher, emerges as the most thoroughgoing historical thinker of all the men we have discussed. Given his insight that all knowledge is historical, the differences among the natural, social, and historical sciences dwindle to insignificance, and the German insistence on a *Geisteswissenschaft*—the crowning glory of the historical school and the stumbling block

229

that led to the crisis of historicism—cease to be formidable. As Edgar Wind so well expressed it,

German scholars have taught for decades that, apart from adherence to the most general rules of logic, the study of history and the natural sciences are to each other as pole and antipole, and that it is the first duty of any historian to forswear all sympathy with the ideals of men who would like to reduce the whole world to a mathematical formula. This revolt was no doubt an act of liberation in its time. Today it is pointless. The very concept of nature in opposition to which Dilthey proclaimed his *Geisteswissenschaft* has long been abandoned by the scientists themselves, and the notion of a description of nature which indiscriminately subjects men and their fates like rocks and stones to its "unalterable laws" survives only as a nightmare of certain historians.[29]

The new science of the twentieth century, after developing a rather sophisticated appreciation of the limits of deterministic thinking, has come to recognize certain issues raised by nineteenth-century historians and philosophers as problems of its own. Dewey's philosophy is especially characteristic of the twentieth century in its proposal of a methodology that makes possible both a unity of knowledge and a harmony between thought and action. It was by means of this historical philosophy that the crisis of historicism was resolved, and that a workable basis for twentieth-century scholarship and science was established.

[29] "Some Points of Contact between History and Natural Science," in Raymond Klibansky and H. J. Paton, eds., *Philosophy and History* (Oxford, 1936), pp. 255–256.

9

A Closing Word

> The problem of restoring integration and cooperation between man's beliefs about the world in which he lives and his beliefs about the values and purposes that should direct his conduct is the deepest problem of modern life. —JOHN DEWEY, 1929

IN this book I have followed certain strands of the history of German scholarship in the nineteenth century as they have been woven into the fabric of scholarship in America. Although I have focused my attention on the last three decades of the nineteenth century, I have not hesitated to move back as far as 1810 and forward into the 1930's whenever such excursions seemed necessary or appropriate. The main field of inquiry has been history and the social sciences, but I have considered religion and philosophy for reasons which I trust need no further justification here. If apologies are in order they must be for what has been omitted, not what has been included. The absence of a chapter on education and psychology may—in fact should—cause raised eyebrows; and that there is nothing on geographical scholarship likewise will not pass unnoticed. By way of explanation I must confess that the quantity of source materials, both primary and secondary, in education and psychology is so vast that I saw no way to deal with them in a single chapter at all proportionate to the rest. In geography the situation is exactly the reverse. For reasons I have suggested elsewhere,[1] geography in American universities never achieved an importance comparable with that of the other social sciences, and the relative scarcity of American academic geographers made it seem hardly fruitful to explore the problems of those who had been trained in Germany.

What I hope to have shown in this study is the complexity of the "transfer of culture." In any society, culture may be said to consist of the interaction of its institutions and ideas. Thus the Americans who went to German universities to acquire the tools of scholarship brought home not only tools but ideas as well. When the ideas proved difficult to assimilate to American conditions, the scholars sought to modify or discard them, only to realize that their scholarly equipment, torn from its ideological setting, would no longer serve until a new context of ideas could be developed. The sociological ethics of Albion Small and the instrumentalism of John Dewey were mainly responsible for this development, and signaled that the transitory dominance of German historicism in America was over.

The question may still be raised whether American scholarship ever fully resolved the crisis of historicism, and whether scholars have altogether discarded its legacy. To the first question I suspect the answer must be both Yes and No. To the extent that the conflict between deterministic thinking on the one hand, and the human affirmation of individuality and capacity for choice on the other, has become an anachronism along with the

[1] "Social Darwinism and the History of American Geography," *Proceedings*, Amer. Philos. Soc. CV (Dec. 15, 1961), 538–544.

feud between natural and social science, the answer is Yes. Science has become a part of history; its unalterable laws are now regarded as historical phenomena, and historical problems viewed as a challenge to inquiry are seen to be in no essential way different from the problems of any scientist.

The answer is No, however, when we remember that not all historical work consists of problem solving but requires of the historian an imaginative understanding and reconstruction of the past. It is No, too, when we consider man's unwillingness to accept the total historization of his existence, his continuing quest for values to live by, and his demand that history reveal its "true" meaning. These issues history cannot resolve until it comes to an end—an event no historical being will be on hand to witness.

To the question whether American scholars forsook the legacy of historicism, the answer is simply that they neither wholly forsook nor wholly retained it, but adapted it to American conditions. They had been stimulated to appraise their scholarship as a body of historical knowledge that needed constant verification under the circumstances of a new and changing environment—a procedure far different from that of old-time college professors who saw as their task the transmission of inherited truths. As a result of the new approach, scholars realized that the data they had acquired in Germany were not exempt either from the need for constant reappraisal, and that the euphoric haze of a German spring did not always survive the crisp air of a New England autumn. Content neither with the "truth" of the college moral philosophers nor with what their German masters revered as "fact," they recognized that scholarship was never at rest; that for the scholar there could never be final knowledge; and that, in the words of John Dewey, intelligent inquiry was both the process and the end of scholarship. But their commitment to inquiry was moral as well as intellectual, and the faith in a meaning both within and beyond history was still alive.

The Americans who absorbed the German *Wissenschaft* were quick to perceive its strengths and to recognize its weaknesses. They instituted graduate and professional schools, but they also kept alive in American colleges the idea of a liberal education. The German university helped lift American colleges out of their provincial complacency; and the same colleges, in their turn, were a check upon the tendency toward overspecialization in the graduate schools. At its best the mutual interpenetration of a liberal and a vocational education helped turn schoolmasters and technical experts into open-minded investigators and teachers. An orthodox moral philosophy and the cult of technology were both transformed and their values preserved in a social science that combined the scientist's discipline with the philosopher's concern for the meaning of human existence.

Bibliographical Notes

1. American Students in German Universities

THE best and most complete survey of seventeenth- and eighteenth-century German-American relations in science and scholarship is Henry A. Pochmann's magisterial *German Culture in America: Philosophical and Literary Influences, 1600–1900* (Madison, 1957), pp. 19–57. Somewhat less detailed summaries may be found in Albert B. Faust's earlier standard work, *The German Element in the United States,* 2 vols. (Boston, 1909), esp. vol. II, pp. 201–210, and in Michael Kraus, *The Atlantic Civilization: Eighteenth Century Origins* (Ithaca, 1949). For a brief account see John A. Walz, *German Influence in American Education and Culture* (Philadelphia, 1936). Thomas N. Bonner has recently reported on *American Doctors and German Universities* (Lincoln, 1963).

On the relative advantages and disadvantages of the universities of Germany, France, and England see Abraham Flexner, *Universities: American, English, German* (N.Y., 1930); and Charles F. Thwing, *The American and the German University* (N.Y., 1928), pp. 69–76. An instructive and often amusing—if not always reliable—source of information on academic life in Germany, the United States, and elsewhere is in the personal memoirs of men who "were there." I especially recommend the following: James M. Baldwin, *Between Two Wars* (Boston, 1926); John W. Burgess, *Reminiscences of an American Scholar* (N.Y., 1934); Nicholas M.

Butler, *Across the Busy Years,* 2 vols., (N.Y., 1939–1940); John R. Commons, *Myself* (N.Y., 1934); Richard T. Ely, *Ground under Our Feet* (N.Y., 1938); G. Stanley Hall, *Aspects of German Culture* (Boston, 1881), and *Life and Confessions of a Psychologist* (N.Y., 1923); Henry Johnson, *The Other Side of Main Street* (N.Y., 1943); Francis G. Peabody, *Reminiscences of Present-Day Saints* (Boston, 1927); Bliss Perry, *And Gladly Teach* (Boston, 1935); and Edward A. Ross, *Seventy Years of It* (N.Y., 1936), *The Autobiography of Lincoln Steffens* (N.Y., 1931), and *The Autobiography of Andrew D. White,* 2 vols. (London, 1905).

The German universities are discussed in Friedrich Paulsen's *The German Universities: Their Character and Historical Development* (N.Y., 1895), originally published as part of Wilhelm Lexis, ed., *Die deutschen Universitäten,* 2 vols. (Berlin, 1893); and in Matthew Arnold's *Higher Schools and Universities in Germany* (London, 1874). Frederic Lilge in *The Abuse of Learning* (N.Y., 1948) gives a valuable history of German scholarship from the days of the Humboldt brothers to the rise of Nazism.

2. The American College and the Problem of Professional Education

American historiography has sadly neglected the field of American higher education. Most college histories suffer from an overdose of academic nostalgia and of denominational apologetics—or else from a desire to tell all, which indiscriminately places the trivial and the significant side by side. Of the few noteworthy books in the field I have used George P. Schmidt's captivating volumes, *The Old Time College President* (N.Y., 1930), and *The Liberal Arts College* (New Brunswick, 1957); Richard Hofstadter and C. DeWitt Hardy's *The Development and Scope of Higher Education in the United States* (N.Y., 1952); Hofstadter and Walter P. Metzger's *The Development of Academic Freedom in the United States* (N.Y., 1955), a work that ranges far beyond the scope of its title to give what amounts to a history of American higher education; R. Freeman Butts' *The College Charts Its Course* (N.Y., 1939), which contains many useful references; W. Carson Ryan's *Studies in Early Graduate Education* (N.Y., 1939); Richard J. Storr's *The Beginnings of Graduate Education in America* (Chicago, 1953), and Frederick Rudolph's *The American College and University* (N.Y., 1962).

The growth of scholarly and scientific associations is best studied from their periodicals, proceedings, and monographs. Among secondary sources I recommend the following: G. Brown Goode, "The Origin of the National Scientific and Educational Institutions of the United States," *Annual Report of the AHA for the Year 1889* (Washington, 1890), pp. 53–161; Ralph S. Bates, *Scientific Societies in the United States* (N.Y., 1945); and G. B. Goode, ed., *The Smithsonian Institution* (1897). Two essays by Richard H. Shryock, "The Academic Profession in the United States," *Bulletin of the American Association of University Professors*, XXXVIII (Spring, 1952), 32–70, and "American Indifference to Basic Science during the Nineteenth Century," *Archives Internationales d'Histoire des Sciences* (Oct., 1948), pp. 50–65, are especially helpful. Arthur E. Bestor, Jr., in "The Transformation of American Scholarship, 1875–1917," *Library Quarterly*, XXIII (July, 1953), 164–179, deals with the rise of professional libraries and the adoption of the Dewey classification, and David D. Van Tassel in *Recording America's Past* (Chicago, 1960) treats the growth of the historical profession before the founding of the American Historical Association in 1884. An evaluation of the seminar is given in Walter P. Webb's "The Historical Seminar: Its Outer Shell and Its Inner Spirit," *MVHR*, XLII (June, 1955), 3–23.

On the subject of college reform I should like to call attention to Russell Thomas' excellent *The Search for a Common Learning: General Education, 1800–1960* (N.Y., 1962), esp. ch. 3. For detailed information, besides the histories of various colleges and universities, Leland L. Medsker's *The Junior College: Progress and Prospect* (N.Y., 1960) should be consulted. The controversial issue of the graduate school's influence on the undergraduate college has recently been discussed from one point of view by Earl J. McGrath in *The Graduate School and the Decline of Liberal Education* (N.Y., 1959), and from another by Bernard Berelson in *Graduate Education in the United States* (N.Y., 1960).

3. German Wissenschaft *and American Philosophy*

For an understanding of college moral philosophy the works I have found most helpful are Herbert W. Schneider's *A History of American Philosophy* (N.Y., 1946); Woodbridge Riley's *American Thought from Puritanism to Pragmatism and Beyond* (N.Y., 1923), especially pp. 118–122 on the Scottish philosophy; and Harvey G. Townsend's *Philosophical Ideas in the United States* (N.Y., 1934), which on pp. 96ff. discusses the relevance of scientific thought. The best recent accounts of the Scottish philosophy are Gladys Bryson's *Man and Society: The Scottish Inquiry of the Eighteenth Century* (Princeton, 1945) and S. A. Grave's *The Scottish Philosophy of Common Sense* (Oxford, 1960). On the influence of this philosophy in American colleges see Wilson Smith's *Professors and Public Ethics: Studies of Northern Moral Philosophers before the Civil War* (Ithaca, 1956) and Ralph H. Gabriel's *Religion and Learning at Yale* (New Haven, 1958), *passim*. The same topic is treated by Sydney E. Ahlstrom in "The Scottish Philosophy and American Theology," *Church History*, XXIV (Sept., 1955), 257–272; by Benjamin Rand in "Philosophical Instruction in Harvard University from 1636 to 1906," *Harvard Graduates Magazine*, XXXVII (1928–1929), 29–47, 188–200,

296–311, and by Edgeley W. Todd in "Philosophical Ideas at Harvard College, 1817–1837," *New England Quarterly*, XVI (March, 1943), 63–90. J. H. Muirhead discusses "How Hegel Came to America" in the *Philosophical Review*, XXXVII (May, 1928), 226–240; William Schuyler gives one of the best short accounts of "The St. Louis Philosophical Movement" in the *Educational Review*, XXIX (May, 1905), 450–467; and Loyd D. Eaton reports on "Hegelianism in Nineteenth-Century Ohio" in the *Journal of the History of Ideas*, XXIII (July–Sept., 1962), 355–378. Excellent for its bibliographies is David F. Bowers, ed., *Foreign Influences in American Life* (Princeton, 1944). A more detailed survey of developments in German academic thinking may be found in the old but still unsurpassed *History of European Thought in the Nineteenth Century* (Edinburgh, 1896) by John T. Merz, esp. Vol. I, pp. 157–225, as well as in Ernst Cassirer's *The Problem of Knowledge: Philosophy, Science, and History since Hegel* (New Haven, 1950), and in Herbert Butterfield's *Man on His Past* (Cambridge, 1955), pp. 32–61.

4. German Theological Science and American Religion

Of the many available secondary sources on German theological scholarship I have found particularly helpful the five volumes of *Die Religion in Geschichte und Gegenwart*. For the period before 1900 the second edition (Tübingen, 1927–1931) is more detailed than later editions. For the history of theology in Germany I recommend Kenneth S. Latourette, *The Nineteenth Century in Europe: The Protestant and Eastern Churches* (N.Y., 1959); Vol. II of I. A. Dorner, *History of Protestant Theology Particularly in Germany* (Edinburgh, 1871); and Otto Pfleiderer, *The Development of Theology in Germany Since Kant* (London, 1880). For a direct acquaintance with the views of nineteenth-century theologians I recommend sampling the works of Schleiermacher and of D. F.

Strauss; Tholuck's *Die Glaubwürdigkeit der Evangelischen Geschichte,* 2nd ed. (Hamburg, 1838); J. R. Beard, ed., *Voices of the Church in Reply to Dr. D. F. Strauss* (London, 1845); and Pfleiderer's *Die Religion, ihr Wesen und ihre Geschichte,* 2 vols. (Leipzig, 1869). The importance of Schleiermacher's hermeneutics for German as well as American theology has been stressed once more by Richard R. Niebuhr in "Schleiermacher on Language and Feeling," *Theology Today,* XVII (July, 1960), 150–167.

Anyone interested in the history of American theology should begin with William W. Sweet, *Religion in the Development of American Culture, 1765–1840* (N.Y., 1952), and Joseph Haroutunian, *Piety versus Moralism: The Passing of the New England Theology* (N.Y., 1932). For material on the history of Congregational theology Daniel D. Williams, *The Andover Liberals: A Study in American Theology* (N.Y., 1941), and *Bibliotheca Sacra,* of which the first volume appeared in 1844, should be consulted. Information on Presbyterianism may be gleaned from the *Presbyterian Quarterly Review* (1852–1862); from Lewis F. Stearns, *Henry Boynton Smith* (Boston, 1892); and from *Henry Boynton Smith: His Life and Work,* edited by his wife (N.Y., 1881). Unitarian theology and history are treated by Earl M. Wilbur in *A History of Unitarianism* (Cambridge, 1945), by Frederick M. Eliot in *Fundamentals of Unitarian Faith* (St. Paul, 1926), and by George H. Williams, ed., in *The Harvard Divinity School* (Boston, 1954). William R. Hutchison illuminates the Transcendentalist controversy in *The Transcendentalist Ministers* (New Haven, 1959). Interesting contemporary documents are given by Eliza Buckminster Lee in her *Memoirs of Rev. Joseph Buckminster* (Boston, 1849); in *The Christian Examiner* (1824–1869); and in Perry Miller's splendid anthology, *The Transcendentalists* (Cambridge, 1950). Arthur M. Schlesinger, Sr., in "A Critical Period in American Religion, 1875–1900,"

Proceed. of the Mass. Hist. Soc., LXIV (June, 1932), 523–547, and Herbert W. Schneider in "Evolution and Theology in America," *Journal of the History of Ideas,* VI (Jan., 1945), 3–18, offer valuable insight into the development of American theology both inside and outside the colleges and seminaries. The role of biblical criticism in theology is suggested by Charles A. Briggs in *Biblical Study: Its Principles, Methods, and History* (N.Y., 1883), and by Orello Cone in *Gospel-Criticism and Historical Christianity* (N.Y. 1891). Anyone interested in the impact of biblical scholarship on the German Reformed and Lutheran churches should read Philip Schaf's *America,* recently republished as edited by Perry Miller (Cambridge, 1961), and James H. Nichols, *Romanticism in American Theology* (Chicago, 1961). Finally, no one should fail to consult *The Shaping of American Religion,* the first volume in Princeton's Religion in American Life series, or its sequel, Nelson R. Burr's *A Critical Bibliography of Religion in America,* 2 vols. (1961).

5. The Science of History and Politics

An entire book could be devoted to the nineteenth-century origins and development of the science of history and politics in the United States. My discussion merely highlights a few of the themes that seem to me crucial for an understanding of the subject. I have focused on the work of Herbert Baxter Adams and John William Burgess because, although their achievements and failures do not illustrate every aspect, they do suggest the kind of problems raised by the transplantation of German academic culture to the universities of the United States.

On the subject of German historiography I have relied heavily on Eduard Fueter, *Geschichte der neueren Historiographie* (München, 1911), on Karl Brandi, *Geschichte der Geschichtswissenschaft,* 2nd ed., (Bonn, 1952); and on Fritz

Wagner, ed., *Geschichtswissenschaft* (München, 1951). Leonard Krieger in *The German Idea of Freedom: History of a Political Tradition* (Boston, 1957) treats the political thought of the idealists; Hajo Holborn in "Der deutsche Idealismus in sozialgeschichtlicher Beleuchtung," *Historische Zeitschrift,* 174 (1952), 359–384, discusses the social factors that led to a differentiation of German idealistic thought from European and American rationalism; and Friedrich Engel-Janosi gives some rather fragmentary sketches of German idealists and historians in his "The Growth of German Historicism," *JHSt.,* LXII (1944), 237–325. Valuable suggestions and points of view are presented in Friedrich Meinecke's classic *Die Entstehung des Historismus* (München, 1936).

For information on individual German scholars see Herbert B. Adams, *Bluntschli's Life Work* (Baltimore, 1884); Burckhardt's *Briefe,* ed. by Fritz Kaphahn (Leipzig, n.d.); Friedrich Meinecke, "Ranke and Burckhardt," in Hans Kohn, ed., *German History: Some New German Views* (Boston, 1954), pp. 141–156, and "Johann Gustav Droysen," *Historische Zeitschrift,* 141 (1930), 249–287. No one should overlook Theodore von Laue, *Leopold Ranke: The Formative Years* (Princeton, 1950), which focuses on Ranke's concept of universal history, or George G. Iggers' illuminating "The Image of Ranke in American and German Historical Thought," in *History and Theory,* II (1962), 17–40—an essay that once and for all sweeps away the one-sided view of the "scientific" and "fact-collecting" Ranke. Another indispensable source concerning German idealistic historiography is Droysen's *Historik,* ed. by Rudolph Hübner, 4th ed. (München, 1960). For an introduction to Prussian political-historical writing I recommend Andreas Dorpalen's *Heinrich von Treitschke* (New Haven, 1957).

General accounts of American historiography include Michael Kraus, *The Writing of American History* (Norman, Okla., 1953); Harvey Wish, *The American Historian* (N.Y.,

1960); and William T. Hutchinson, ed., *Marcus W. Jernegan Essays in American Historiography* (Chicago, 1937). On Herbert Baxter Adams see John Martin Vincent in Howard W. Odum, ed., *American Masters of Social Science* (N.Y., 1927), pp. 99–127; also W. Stull Holt, "Historical Scholarship in the United States, 1876–1901, as revealed in the correspondence of Herbert B. Adams," *JHSt.*, LVI (1938), 399–706.

The development of political science as an academic discipline in America is covered by Anna Haddow, *Political Science in American Colleges and Universities, 1636–1900* (N.Y., 1939), and by Bernard Crick, *The American Science of Politics* (Berkeley, 1959). Recent evaluations of Burgess may be found in Edward N. Saveth, *American Historians and European Immigrants, 1875–1925* (N.Y., 1948); in Bernard E. Brown, *American Conservatives: The Political Thought of Francis Lieber and John W. Burgess* (N.Y., 1951), and in Bert James Loewenberg, "John William Burgess, the Scientific Method, and the Hegelian Philosophy of History," *MVHR,* XLII (Dec., 1955), 490–509. Much information on Burgess is given by Ralph G. Hoxie in "John W. Burgess, American Scholar" (Columbia U. dissertation, 1950), and by Charles B. Robson in "The Influence of German Thought on Political Theory in the United States in the Nineteenth Century" (U. of North Carolina dissertation, 1930).

6. The Sciences of Society: Political Economy and Sociology

For a general introduction to the history of economic thought the reader may turn to Joseph A. Schumpeter, *History of Economic Analysis* (N.Y., 1954), and Gerhard Stavenhagen, *Geschichte der Wirtschaftstheorie,* 2nd ed. (Göttingen, 1957). German developments of the period under discussion are treated by Wilhelm Roscher in *Geschichte der National-Oekonomik in Deutschland* (München, 1874); by Karl Diehl in "Volkswirtschaft und Volkswirtschaftslehre," *Wörterbuch der Volkswirtschaft,* 4th ed., III (Jena, 1933), 818–884; in the essays by H. Dietzel, E. Gothein, and W. Lexis in W. Lexis, ed., *Die deutschen Universitäten,* I (Berlin, 1893), 566–606; and by Adolph Wagner in *Die akademische Nationalökonomie und der Socialismus* (Berlin, 1895). The German historical school of national economy is critically evaluated by F. Lifschitz in *Die historische Schule der Wirtschaftswissenschaft* (Bern, 1914). For information on German influences on American economics see Joseph Dorfman's "The Role of the German Historical School in American Economic Growth," *American Economic Review: Papers and Proceedings,* XLV (May, 1955), 17–28; also Henry Carter Adams, *Relation of the State to Industrial Action,* republished and edited by Dorfman in 1954. The third volume of Dorfman's *The Economic Mind in American Civilization* (N.Y., 1949), covering the years from 1865 to 1918, constitutes the best available survey.

Harry Elmer Barnes, ed., *Introduction to the History of Sociology* (Chicago, 1948) and Albion W. Small, *Origins of Sociology* (Chicago, 1924), should be read together with Leon Bramson's fine study, *The Political Context of Sociology* (Princeton, 1961), which offers an illuminating interpretation of the data collected by Barnes and Small. For further insight into the history and philosophy of the social science movement I would recommend—in addition to the works cited in the footnotes—Ernst Cassirer's *The Logic of the Humanities,* trans. C. S. Howe (New Haven, 1961); Carlo Antoni's *From History to Sociology: The Transition in German Historical Thinking* (Detroit, 1959); and H. Stuart Hughes' *Consciousness and Society: The Reorientation of European Social Thought, 1890–1930* (N.Y., 1958). Two works, one old and one recent, that will help orient the reader in the field of statistics are Karl G. A. Knies, *Die Statistik als selbstständige Wissenschaft* (Kassel, 1850), and George A. Lundberg, "Statistics in Modern Social Thought," in Barnes, Becker, and Becker, eds., *Contemporary Social Theory* (N.Y., 1940), pp. 110–140. For an understanding of the history of American sociology, Albion Small's "Fifty Years of Sociology in the United States (1865–1915)," *American Journal of Sociology,* XXI (May, 1916) is indispensable as both a primary and secondary source. Finally, no reader should fail to look into Lester F. Ward's *Dynamic Sociology,* 2 vols. (N.Y., 1883).

7. Scholarship and Social Action

A thoughtful case study of the problem of thought and action is Arthur Schlesinger, Jr., "Walter Lippmann: The Intellectual v. Politics," in Marquis Childs and James Reston, eds., *Walter Lippmann and His Times* (N.Y., 1959), pp. 189–225. Schlesinger's essay is relevant because of Lippmann's association with Herbert Croly on the staff of the *New Republic.* On reform proposals involving scholars in public affairs see Charles McCarthy, *The Wisconsin Idea* (N.Y., 1912), and compare with Ely's views as given in *Ground under Our Feet,* pp. 208ff, as well as with Commons' opinion in *Myself,* pp. 107–111. Other sources are Edgar B. Wesley, *Proposed: The University of the United States* (Minneapolis, 1936), and Leonard D. White, *Trends in Public Administration* (N.Y., 1933), pp. 259–266. The standard works on the early development of the Social Gospel in America are James Dombrowski, *The Early Days of Christian Socialism in America* (N.Y., 1936), and Charles H. Hopkins, *The Rise of the Social Gospel in American Protestantism, 1865–1915* (New Haven, 1940). For its academic and theological aspects see Henry F. May, *Protestant Churches and Industrial America* (N.Y., 1949), pp. 136–153, and W. A. Visser't Hooft, *The Background of the Social Gospel in America* (Haarlem, 1928). The involvement of ministers and professors in social reform is summarized by Sidney Fine in his *Laissez-Faire and the General-Welfare*

State (Ann Arbor, 1956), pp. 169–286. Peabody and the New England reformers receive particular attention in Arthur Mann's *Yankee Reformers in the Urban Age* (Cambridge, 1954), esp. pp. 102–125.

For relevant discussions of progressivism see Russel B. Nye's *Midwestern Progressive Politics: A Historical Study of Its Origins and Development, 1870–1958* (East Lansing, 1959); Eric F. Goldman's *Rendezvous with Destiny* (N.Y., 1952); George E. Mowry's *Theodore Roosevelt and the Progressive Movement* (Madison, 1946) and *The Era of Theodore Roosevelt: 1900–1912* (N.Y., 1958); Arthur Link's *Woodrow Wilson and the Progressive Era, 1910–1917* (N.Y., 1954); Daniel Aaron's *Men of Good Hope* (N.Y., 1951, 1961), John M. Blum's *The Republican Roosevelt* (Cambridge, 1954); David W. Noble's *The Paradox of Progressive Thought* (Minneapolis, 1958); and Charles Forcey's *The Crossroads of Liberalism* (N.Y., 1961).

8. The German Influence and American Social Science

The St. Louis Congress has twice received scholarly attention—in George Haines IV and Frederick H. Jackson, "A Neglected Landmark in the History of Ideas," *MVHR*, XXXIV (Sept., 1947), 201–220, and in A. W. Coats, "American Scholarship Comes of Age: The Louisiana Purchase Exposition of 1904," *Journal of the History of Ideas*, XXII (July–Sept., 1961), 404–417. The latter essay throws a revealing light on A. W. Small's original opposition and subsequent acquiescence to Münsterberg's "ground plan."

On the American response to historicism the reader should consult Philip P. Wiener's *Evolution and the Founders of Pragmatism* (Cambridge, 1949), as well as Morton White's *The Origin of Dewey's Instrumentalism* (N.Y., 1943) and *Social Thought in America: The Revolt against Formalism*

(N.Y., 1947). See also Lloyd R. Sorenson, "Charles A. Beard and German Historiographical Thought," *MVHR*, XLII (Sept., 1955), 274–287, and David W. Noble, "Carl Becker: Science, Relativism, and the Dilemma of Diderot," *Ethics*, LXVII (July, 1957) 233–248. Becker and Beard are evaluated together by Cushing Strout in *The Pragmatic Revolt in American History* (New Haven, 1958); the former is the subject of biographies by Charlotte W. Smith—*Carl Becker: On History and the Climate of Opinion* (Ithaca, 1956)—and Burleigh T. Wilkins—*Carl Becker* (Cambridge, 1961), and the latter has been portrayed by Bernard C. Borning in *The Political and Social Thought of Charles A. Beard* (Seattle, 1962). "John Dewey's Theory of History" is discussed by Joseph L. Blau in *The Journal of Philosophy*, LVII (Feb. 4, 1960), 89–100, and by Sidney Ratner in Sidney Hook, ed., *John Dewey: Philosopher of Science and Freedom* (N.Y., 1950), pp. 134–152. An evaluation of Dewey's historical thought (with which the present author does not agree), is given by B. T. Wilkins in "Pragmatism as a Theory of Historical Knowledge: John Dewey on the Nature of Historical Inquiry," *AHR*, LXIV (July, 1959), 878–890. Finally, I should like to call attention to Gordon D. Kaufman's admirably lucid exposition of the problem of historical relativism in *Relativism, Knowledge, and Faith* (Chicago, 1960).

Index

Academic freedom: *Lernfreiheit*, 19–22, 23, 29; *Libertas philosophandi*, 30, 32, 49, 50; *Lehrfreiheit*, 30, 163–173
Achenwall, Gottfried (1719–1792), 104
Adams, Charles Kendall (1835–1902), 35, 41, 100, 113
Adams, Henry Brooks (1838–1918), 35, 100, 103, 106–108, 118, 124, 217
Adams, Henry Carter (1851–1921), 14, 36, 129, 134–135, 149–151, 192–193, 213
Adams, Herbert Baxter (1850–1901): on education in France, 11; as student in Germany, 18, 115; on seminar instruction, 36–37, 106; and American Historical Association, 41–44; change in his views, 43–44, 114; on history as past politics, 112–113; and Bluntschli, 115, 119; and germ theory, 115–120, 179, 180; and Social Contract theory, 119; on Aryan race, 121; criticism of, 125; and English scholars, 126–127, 179–181; as teacher of Small, 154; and civil service, 175–176, 178; on popular education, 178–182; on charities, 183; on municipal reforms, 192
Adler, Felix (1851–1933), 210
American Association of University Professors, 173
American Economic Association, 39, 44–45, 134, 139, 142, 148, 174
American Historical Association, 39, 41–44, 46, 67, 100, 124
American Political Science Association, 40, 45–46
American Social Science Association, 39, 41–45
American Sociological Society, 40, 46–47
American students in Germany, 1–22
Amherst College, 27, 29, 66, 67
Ammon, Christoph Friedrich von (1766–1850), 82
Andover Theological Seminary, 80–83, 89–91
Andrews, Charles McLean (1863–1943), 118
Andrews, Elisha Benjamin (1844–1917), 210
Anti-Semitism, 185–186; *see also* History, race theory of
Arnold, Thomas (1795–1842), 183
Arons, Martin Leo (1860–1919), 167

Aryanism, *see* History, race theory of

Association of American Universities, 48–49

Associations, scholarly, 39–49; *see also under names of individual associations*

Baldwin, James Mark (1861–1934), 198–199, 209

Bancroft, George (1800–1891), 4, 14, 15, 35, 66–67, 70, 75–79, 92, 100–103

Barnard, Frederick Augustus Porter (1809–1889), 2

Barth, Ernst Emil Paul (1858–1922), 153–155, 161

Bascom, John (1827–1911), 29

Baur, Ferdinand Christian (1792–1860), 82

Beard, Charles Austin (1874–1948), 114, 204, 220–226, 229

Becker, Carl Lotus (1873–1945), 204, 219–221, 224–226, 229

Bellamy, Edward (1850–1898), 187

Bentley, William (1759–1819), 14

Berlin, University of, 5, 9, 16–18, 54, 76, 122, 164, 167

Bernhardi, Friedrich Adam Julius von (1849–1930), 169

Bismarck, Otto Eduard Leopold von (1815–1898), 146, 164, 190, 191, 194

Bluntschli, Johann Caspar (1803–1881), 18, 36, 115, 119–121, 164, 192

Boas, Franz (1858–1942), 214

Böhm-Bawerk, Eugen Ritter von (1851–1914), 131

Boltzmann, Ludwig Eduard (1844–1906), 212, 215

Bonn, University of, 17, 18, 162, 165

Bowen, Francis (1811–1890), 61, 62, 93

Bowne, Borden Parker (1847–1910), 211

Breslau, University of, 162, 164

Brown University, 61

Brownson, Orestes Augustus (1803–1876), 87, 88

Bryce, Lord James (1838–1922), 12, 99, 100, 124, 214

Burckhardt, Jacob Christoph (1818–1897), 102–103, 111

Burgess, John William (1844–1931): in Germany, 3, 115; on American college, 26–27, 49–50; on philosophical faculty, 30; on fellowships, 33; at Columbia, 35, 175–176; as Hegelian, 67, 126, 127; on science of politics, 112–115, 150; his *Political Science and Comparative Constitutional Law*, 113, 121–122; view of history, 115; on crime of war, 116–117; on natural rights philosophy, 119; on Aryan race, 121–123; on immigration, 122; and Wilhelm II, 122, 123, 127; and World War I, 123; on Edward VII, 123; criticism of, 125; declining influence of, 127–128; on academic freedom, 169, 172; on socialism, 169, 189; on nationalism, 191–192; as defender of Germany, 194

Bushnell, Horace (1802–1876), 79, 90

Butler, Joseph (1692–1752), 85

INDEX

Butler, Nicholas Murray (1862–1947), 11, 47

California, University of, 48
Cambridge Prospect Union, 184
Caprivi, Georg Leo Graf von (1831–1899), 164
Catholic University, 48, 49
Cattell, James McKeen (1860–1944), 209
Certainty, quest for, 158, 206, 226–229
Channing, Edward (1856–1931), 35, 36, 101, 117–118
Channing, William Ellery (1780–1842), 80
Chartism, 187
Chautauqua, 178–181, 184
Chicago, University of, 40, 48, 49, 170
Christian Social Union, 184
Christian socialism, *see* Socialism
Churches, German state, 185–186
Civil Service, 165–168; examinations, 22, 166, 178; reform, 42, 43, 175–178
Clark, John Bates (1847–1938), 210
Clark University, 48, 49
Cogswell, Joseph Green (1786–1871), 3–4, 14, 15, 70
Collectivism, 66–68, 145, 163, 188, 193–197, 201
College, American, 23–29
College reform, 48–50
Columbia University, 40, 48, 49, 175–176
Commons, John Rogers (1862–1945), 177
Common-sense realism, 59–64, 66, 74, 84, 86, 87, 88, 93, 106; *see also* Philosophy, moral
Comparative method, 18, 54, 115–118, 133–137, 154
Comte, Auguste (1798–1857), 68, 69, 153, 196
Congregationalism, 79, 80–84, 89–92
Conrad, Johannes Ernst (1839–1915), 10, 14, 131, 144, 147–148, 164, 201–202, 209
Constant de Rebecque, Henry-Benjamin (1767–1830), 88
Cooley, Charles Horton (1864–1929), 198
Coolidge, Archibald Cary (1866–1928), 36
Cooperation, 180, 184, 189-192, 197
Cornell University, 48, 73
Cousin, Victor (1792–1867), 88
Criticism: biblical, 55, 76–96; higher, 7, 55, 57, 62, 77, 78, 84, 85, 87, 89, 91, 93, 96, 108, 132, 134; historical, 15, 54–55, 57, 62, 76, 78, 85, 89, 91–94, 96, 104; in philosophy, 54, 57, 62; lower, 55, 76–77, 80–85, 89
Croce, Benedetto (1866–1952), 222

Croly, Herbert David (1869–1930), 196–201
Curtius, Ernst (1814–1896), 16

Dartmouth College, 29
Darwin, Charles Robert (1809–1882), 68, 69
Darwinism, 68, 129, 142, 143, 156
Davis, William Morris (1850–1934), 211
Debs, Eugene Victor (1855–1926), 198
Delitzsch, Franz Julius (1813–1890), 18
De Wette, Wilhelm Martin Leberecht (1780–1849), 82, 88
Dewey, John (1859–1952), 157–159, 161, 195, 199, 204, 206, 214,
    223, 224–234
Dissen, Georg Ludolph (1784–1837), 15
Doctorate, 4, 9, 11, 22, 48, 100, 131
Droysen, Johann Gustav Bernhard (1808–1884), 10, 16, 110–113, 115,
    125, 126, 164
Du Bois-Reymond, Emil Heinrich (1818–1896), 10, 16
Dunbar, Charles Franklin (1830–1900), 36
Dunning, William Archibald (1857–1922), 214

Eaton, John (1829–1906), 41, 42
Ebeling, Christoph Daniel (1741–1817), 14
Ecole Libre des Sciences Politiques, 175
Economics, *see* Political Economy
Educational reforms of scholars, 174–182
Edwards, Jonathan (1703–1758), 13, 92, 159
Eichhorn, Johann Gottfried (1752–1827), 15, 75, 82
Eliot, Charles William (1834–1926), 6, 33, 47, 48, 50, 65
Ely, Richard Theodore (1854–1943): at Johns Hopkins, 4; in Germany,
    14, 18; and academic freedom, 19, 169, 171–173; and American
    Economic Association, 44–45; on German scholarship, 53; as
    Hegelian, 67; and Science-Economic discussion, 134–135; on role of
    state, 149; on economics as branch of sociology, 150; as new econo-
    mist, 161; on scholar as aristocrat, 172; as reformer, 174, 181; on
    training for civil service, 175–176; and Wisconsin Idea, 176–178;
    and Social Gospel, 182–184; on German state churches, 185–186;
    under attack, 188; on socialism, 189–190; on cooperation and na-
    tionalization, 190; and Croly, 199; and Theodore Roosevelt, 199–201;
    at St. Louis Congress, 213
Emerson, Ralph Waldo (1803–1882), 63, 65, 87, 94, 96
Emerton, Ephraim (1851–1935), 35, 94
Empiricism, 54–61, 68, 70, 92, 93, 101–106, 132–134, 153–155, 207,
    216, 223, 227, 229; *see also*, Idealism, empirical
Engel, Christian Lorenz Ernst (1821–1896), 138, 139, 142, 145, 175

Engels, Friedrich (1820–1895), 187
Erdmannsdörffer, Bernhard (1833–1901), 18, 115
Ethical school, see Political economy
Ethics, sociological, 68, 95–96, 156–159, 196, 232; see also Philosophy, moral
Everett, Charles Carroll (1829–1900), 93–94
Everett, Edward (1794–1865), 3–4, 14, 15, 70
Evolution, 68, 73, 93, 96, 115–119, 132, 145, 156

Faculty psychology, 25–26, 74, 195
Falkner, Roland Post (1866–1940), 14
Farnam, Henry Walcott (1853–1933), 130–131
Fellowships, 32–34
Ferguson, Adam (1723–1816), 59, 69
Fetter, Frank Albert (1863–1949), 14, 210
Fichte, Johann Gottlieb (1762–1814), 16, 93
Fiske, John (1842–1901), 206
Follen, Charles (1796–1840), 86
Fourier, François Marie Charles (1772–1837), 187
Francke, August Hermann (1663–1727), 13, 14
Franklin, Benjamin (1706–1790), 14, 38, 221
Freeman, Edward Augustus (1823–1892), 117, 118, 121, 122
Fremantle, William Henry (1831–1916), 184

Gatterer, Johann Christoph (1727–1799), 15, 104
Gauss, Karl Friedrich (1777–1855), 15
Geisteswissenschaft, 55–58, 64, 136, 216, 222, 229–230
George, Henry (1839–1897), 187, 188
Gibbs, Josiah Willard (1839–1903), 62
Giddings, Franklin Henry (1855–1931), 209
Gildersleeve, Basil Lanneau (1831–1924), 35
Gilman, Daniel Coit (1831–1908), 28
Gneist, Heinrich Rudolf Hermann Friedrich von (1816–1895), 16, 164
Goethe, Johann Wolfgang (1749–1832), 4, 88
Göttingen, University of, 3–4, 7, 9, 13–15, 75–77, 104, 115
Graduate School of Arts and Science, 4–5, 30; see also Philosophical faculty
Grammar, science of, 76, 80–82, 85
Green, Nicholas St. John (1835–1876), 206
Grimm, Hermann Friedrich (1828–1901), 16
Grimm, Jacob Ludwig Karl (1785–1863), 16
Grimm, Wilhelm Karl (1786–1859), 16
Gross, Charles (1857–1909), 36
Gymnasium, German, 21–22, 23, 49

Hadley, Arthur Twining (1856–1930), 134–136, 213

Haeckel, Ernst Heinrich (1834–1919), 93

Hall, Granville Stanley (1844–1924), 21, 31, 34, 53, 69–70, 214

Halle, University of, 13–14, 54, 91, 94

Hamilton, Sir William (1788–1856), 12

Hart, Albert Bushnell (1854–1943), 36, 118

Harvard Divinity School, 65, 86, 93–96

Harvard University, 6, 29, 35, 36, 40, 48, 49, 61, 79, 95

Hayek, Friedrich August von (1899–), 215

Hedge, Frederic Henry (1805–1890), 92–93

Hedge, Levi (1766–1844), 61

Heeren, Arnold Hermann Ludwig (1760–1842), 15

Hegel, Georg Wilhelm Friedrich (1770–1831), 10, 16, 57, 69, 70, 92–94

Hegelianism, 65–68, 85–86, 94, 126, 127, 195, 223; *see also* Idealism, speculative, *and* Philosophy, speculative

Heidelberg, University of, 17–18

Heinrichs, Johann Heinrich (c. 1750–1830), 82

Helmholtz, Hermann Ludwig Ferdinand (1821–1894), 10, 16

Henry, Joseph (1797–1878), 62

Herbart, Johann Friedrich (1776–1841), 69

Herder, Johann Gottfried (1744–1803), 86, 88

Heussi, Karl (1877–1961), 222, 223

Hildebrand, Bruno (1812–1878), 132, 137, 143, 145

Historical school: of jurisprudence, 7, 111, 132; at Göttingen, 14–15; of national economy, the older, 18, 55, 132, 146; attacks speculative philosophy, 56–57; evaluation of German-trained Americans of, 123–128; in the social sciences, 130–131; connection of its empiricism with reform, 143–144, 156; absorbed by American pragmatism, 158; supporting German collectivism, 187–192, 194; suspected of supporting socialism, 188; defeated by speculative philosophy, 195; and the New Nationalism, 195–201; irony of, in America, 202; its bequest to American scholarship, 204–205; at high tide, 207–215; *Weltanschauung* of, 208, 215–217; problem of, 216–217

Historicism, 163, 205, 215–216, 232–234; crisis of, 202, 204, 205, 207, 215–219, 222–224, 227, 230, 232

History: scientific character of, 37, 99–105, 205; Hegel's philosophy of, 56, 71, 102; as successor to moral philosophy, 66–67, 96; as vindication of faith, 91–92; establishment of an American science of, 99–128; auxiliary branches of, 104–105; dissatisfaction with science of, 106–108, 219–224; Droysen on nature of, 110–111; relation of politics to, 111–115; the "new" social or cultural, 111, 114, 126, 151, 208–209, 220, 222; comparative institutional and constitutional, 115–117; germ theory of, 115–120, 179, 180; biological basis of, 118–120; race theory of, 117, 120–123; and sociology, 151–159; as applied psychology,

152–153; as science of man, 204–205; meaning in, 217–219, 221, 223, 227–230, 233–234; nature of, 228–230, 233
Hofer, Walther (1920–), 215
Holmes, Oliver Wendell (1841–1935), 206
Holt, William Stull (1896–), 126
Hopkins, Mark (1802–1887), 29
Hopkins, Samuel (1721–1803), 79
Howison, George Holmes (1834–1916), 211
Humboldt, Friedrich Wilhelm Christian Karl Ferdinand von (1767–1835), 22, 108–110, 125, 128, 164, 165
Humboldt, Friedrich Wilhelm Heinrich Alexander von (1769–1859), 57
Hume, David (1711–1776), 59
Hutcheson, Francis (1694–1746), 59, 69

Idealism, empirical: of Schleiermacher, 78; replaces Hegelian philosophy of history, 102; as philosophy of German historians, 108–111; of Humboldt and Ranke, 108–110; in social science, 130; rejects both speculation and positivism, 136; dominates in both Europe and America, 210–211; as methodology and ideology, 216; see also Empiricism
Idealism, speculative, 62, 86, 88, 89; see also Hegelianism, and Philosophy, speculative, and Transcendentalism
Ideengeschichte, 109, 111, 128, 222; see also Idealism, empirical
Instrumentalism, 158, 232
International Congress of Arts and Science, 207–215

James, Edmund Janes (1855–1925), 14, 134–135, 149
James, William (1842–1910), 196, 206
Jameson, John Franklin (1859–1937), 43, 106–107, 116–118
Jena, University of, 18
Johns Hopkins University, 4, 6, 33, 35, 36, 40, 48, 49, 112–114, 181, 203
Johnson, Joseph French (1853–1925), 14
Jordan, David Starr (1853–1931), 33, 34, 48, 50
Jouffroy, Théodore (1796–1842), 88
Judson, Harry Pratt (1849–1927), 33

Kant, Immanuel (1724–1804), 10, 54, 56, 70, 88
Kathedersozialismus, 146–147, 150, 169, 187, 192
Ketteler, Wilhelm Emanuel (1811–1877), 186
Kimball, Arthur Lalanne (1856–1922), 211
Kingsley, Charles (1819–1875), 183
Kinley, David (1861–1944), 5
Kirkland, John Thornton (1770–1840), 75

Knies, Karl Gustav Adolf (1821–1898), 18, 115, 131–133, 136–139, 145, 146, 164, 194
Knowledge, nature of, 159, 228–230
Koch, Robert (1843–1910), 10
Kunze, John Christopher (1744–1807), 13

La Follette, Robert Marion (1855–1925), 178, 201
Lamprecht, Karl Gotthard (1856–1915), 152–153, 154, 213
Legal education, 6–7
Legaré, Hugh Swinton (1797–1843), 7
Lehrfreiheit, see Academic freedom
Leipzig, University of, 17–18, 94
Lepsius, Karl Richard (1810–1884), 16
Lernfreiheit, see Academic freedom
Lessing, Gotthold Ephraim (1729–1781), 91
Libertas philosophandi, see Academic freedom
Lindsay, Samuel McCune (1869–1959), 14
Locke, John (1632–1704), 60, 63, 66, 69, 84, 85, 87, 88, 93, 120
Lotze, Rudolf Hermann (1817–1881), 15
Lowell, Abbott Lawrence (1856–1943), 214

McCarthy, Charles (1873–1921), 176–177, 182
McCosh, James (1811–1894), 61, 69
Mannheim, Karl (1893–1947), 218, 222, 228, 229
Marx, Karl (1818–1883), 187
Massachusetts Institute of Technology, 29, 139
Mather, Cotton (1663–1728), 13
Maurice, Frederick Denison (1805–1872), 183
Mayhew, Jonathan (1720–1766), 79
Mayo-Smith, Richmond (1854–1901), 134–135, 140–141
Mayr, Georg von (1841–1925), 140–141
Medical education in America, 6
Meinecke, Friedrich (1862–1954), 218–219
Menzel, Wolfgang (1798–1873), 88
Meyer, Gottlob Wilhelm (1768–1816), 82
Michigan, University of, 35, 36, 48
Mill, John Stuart (1806–1873), 68
Miracles, debate over, 86–87
Mommsen, Theodor (1817–1903), 16, 111, 115, 164
Moral science, *see* Common-sense realism
Morrill Act, 29
Mühlenberg, Henry Melchoir (1711–1787), 13
Müller, Johannes von (1752–1809), 15
Mueller-Armack, Alfred (1901–), 222

München, University of, 18, 165
Münsterberg, Hugo (1863–1916), 207–208, 211, 213, 214

Nairne, Charles Murray (1808–1882), 29
National economy, *see* Political economy
National Education Association, 47
Natural rights philosophy, 119, 120
Naturphilosophie, see Philosophy, natural
Neology, 77, 90, 91
New Freedom, *see* Wilson, Woodrow
New Nationalism, *see* Roosevelt, Theodore
Newcomb, Simon (1835–1909), 134–136, 141–142, 148, 149, 188, 207
Newton, Sir Isaac (1642–1727), 58, 63, 83, 216
Nichols, Edward Leamington (1854–1937), 211
Niebuhr, Barthold Georg (1776–1831), 7, 164
Norton, Andrews (1786–1853), 84–89, 93
Noyes, William Albert (1857–1941), 211

Objectivity, 163, 166, 170, 173, 206, 215, 219–223, 225
Osgood, Herbert Levi (1855–1918), 118
Ostwald, Wilhelm (1853–1932), 212
Owen, Robert (1771–1858), 187

Paley, William (1743–1805), 58, 60, 63, 69, 85
Palmer, George Herbert (1842–1933), 196
Park, Edwards Amasa (1808–1900), 89–91
Parker, Theodore (1810–1860), 86, 87
Patten, Simon Nelson (1852–1922), 14, 45, 149, 209
Paulsen, Friedrich (1846–1908), 167–169
Peabody, Andrew Preston (1811–1893), 28–29
Peabody, Francis Greenwood (1847–1936): at Halle, 14; on American college, 27; on Harvard Divinity School, 94; and Emerson, 94; introduces German theology at Harvard, 94–95; as theologian of the Social Gospel, 95–96; on scholarship and reform, 174; his reliance on English methods of philanthropy, 184; on German state churches, 185, 186; on socialism and cooperation, 189–191; and Croly, 199
Peirce, Charles Sanders (1839–1914), 62, 158, 206
Penck, Albrecht (1858–1945), 214
Pennsylvania, University of, 48
Periodicals, *see* Publications
Perry, Bliss (1860–1954), 3
Pfleiderer, Otto (1839–1908), 16, 69, 94, 212
Philosophical faculty, 30–31, 165
Philosophy: instruction in, 9, 54, 58–71; moral, 25, 57–64, 66, 71, 112, 142, 150, 159, 233–234; natural, 55–57, 102; Scottish, *see* Common-

sense realism; speculative, 55–57, 62, 84–86, 92, 102–103, 109–110, 207, 222; *see also* Hegelianism, *and* Idealism, speculative
Planck, Gottlieb Jacob (1751–1833), 15
Pochmann, Henry August (1901–), 70
Poincaré, Henri (1854–1912), 214
Political activity of scholars, 112, 162–174
Political economy, 129–152; and ethics, 134–135, 143–144, 145; new school of, 14, 44, 45, 134–137, 139, 142–143, 148–150, 161–162, 196; old school of, 44, 45, 129, 134, 139, 148, 188
Popper, Karl Raimund (1902–), 215
Porter, Noah (1811–1892), 23–24, 29, 50, 51, 61
Pragmatism, 130, 157–159, 206, 207
Presbyterianism, 83, 92
Presentism, 205, 225
Princeton University, 40, 48, 61
Privatdozent, 33, 166–168
Probability, *see* Statistics
Professional education, 6–8, 12, 19, 23–51, 178
Professorial socialism, see *Kathedersozialismus*
Prussia, American sympathy for, 10, 112
Publications, scholarly, 37–40

Racism, *see* History, race theory of
Ranke, Leopold von (1795–1886), 16, 102, 103, 108–111, 113, 125, 128, 164, 221–222
Ratzenhofer, Gustav (1842–1904), 155, 209
Rauch, Frederick Augustus (1806–1841), 65
Reform, *see* Scholarship and Reform, *and* Educational reforms
Reid, Thomas (1710–1796), 59, 69
Rein, Wilhelm (1847–1929), 210
Relativism, ethical, *see* Ethics, sociological
Relativism, historical, 157–159, 205, 218; *see also* Historical school
Research, 30–37, 45, 46, 50; *see also* Teaching
Riezler, Kurt (1882–1955), 222
Ripley, George (1802–1880), 86–88
Robins, Henry Ephraim (1827–1917), 29
Robinson, James Harvey (1863–1936), 209
Rohrbach, Paul (1869–1956), 194–195
Roosevelt, Theodore (1858–1919), 162, 163, 198–201
Roscher, Wilhelm Georg Friedrich (1817–1894), 18, 111, 131–134, 137, 138, 143, 145, 146, 152
Ross, Edward Alsworth (1866–1951), 170–171, 213
Royce, Josiah (1855–1916), 196, 211
Rutherford, Ernest (1871–1937), 214

Saalfeld, Friedrich (1785–1834), 15

Sadler, Sir Michael Ernest (1861–1943), 214

St. Louis Congress, *see* International Congress of Arts and Science

Sanborn, Franklin Benjamin (1831–1917), 41, 42

Santayana, George (1863–1952), 196

Savingy, Friedrich Karl von (1779–1861), 7, 111, 132

Schäffle, Albert Eberhard Friedrich (1831–1903), 153–155, 161

Schelling, Friedrich Wilhelm Joseph (1775–1854), 16, 55

Schiller, Johann Christoph Friedrich (1759–1805), 88

Schleiermacher, Friedrich Daniel Ernst (1768–1834), 16, 76–79, 84, 86–96

Schlözer, August Ludwig (1735–1809), 15, 104–105

Schmoller, Gustav (1838–1917), 131, 137–139, 143, 145, 147, 148, 152, 164

Schneider, Herbert Wallace (1892–), 61

Scholarship, German: specialization of, 19, 71, 105–106, 124–125; as profession, 19; vocationalism of, 22, 31, 50–51; in America, 53–71, 123–128, 201–234; development of, 54–58; at St. Louis International Congress, 213–214; *see also* Historical School

Scholarship and reform, 42–46, 63, 95, 141–152, 158–159, 161–202, 230

Schurman, Jacob Gould (1854–1942), 39

Science: as crowning subject of curriculum, 70; as most significant contribution of Germany to American college, 70; as arbiter of ethical questions, 71; its impact on religion, 73–97; its appeal to Americans, 105–106; historical nature of, 228–230

Science, economic discussion in, 134–136

Scientific schools in America, 29

Scott, Austin (1848–1922), 35

Scottish philosophy, *see* Common-sense realism

Seager, Henry Rogers (1870–1930), 14

Seelye, Julius Hawley (1824–1895), 29, 66, 67

Seligman, Edwin Robert Anderson (1861–1939), 134–135, 213

Seminar, 34–37, 94, 105–107

Settlement houses, 95, 180, 184

Siegfried, Jules (1837–1922), 179

Small, Albion Woodbury (1854–1926): on American Economic Association, 45, 174; on science of human welfare replacing theology, 64; applies Hegelian dialectic, 67; on social science, 154–159; and Dewey, 156–159, 195–196; on sociological ethics, 156–158, 232; on marriage of thought and action, 158, 161; on *Verein für Sozialpolitik*, 169, 174; on German militarism, 169; on academic freedom, 169–172; on German state churches, 185; on Social Gospel, 185; on socialism, 189; and Bluntschli, 192; *The Cameralists*, 192–194; *The Origins of*

Sociology, 192–194; censors aberrations of German scholarship, 194–196; and Croly, 197–199; at International Congress, 207, 214

Smith, Henry Boynton (1815–1877), 14, 91–92, 94

Smyth, Egbert Coffin (1829–1904), 91

Social ethics, 95, 184

Social Gospel, 95, 174, 182–187

Social process, 155–159, 161

Social Science: as "all embracing science of human association," 18, 150–159; a "true" historical, 130; as science of reform, 151, 155–159; historical approach to, 154; field of and rationale for, 156; pragmatism in, 158–159; lack of unified field theory for, 161; *see also* Political economy *and* Sociology

Socialism, 135, 145–147, 184, 186–192, 197–198; *see also* State socialism

Society, as organizing concept for political economy, 130, 150

Sociology, 68, 130, 135, 141, 151–159, 174, 195, 209, 220; *see also* Social Science

Solidarism, *see* Socialism

Sombart, Werner (1863–1941), 213

Sorley, William Ritchie (1855–1935), 212

Spalding, John Lancaster (1840–1916), 214

Specialization, 19, 29–30, 47, 124, 159

Spencer, Herbert (1820–1903), 68, 69, 93, 153

Spranger, Eduard (1882–), 165–166

Stanford, Mrs. Jane Lathrop (1825–1905), 171

Stanford University, 33, 48, 171

State, role of, 131, 134, 135, 144–150, 164–168, 171, 190–193, 198

State socialism, 139, 142, 146, 169, 190; *see also* Socialism

Statistical Bureau of Prussia, Royal, 17, 138, 142, 175

Statistics, 104–105, 135–142, 209, 217

Stewart, Dugald (1753–1828), 59, 69

Stoecker, Adolf (1835–1909), 185–186

Strassburg, University of, 18, 175

Stuart, Moses (1780–1852), 80–84, 89

Sumner, William Graham (1840–1910), 68, 129, 188

Sybel, Heinrich von (1817–1895), 111, 125, 164

Taussig, Frank William (1859–1940), 36, 134–136

Taylor, Nathaniel William (1786–1858), 64, 79

Teaching, 28–29, 32, 34, 46–47, 50, 64

Theological education, 6–7

Theology, 8, 9, 75–79, 89–90, 95

Thiess, Johann Otto (1762–1810), 82

Tholuck, Friedrich August Gottreu (1799–1877), 14, 94, 96

Thoreau, Henry David (1817–1862), 63

Thought and action, *see* Scholarship and reform
Ticknor, George (1791–1871), 3–4, 9, 14, 15, 70
Tönnies, Ferdinand (1855–1936), 214
Toynbee, Arnold (1852–1883), 183
Transcendentalism, 62–66, 85, 87–89, 91; *see also* Idealism, speculative
Treitschke, Heinrich Gotthard von (1834–1896), 10, 16, 111–112, 115, 119, 125, 146, 147, 164, 169, 179
Treitschke-Schmoller debate, 146–147
Trendelenburg, Friedrich Adolf (1802–1872), 16
Troeltsch, Ernst (1865–1923), 212, 218–219
Tübingen school, 85
Turner, Frederick Jackson (1861–1932), 114, 126, 181–182, 209
Tuttle, Herbert (1846–1894), 35
Tyler, Moses Coit (1835–1900), 35, 41, 100

Union Theological Seminary, 89, 91, 94
Unitarianism, 64–65, 79–80, 83–89, 91–96
Unity of knowledge and of science, 55, 56, 154, 207, 208, 211, 212, 214, 215, 224, 226, 230
Universities: English, 8, 11–13; French, 8–11; German, 1–22; *see also under individual names*
University extension, 178–183

Valla, Laurentius (1406–1457), 104
Value, 57, 155, 159, 205, 206, 212, 223–224, 227–230, 233
Verein für Sozialpolitik, 144–148, 156, 169, 174
Vincent, George Edgar (1864–1941), 209
Virchow, Rudolf Ludwig Karl von (1821–1902), 16, 57, 104
Vocational education, 29
Voigt, Georg (1827–1891), 18, 115

Wagner, Adolph Heinrich Gotthilf (1835–1917), 10, 16, 131, 138–139, 142, 145, 146, 164, 169, 190, 192, 194
Waitz, Georg (1813–1886), 15, 115, 164
Walker, Francis Amasa (1840–1897), 139–140, 141
Walker, James (1794–1874), 28, 61, 64
Wappäus, Johann (1812–1879), 15
Ward, Lester Frank (1841–1913), 46, 214
Ware, Henry (1764–1845), 79, 84
Warner, Joseph Bangs (1848–1923), 206
Wayland, Francis (1796–1865), 60, 61, 69
Weber, Max (1864–1920), 213, 218–219, 228, 229
Weber, Wilhelm Eduard (1804–1891), 15
Welcker, Friedrich Gottlieb (1784–1868), 15

Wellek, René (1903–), 38
White, Andrew Dickson (1832–1918), 26, 73–74, 100
White, Morton Gabriel (1917–), 129
Whitefield, George (1714–1770), 13
Wiener, Philip Paul (1905–), 203
Willoughby, Westel Woodbury (1867–1945), 210
Wilson, Woodrow (1856–1924), 106, 118, 127, 163, 200–201, 209
Wind, Edgar (1900–), 230
Winkelmann, Eduard (1838–1896), 115
Winsor, Justin (1831–1897), 114
Wisconsin, University of, 48
Wisconsin Idea, 176–178
Wissenschaft, see Scholarship, German
Wöhler, Friedrich (1800–1882), 15, 56
Woodbridge, Frederick James Eugene (1867–1940), 211
Woods, Leonard (1774–1854), 83, 84
Woodward, Robert Simpson (1849–1924), 211, 214
Woolsey, Theodore Dwight (1801–1889), 29
World War I, 123, 128, 163, 166, 186, 195, 203–204
Wright, Carroll Davidson (1840–1909), 142
Wright, Chauncey (1830–1875), 206
Wundt, Wilhelm (1832–1920), 69
Wuttke, Johann Karl Heinrich (1818–1876), 18, 115

Yale College, 26, 29, 48, 49
Yale Report of 1827, 24, 26, 27

Zachariä, Heinrich Albert (1806–1875), 15
Zeller, Eduard (1814–1908), 16

RENEWALS: 691-4574

DATE DUE

DEC 11			

Demco, Inc. 38-293